Social Anthropology and Human Origins

The study of human origins is one of the most fascinating branches of anthropology. Yet it has rarely been considered by social or cultural anthropologists, who represent the largest subfield of the discipline. In this powerful study Alan Barnard aims to bridge this gap. Barnard argues that social anthropological theory has much to contribute to our understanding of human evolution, including changes in technology, subsistence and exchange, family and kinship, as well as to the study of language, art, ritual and belief. This book places social anthropology in the context of a widely conceived constellation of anthropological sciences. It incorporates recent findings in many fields, including primate studies, archaeology, linguistics and human genetics. In clear, accessible style Barnard addresses the fundamental questions surrounding the evolution of human society and the prehistory of culture, suggesting a new direction for social anthropology that will open up debate across the discipline as a whole.

ALAN BARNARD is Professor of the Anthropology of Southern Africa at the University of Edinburgh, where he has taught since 1978. He has undertaken a wide range of ethnographic fieldwork and archaeological research in Botswana, Namibia and South Africa, is a participant in the British Academy Centenary Research Project 'From Lucy to language: the archaeology of the social brain' and serves as Honorary Consul of the Republic of Namibia in Scotland. His numerous publications include *History and theory in anthropology* (2000) and *Anthropology and the Bushman* (2007).

Social Anthropology and Human Origins

Alan Barnard

Professor of the Anthropology of Southern Africa
University of Edinburgh

CAMBRIDGE
UNIVERSITY PRESS

CAMBRIDGE
UNIVERSITY PRESS

Shaftesbury Road, Cambridge CB2 8EA, United Kingdom

One Liberty Plaza, 20th Floor, New York, NY 10006, USA

477 Williamstown Road, Port Melbourne, VIC 3207, Australia

314–321, 3rd Floor, Plot 3, Splendor Forum, Jasola District Centre, New Delhi – 110025, India

103 Penang Road, #05–06/07, Visioncrest Commercial, Singapore 238467

Cambridge University Press is part of Cambridge University Press & Assessment, a department of the University of Cambridge.

We share the University's mission to contribute to society through the pursuit of education, learning and research at the highest international levels of excellence.

www.cambridge.org
Information on this title: www.cambridge.org/9780521749299

First published 2011

A catalogue record for this publication is available from the British Library

Library of Congress Cataloging-in-Publication data
Barnard, Alan (Alan J.)
    Social anthropology and human origins / Alan Barnard.
        p.   cm.
    ISBN 978-0-521-76531-2 (hardback) – ISBN 978-0-521-74929-9 (paperback)
    1. Human beings–Origin.   2. Human evolution.   I. Title.
    GN281.B369   2011
    301–dc22
    2010051877

ISBN   978-0-521-76531-2   Hardback
ISBN   978-0-521-74929-9   Paperback

For my mother and for Mother Africa

Contents

Figures

Tables

Preface

As an undergraduate in an American four-field anthropology department, I came to regard the study of human origins as part of archaeology or physical anthropology. In my subsequent career in British social anthropology, little has changed. The people with trowels and callipers do human origins, and 'we' do ethnography.

However, the fact is that archaeology and biological anthropology (as the old physical anthropology has become) have little to say about the social or the cultural. Of course, I exempt the archaeological concern with specifically material culture, and I also exempt some rock art studies, with their concern with the richness of symbolic culture. I recognize too the odd archaeologist with an interest in music and human origins, or mathematics and human origins, and so on. These, though, are not the 'bread and butter' of their field. If you want an expert in ritual or symbolism, in kinship or reciprocity, or in political organization, or even in the utilization of resources and communication of environmental knowledge, why not turn to a social or cultural anthropologist? These are our areas of expertise.

My reintroduction in later life to 'early man' studies came through the fourth of the classic four fields of American anthropology: linguistics, where, as in Palaeolithic archaeology, there is much interest in some circles in early phases of human culture. I have long been interested in, and been writing on, theories of the origin of language and of the evolution of humankind from ape-like creatures. That interest, though, had been largely historical, that is, in terms of the history of anthropological thought – especially eighteenth-century anthropological thought. I had also long been writing on the evolution and transformation of kinship systems, but until recently not really with human origins as my focus. An invitation to the Cradle of Language Conference, held in Stellenbosch in 2006, encouraged me to develop some of my ideas in this area. A request to contribute to a book on early kinship further sharpened my theoretical understanding of the structural arrangements of human and proto-human interaction in the distant past. This in turn suggested to me that social anthropological theory has as much to contribute as comparative ethnography to the study of human prehistory.

For any readers unfamiliar with the phrases 'cultural anthropology' and 'social anthropology', let me simply explain that in general they refer to the same thing. For historical reasons, in some countries one is used, while in other countries the other. It is meaningful to think in terms of both 'society' and 'culture' as the things that this discipline, or this branch of a larger anthropological science, can have something to say about. For now, let me say only that while both 'society' and 'culture' are contested abstractions, nevertheless, the social and the cultural are taken as broadly meaningful in the field of what is sometimes called 'social and cultural anthropology'. In this book I will generally use the term 'social anthropology', which is the more common term in the United Kingdom, but this can be taken as comprising also what, especially in North America, is included under the heading 'cultural anthropology'.

Social anthropology is a discipline that advances, like any other. Yet it is slower in this respect than, say, genetics, linguistics or archaeology. For that reason, among others, the material cited here from social anthropology is often older than that of other disciplines, genetics in particular. Social anthropology is built on firm foundation, and classic ethnography, and even classic theory, guide present-day concerns. The vast majority of citations to works in genetics are very recent; those to works in social anthropology, less so. Also, it is worth noting that a good deal of the material discussed here is in works written by others, in a vast number of disciplines. The study of human origins yields hundreds of publications each year. I have read thousands in the course of preparing this monograph, but have room to discuss and cite only a small percentage. Otherwise, there would have been little room for my own ideas. This, among other things, highlights the relevance of my main reason for writing: to help to establish a social anthropology of human origins.

One facet of my argument throughout the book is that the social and the cultural either have been neglected, or have been poorly treated, by colleagues in archaeology, biological anthropology and even linguistics. Indeed, one might throw in primatology, evolutionary psychology, human genetics, or whatever, as related disciplines in which the same problem may be found. The other facet of my argument is that we social anthropologists are, in fact, very much to blame for this. Few of us bother to learn the basics of these related disciplines, or to engage in the debates which surely are the essence of a wider field of 'anthropology' in its literal sense. But frankly, few of my friends in archaeology, linguistics or the biological branches of modern anthropology can hold their own with proper social anthropologists in theories of sociality, kinship, totemism,

symbolism or ethnicity. Social anthropologists have a wealth of knowledge of these things, with ethnography to back it up; and equally, we
have a magnificent range of theoretical perspectives, from the nineteenth
century right up to the present, which can provide insights.

In short, this book aims to fill a big gap in anthropological studies.
In order to enable a better understanding of prehistory, a good dose of
real social anthropology is needed. It is my hope both that some social
anthropologists will develop a specialist interest in human origins, and
that the discipline of social anthropology as a whole can contribute significantly to filling the great cultural and social gap in human origins
studies.

I would like to thank Robin Dunbar for encouraging me to write this
book, and my many colleagues in social anthropology in Edinburgh and
elsewhere for sharing ideas on its theme. I am grateful to my wife Joy for
harsh criticism of my more fanciful ideas. All figures and tables are my
own, except, figure 3.2 which is in the public domain, and figure 4.1,
which is courtesy of Robin Dunbar.

Social anthropology and human origins is dedicated to the memory of
my mother, Doris Pinder Barnard (1924–2010), and to Africa, mother
of us all.

1   Introduction

Social anthropology is a discipline largely missing from the study of human origins. Until now, the discipline has sidelined itself. Yet its central concerns with notions like society, culture and cross-cultural comparison make it of the utmost relevance for understanding the origins of human social life, and relevant too as an aid for speculation on the kinds of society our ancestors inhabited. Like archaeologists, social anthropologists can dig backwards through layers of time, into the origins of language, symbolism, ritual, kinship and the ethics and politics of reciprocity.

When did human origins begin? That is a trick question. Of course, human origins began when humanity began, but in another sense human origins began when origins became an intellectual issue. There is no real history of engagement between social anthropology and early humanity, so one must be created here. Social anthropology's ancestral disciplines, like moral philosophy and jurisprudence, natural history and antiquarianism, travelogue and philology, all fed into post-medieval developments in building a picture of 'early man'. Yet, as I have implied, social anthropology proper has been absent. Since the days of Franz Boas at the dawn of the twentieth century, the study of human origins has been seen instead as the preserve of biological or physical anthropology. While not wishing to encroach too deeply into biological territory, in this book I want to carve out within social anthropology a new subdiscipline. I see this as a subdiscipline that touches on the biological and makes full use too of a century and a half of social anthropology – its accumulated experience and especially some of its more recent, and relevant, developments.

Scientific interest in human origins in fact has quite a long history. Seventeenth-century European thinkers such as Hobbes and Locke speculated on the 'natural' condition of 'man', and its relation to the earliest forms of human society. Eighteenth-century thinkers continued this tradition, and archaeological and linguistic concerns were added at that time. In the nineteenth century, the theory or theories of evolution, as well as important fossil finds like the first Neanderthal in 1857 and *Pithecanthropus* in 1891, provided much added impetus. Indeed, the later supposed 'discovery' of 'Piltdown Man' in 1912 had the same effect. Piltdown, classified originally as *Eoanthropus dawsoni*, was exposed as a hoax only in 1953. Until then, although its importance was doubted by some (most notably Franz Weidenreich, from as early as 1923), its place in human evolution had to be counted. From *Australopithecus africanus* (unearthed in 1924 and described in 1925), discoveries through the twentieth century were eventually of great significance in understanding the place of Africa in human evolution, and later the spread of humankind from Africa throughout the world. That said, we must not read too much of what we know now into our understanding of the past: just as for several decades Piltdown was not known to have been a hoax, so too 'Dart's child' (*Australopithecus*) was not in the first decades after its discovery universally accepted as a human ancestor.

In each of these centuries, scholars of course debated the significance of what they found, and the debates too formed part of several emerging disciplines, including anthropology, archaeology, psychology, linguistics and philosophy. Yet we should not forget that both the fossils and the anthropological ideas in fact preceded, and in some cases long preceded, the academic disciplines as we know them today. This introductory chapter briefly traces the long history of relevant ideas, and then explores the potential for contributions from social and cultural anthropology. Its purpose is to highlight not only the trajectory of discovery and knowledge, but also the dependence of knowledge on theory, especially social theory in its widest sense. I am not aiming for a 'history of science' treatment of the topic, much less a history of some specific science, but rather a brief and, I hope, enlightening narrative of relations between some relevant ideas.

A short history of human origins

The seventeenth century

Archaeology, or more accurately its predecessor, antiquarian studies, emerged as an amateur pursuit in the seventeenth century. Even before that, in the early sixteenth century, Italian geologists had speculated on the idea of stone tools as antecedents of iron ones (Trigger 1989: 53). However, the great social thinkers like Grotius, Hobbes, Pufendorf and even Locke were *not* among those who had such notions. Social theory in the seventeenth century seemed almost completely oblivious to such insights and to the growing interest, throughout much of Europe, in early technology and in comparisons between Europeans of the past and the inhabitants of Africa or the Americas at the time. In retrospect, it is as if Europe were emerging only very slowly from its medieval belief that the inhabitants of the other continents were degenerate remnants of Near East civilizations of the past (see Malina and Vašíček 1990: 12–15; Trigger 1989: 45–55).

It is true that Locke (e.g. 1988 [1690]: 339–40) speculated on Amerindian society as analogous to earlier Asian and European forms of social organization. Yet he failed to develop an evolutionary understanding of society in the abstract. He seems to suggest that 'man in the state of nature' possessed sheep and cattle, and that the earliest stages of society might be characterized by the exchange of wool for other goods (Locke 1988: 300). Hobbes's (1996 [1651]: 86–90) notion of the natural condition of the human species is well known: competition for resources, fear of one's neighbours, no domestication of plants, no true sociality and a state of war (or cold war) of all against all. Neither Hobbes nor Locke, nor any of their contemporaries, had any idea of biological evolution; and their notions of social evolution were not coupled with any appreciation of the universality of human advancement, of stages of development or of a relation between the social and the material. Neither of them, for example, seems to have developed anything approaching the modern notion of *hunter-gatherer society*, which had to wait until the following century to come into existence (see Barnard 2004). In short, although we may reasonably look to seventeenth-century philosophy as the basis for modern, post-medieval, European secular thought in many respects, nevertheless, the greatest names of the seventeenth century had virtually no understanding of prehistory, nor, apparently, much interest in the ethnographic discoveries then beginning to inform the European intellectual elite. I shall not dwell further on seventeenth-century political thought. The building blocks of at least social evolutionary theory were there, but they had yet to be put together.

On the biological side, there was one significant development relevant to human evolution. In 1698, London physician Edward Tyson dissected the body of a young chimpanzee, which had died soon after arrival in England from Angola. Tyson's (1699) famous treatise became widely known. Tyson's careful dissection showed unexpected similarities between what we now call the chimpanzee and the human, especially with regard to the brain, and he concluded that the specimen was neither human nor monkey but something in between: 'our *Pygmie* [chimpanzee] is no *Man*, nor yet the *Common Ape* [monkey]; but a sort of *Animal* between both; and tho' a *Biped*, yet of the *Quadrumanus-kind*' (Tyson 1699: 91). Although Tyson's treatise was well known, much less well known, and of course without support from the scientific establishment, was the idea that humans are descended from apes. The Italian free-thinking philosopher Lucilio Vanini apparently suggested the idea in 1616, and was executed for the suggestion in 1619 (Thomas 1995: 19).

The eighteenth century

The eighteenth century was quite different from the seventeenth. In the early part of the century, the revolutionary thinker Giambattista Vico became perhaps the first 'major' figure to tackle social evolution in any serious way. This he did through the three, quite different, editions of his *Scienza nuova*, which were published in 1725, 1730 and 1744. His schemes were both social and material: 'Thus did the order of human things proceed: first there were forests, then isolated dwellings, whence villages, next cities, and finally academies' (Vico 1982 [1744]: 180). Vico conceived of world history as a sequence of recurring ages: *divine* (characterized by religion, as well as poetry and imagination), *heroic* (by noble heroes, perceived as divine) and *human* (by reason and by civil duty). Rejecting Hobbes's apparent atheism, he did, however, return to the medieval concern with divine providence as an evolutionary inducement. And while his works were important in Neapolitan thought, they were hardly read at all beyond Naples until long after his death. They became 'important' only in the twentieth century, and in terms of the eighteenth century are best understood as products of their time, however original, and not as carrying much influence.

The latter half of the eighteenth century saw developments in social theory, or 'moral philosophy' as it was called, and also in natural history. It also saw much better lines of communication among scientists and scholars across Europe. Yet it is important not to take for granted what we know today. For example, many intellectuals, including Vico, believed that 'giants' had once roamed the earth, but denied travellers' reports of 'pygmies' in Africa or Asia. And very importantly, eighteenth-century writers often used words like 'species', 'nature', 'savage' or even 'man' in senses quite different from our usage today.

Take the term 'Orang Outang', whose usage, especially in the works of Scottish judge Lord Monboddo (e.g. 1793), is revealing (and I use his eighteenth-century spelling to designate his concept, which was not at all the same as the modern notion of an orang-utan). 'Orang Outang' was in the eighteenth century widely employed to mean great apes generally: chimpanzees and orang-utans (gorillas were then unknown in Europe), while the word 'ape' usually meant what we refer to today as the baboon. Furthermore, the eighteenth-century image of such creatures was coloured by stories of their habits, which may or may not have been true descriptions: hut-building, tool use, fire-making and even 'a sense of honour' in the case of Orang Outangs (e.g. Monboddo 1795: 27). Monboddo was famous among commentators on the *humanity* of Orang Outangs. He wrote twelve rambling volumes on a variety of subjects, and several of these touch on the issue. His arguments tested questions such as the relative importance of language and tool-making as defining characteristics of humanity, and they probed problems in what today would be called theories of mind. Arguably, Rousseau and Linnaeus also believed the Orang Outang to be 'a man', or at least, in Linnaean terms, of the genus *Homo* (see Barnard 2000: 18–22), although these far more famous writers never probed this issue quite as far as did Monboddo (Barnard 1995a, 1995b).

Feral children were perceived as both *pre*-linguistic and *a*-social. They occupied much attention in the semi-popular writings of the day, and also offered tests for any number of theories of the nature of the human species. Wild Peter of Hanover was the most celebrated (see, e.g. Monboddo 1795: 25–34). Peter was found in 1725, was brought to England, and lived to an old age on a pension provided by George I, George II and George III. He never did learn to say more than a few words, but was studied by intellectuals of the time in order to give them insight into natural, pre-linguistic thought. Memmie Le Blanc, the 'wild girl' of Champagne, was equally interesting, being both feral and 'savage'. She is believed to have been a Native North American, brought as a child-slave first to the West Indies and subsequently to France. In the 1760s, she dictated her memoirs, and parts were published in the fourth volume of Monboddo's *Antient metaphysics* (1795: 403–8).

The first presumed prehistoric ape-man to be found was *Homo diluvia testis* (literally 'Man, witness of the flood'), unearthed in Baden in 1726 (see, e.g., Haddon 1910: 70). Yet this creature turned out not to be a man at all, but a giant salamander. A hundred years later the specimen was to be renamed first *Salamandra scheuchzeri* and then *Andrias scheuchzeri* ('Image of man, of Scheuchzer'), after the discoverer. The story is of interest because it shows the state of understanding at the time. Fossils were, simply, not important in a world where living apes, feral children and 'savages' defined the boundary between our species and others, and gave the clues scholars needed as to whether humans are naturally social or naturally solitary. The *solitary* versus *social* debate on human nature dominated discussion in what would today be called political philosophy, from Hobbes (e.g. 1996 [1651]) to Rousseau (e.g. 1973 [1750–62]) and after. In a certain sense, then, the social anthropology of human origins actually preceded mainstream biological concerns with origins. Linnaeus, Buffon, Camper, Blumenbach, Cuvier and others in the eighteenth and early nineteenth centuries all lacked the comparative evolutionary understanding we take for granted today, and the very idea of fossils of long-extinct animals was far more alien to eighteenth-century thought than was that of a feral child found alone, or in the company of wolves.

The nineteenth century

As naturalist on the voyage of HMS *Beagle*, Charles Darwin spent nearly five years from 1831 to 1836 sailing around the world recording what he encountered and collecting specimens. He published his theory of natural selection in his most famous work, *On the origin of species* (Darwin 1859), and twelve years later turned his attention to its implications for human evolution in *The descent of man* (Darwin 1871). In the latter, Darwin argued that human social life is rooted in that of the primates, and that from this basis humanity has evolved the cognitive skills that produced language, complex and co-operative forms of social organization and increasing moral awareness. He believed that some branches of the human species were superior to others, and that environmental adaptation and natural selection have produced 'racial' variation in these respects. This 'Darwinian' or 'evolutionist' view is often contrasted to the medieval and indeed eighteenth-century understanding of the 'Great Chain of Being' (see, e.g., Lovejoy 1936), which was hierarchical but static – lacking any mechanism or even any possibility for moving from a more primitive to a more advanced biological form.

Darwin's approach may also be contrasted to that of Jean-Baptise Lamarck. Like others of his time, Lamarck accepted the notion that acquired characteristics could be inherited. This 'Lamarckian' view is expressed most clearly in his 'second law of nature':

All the acquisitions or losses wrought by nature on individuals, through the influence of the environment in which their race has long been placed, and hence through the influence of the predominant use or permanent disuse of any organ; all these are preserved by reproduction to the new individuals which arise, provided that the acquired modifications are common to both sexes, or at least to the individuals which produce the young. (Lamarck 1914 [1809]: 113)

Darwinian theory, though, might as easily be contrasted to Monboddo's. Far from being a 'forerunner of Darwin', as is often said, Monboddo embodies an otherwise never-fully realized eighteenth-century vision which is the antithesis of Darwin. If in probing the boundaries of 'man' Monboddo defined the 'Orang Outang' as part of the category, Darwin did the opposite: he defined 'man' as an 'ape' (figure 1.1). Linnaeus came close to seeing both sides of the problem that would haunt Darwin when

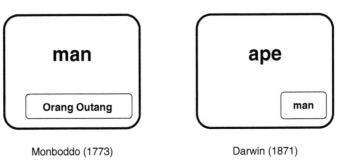

Figure 1.1 Images of the relation between 'man' and 'Orang Outang' (ape)

the former wrote, in a letter: 'But, if I had called man an ape, or vice versa, I should have fallen under the ban of all the ecclesiastics. It may be that as a naturalist I ought to have done so' (Linnaeus to J. G. Gmelin, 14 Feb. 1747; quoted in Slotkin 1965: 180).

The most famous find of human palaeontology was also the first to be generally recognized, and the most disputed. In 1856 workmen quarrying lime discovered a skeleton they presumed to be that of a cave bear in the Neander Valley near Düsseldorf. At first they discarded the bones, but the quarry manager saved them and showed them to a local teacher named Johann Carl Fuhlrott. Fortunately, Fuhlrott had read of the discovery, in 1847, of specimens of what is now known as the gorilla. Like the gorilla, the Neander skull had high brow ridges but was otherwise human-looking. Fuhlrott and anatomist Hermann Schaaffhausen announced the discovery of *Homo neanderthalensis* in 1847 (see, e.g. Trinkaus and Shipman 1994). The common name is either Neanderthal, or using modern German orthography, Neandertal (meaning 'Neander Valley'). Specimens had been discovered but not recognized, earlier in the century in Belgium and in Gibraltar, and by the end of the century hundreds of bones had been found, often in association with flint hand axes and points of the Mousterian tool industry. Some scholars doubted the authenticity of the finds, not least because the implied biological evolution did not seem to accord with biblical expectation. Neanderthal was variously said to have been an ape, a deformed member of *H. sapiens* or a recently deceased Cossack soldier from the Napoleonic Wars. In the twentieth century, the species name *Homo sapiens neanderthalensis* came into common use, as its similarities to *H. sapiens sapiens* became clear. The tendency in recent years, however, is to return to the traditional designation *H. neanderthalensis* (and the Linnaean Latin is not altered by the German spelling change). The first draft of the Neanderthal genome was completed only in 2009, and it suggests that the two species remained quite separate through a long history of coexistence.

Among other important fossil discoveries in Europe was 'Cro-Magnon Man', in 1868. Cro-Magnon is a rock shelter in the Dordogne Valley of France. The name no longer has any scientific significance, because 'Cro-Magnon' people are now known to have been fully modern *H. sapiens* – albeit *H. sapiens* who lived at the same time as Neanderthals. Yet in the nineteenth century, the find was deemed important, not least because the skeletons of five 'cave people' had been unearthed, buried in association with ivory pendants and carved antlers, as well as stone tools. It also seemed to show France as an early point of origin for humanity, and debates ensued on the relative significance of Neanderthal and Cro-Magnon for building a picture of human evolution (see Trinkaus and Shipman 1994: 110–11, 178–9).

It is worth noting that the debate was then still alive between monogenesis (a single origin for all humankind) and polygenesis (a multiple origin). In England, monogenic theory emerged as victorious with Darwin's *Descent of man* (published in 1871) and with the merger of the mainly polygenist Anthropological Society of London and the mainly monogenist Ethnological Society of London to form the Anthropological Institute (also in 1871). Darwin himself was not just a naturalist, but also a member of the Ethnological Society, and indeed one who had a personal objection to the perceived polygenist term 'anthropological'. However, polygenic theory was still strong on the Continent, where Darwinian thought had yet to penetrate as deeply as in England and Scotland. Evolutionism as we know it is dependent on acceptance of the monogenic thesis: one origin for humankind. British, and, to a lesser extent, American, French, German and Swiss, social anthropologists, through the last half of the nineteenth century, debated such things as: which came first, matrilineal descent or patrilineal? What was the earliest religion, animism or fetishism? Is early religion a reflection of early society, or does religious belief mould the social order?

Social anthropology or ethnology (as it was more usually known) was emerging as a discipline, but it was almost entirely composed of amateurs. Amateurs were not constrained by the boundaries of academic subjects in the way that professionals were. Some of the individuals who practised ethnology, most famously the banker Sir John Lubbock (later Lord Avebury), were also prominent in archaeology. Among other twists of fate, the foremost ethnologist of the late nineteenth century, Sir Edward Burnett Tylor, met Henry Christie while travelling in Cuba in 1856, and Christie persuaded him to accompany him to Mexico. Christie, like Lubbock a banker, ethnologist and archaeologist, was among the first to suggest that extinct ice-age mammals (whose bones were found alongside stone tools on cave floors) had lived at the same time as our prehistoric human ancestors. (He was also, incidentally, the banker who helped pay for excavations that led to the discovery of Cro-Magnon Man.) Ethnology, unlike archaeology, had not yet developed as a fieldwork subject, and the theorists rarely had experience of the peoples they wrote about. Ethnographic observation depended instead on travellers' reports, but perhaps for this reason the separation of theory and ethnography favoured the development of the speculative science of imagined social evolution (see also Barnard 2000: 27–46).

In 1879, an amateur archaeologist uncovered the magnificent Upper Palaeolithic paintings of Altamira Cave in northern Spain. Their significance was rejected by many, who assumed either that they were more recent than Palaeolithic or even that they were forgeries. Yet other discoveries followed, and the archaeological establishment retracted their objections in the early years of the twentieth century (see, e.g., Lewis-Williams 2002: 18–40). It was not until 1940 that the site of Lascaux, in the Dordogne, gave France a site of equal brilliance. Rock art, though, had already come into its own in the early twentieth century, and gained in prominence in the study of human origins with late twentieth-century concerns with the origin of symbolic culture among early *Homo sapiens*, especially in Africa.

In the second half of the nineteenth century, much interest rested on which was the origin of humankind before *H. sapiens*: Asia, Africa or indeed a now-submerged continent in between. Europe was not really in the running. Darwin favoured Africa, but he was in the minority. Ernst Haeckel famously championed Asia, and that theory held sway. In the absence of fossil evidence, Haeckel speculated on the hypothetical 'missing link', which he called *Pithecanthropus alalus*. He was also responsible for the notion that 'ontogeny replicates phylogeny', for popularizing the idea of human evolution as a line of progress from earlier forms to *H. sapiens*, and even for helping to shape the public image of Darwinism in Britain (Bowler 1989: 154–8). Haeckel's hypothetical creature became reality in 1891, with Eugène Dubois's find 'Java Man'.

Eugène Dubois was a Dutch medical doctor. When he seemed destined for a professorship in anatomy, Dubois realized that 'he loathed teaching and was becoming disenchanted with anatomy' (Trinkaus and Shipman 1994: 134). He set off for East Indies and arrived on Sumatra in late 1887. He published on evolutionary theory, and soon began examining fossils on Java. His break came when, in 1891, he discovered fossils of the species first, briefly, labelled *Anthropithecus erectus*, then *Pithecanthropus erectus*, which he believed stood in evolutionary terms between the apes and *H. sapiens*. They are now known as *Homo erectus*. One fossilized femur and a skull (not necessarily from the same individual) remained virtually intact, and Dubois kept them under his bed for many years. He died in the Netherlands in 1940, and his grave is marked with a tombstone depicting the skull of *Pithecanthropus* and *both* femurs, crossed (Leakey and Slikkerveer 1993: 162).

The twentieth century

When the 'discovery' of Piltdown Man was announced in December 1912 (Smith Woodward 1913), England could lay claim to the missing link. Those who were soon to comment so favourably on Piltdown knew perfectly well that a human-like skull had been found in association with an ape-like jaw, but it took decades before anyone suggested, let alone proved, that they could not have been from the same animal. The early debate was not on forgery, but on the significance of the Piltdown bones for human prehistory. The earliest challenges, in a way, actually preceded the 'discovery': the eminent archaeologist Sir John Evans had in 1877 urged 'caution, caution, caution' in any dealings with the Eolithic or 'Dawn Stone Age': 'It is now no longer difficult to get evidence accepted as to the antiquity of man. The danger rather lies in the other direction, and we are liable to have evidence brought forward relating to discoveries bearing upon the subject which is hardly trustworthy' (quoted in Spencer 1990: 13).

The direct challenge to Piltdown was not from within British archaeology but from a foreign camp. Just over a decade later, Raymond Dart, an Australian anatomist working in South Africa, announced the discovery of *Australopithecus africanus* (Dart 1925). Perhaps he had a vested interest in finding the earliest human ancestor outside of Britain, but the British archaeological establishment had a vested interest in finding it in their own soil. They hailed Piltdown as overthrowing the ancestral claims of Neanderthal Man and Java Man, and they denounced the new foreign rival in similar terms. 'Dart's child', they said, was simply a juvenile ape and not a human ancestor at all (Keith *et al.* 1925). As Robert Ardrey (1963: 26) wrote: 'Piltdown Man combined perfectly the elements visualized by anthropology – by English anthropology in particular – as essential to threshold man. There was the ape jaw, and there was the bulging human cranium, source of all future evolutionary glory. The unknown perpetrator of the fraud had provided science with just what science wanted.' The British archaeological establishment was not about to abrogate the title 'noblest savage' to an African ape. We now know that Dart was right and the British were wrong. Even if we take the debate at face value and admit the likelihood that each protagonist was acting as a dispassionate observer, we must nevertheless admit that the theories these scientists maintained conjure images as well as connect facts. These images, in turn, become internalized and today form part of both the folklore and the science of the story of human origins (see, e.g., Lewin 1989: 47–84; Reader 1988: 79–90, 112–31).

It would take until 1974 to give final proof of *bones before brain* – when a member of Donald Johanson's team found 'Lucy', with her ape-like skull atop a modern skeleton, in the low-lying Afar Region of northern Ethiopia. Johanson's first book on 'Lucy' (Johanson and Edey 1981) gives a splendid account not only of that discovery, but also of the complications of palaeo-anthropological field research, post-excavation work and interpretation of the results. In the end, 'Lucy', or *Australopithecus afarensis*, appeared to be ancestral both to *A. africanus* and to the various species of *Homo*. It also confirmed Dart's belief that australopithecines walked upright. Apart from 'Lucy', several other australopithecine species have been discovered and described. All were found in southern or eastern Africa, and nowhere else. Palaeo-anthropologists now usually classified them as members of two separate genera *Australopithecus* (gracile australopithecines, some five species including *A. africanus* and *A. afarensis*) and *Paranthropus* (robust australopithecines, some three species). The designations have shifted as 'lumpers' and 'splitters' have battled out not only the names but also the classifications of fossils, according to greater or lesser resemblances to other fossils.

There are three main areas where hominin fossils have been found: South Africa and neighbouring countries, the Rift Valley of Tanzania and Kenya (including Olduvai or Oldupai Gorge) and Ethiopia (especially the Afar Region). South Africa came to prominence in human palaeontology through Dart's work and that of his successor as Professor of Anatomy at the University of the Witwatersrand, Phillip Tobias. What is usually called Olduvai Gorge became known to Western science only in 1911, when a German butterfly collector fell upon it. It was officially renamed Oldupai (which is phonetically more correct) in 2005, although among palaeontologists the old spelling still seems to dominate. Through the twentieth century a succession of fossil and stone tool discoveries were made in the layers along this forty kilometre ravine, which lies in northern Tanzania. Most prominent among its field researchers are members of the Leakey family, including Louis (who started work there in 1931) and Mary, and their son Richard. Afar is an administrative region of Ethiopia, and much of it comprises a deep depression which is an extension of the Rift Valley. Johanson and a number of others have worked there since the early 1970s.

The fossil finds and associated archaeological discoveries will be described in slightly more depth in chapter 3, but the issues of classification deserve brief mention here. In the early 1960s the Leakeys discovered fossils that became known as *Homo habilis* (Leakey, Tobias and Napier 1964). This was the supposedly first tool-making species, although later developments were to call this into question. The subsequent *H. erectus* came to be recognized as the longest-lived hominin species (roughly from 1,800,000 to 1,000,000 years ago). Eventually, its earliest, African form was given the separate species name of *H. ergaster*, and debates ensued about whether to separate the African form as a distinct species (as advocated by Ian Tattersall, for example), or to classify African, Southeast Asian, Eastern Asian and European forms all as *H. erectus* (as advocated by Richard Leakey). Debates also ensued as to whether early *Homo* was more like *Austalopithecus* or more like modern *Homo* in social organization and cognitive abilities (see, e.g., Coolidge and Wynn 2009: 107–50).

Meanwhile, social and cultural anthropology were developing in Europe and North America. These developments were to a large extent quite separate from the activities of palaeo-anthropologists working in Africa. Or indeed in Asia, where discoveries, for example, of the *Homo erectus* specimens of 'Peking Man' in the 1920s kept the idea of Asian origins alive. In Europe, ethnology or social anthropology became quite distinct disciplines from palaeo-anthropology. The two fields were rarely taught within the same university department, and unlike in the nineteenth century, in the twentieth very few practitioners became competent in both. Especially in German-speaking countries (and to some extent in England), diffusionism became a dominant theoretical force. In terms of its explanation of social development, diffusionism is logically the opposite of evolutionism. Social evolutionists assume a progressive chain of events which may occur in different places, either simultaneously or not. Diffusionists look for common points of origin, and assume that things are invented only once (see Barnard 2000: 47–60).

One outgrowth of diffusionism was the idea of the 'culture area'. This became a common focus in North American anthropology, which owes its origins to Franz Boas and several other German immigrants, and children of German immigrants who had been exposed to German-language ideas in their reading, if not in their early training. Boas taught at Columbia University from 1896 to 1936. His department there included both cultural anthropology and physical anthropology, and Boas took an interest in both, although his main specialization was the culture area known as the Northwest Coast, including its art, material culture and mythology. 'Cultures', it was noted, do not occur randomly, but in areas found along with similar 'cultures' – often in a specific environmental region. Each will be similar to its neighbours, perhaps with similar subsistence (for example, hunting, gathering and salmon-fishing in the Northwest Coast), similar social organization (hierarchical, with chiefs), similar religion (totemism and a rich mythology), similar customs (the ceremonial feasting-giving system known as the potlatch), and so on. Apart from the idea of the culture area, Boasian anthropology also introduced a theoretical perspective (or set of perspectives) known as relativism (Barnard 2000: 99–119). Among its varieties, linguistic relativism emphasized the fact that languages were complex in diverse ways and 'primitive' peoples such as hunter-gatherers did not necessarily speak primitive languages.

In the United Kingdom and a number of other countries, functionalist and structural-functionalist traditions came to dominate for at least the first half of the twentieth century, with structuralism and allied traditions coming later. As with Boasian relativism, the emphasis was on understanding contemporary society, but with social action and organization, or relations between institutions, or (in the case of structuralism) relations between symbolic forms, the key foci. Interpretivism followed, with its emphasis of the 'translation' of culture, and social anthropology thus drifted further away from scientific credibility (see Barnard 2000: 158–77).

Among the most important scientific developments in the later twentieth century were advances in genetics. These showed quite definitively that *Homo sapiens* originated in Africa, and did not emerge from previous migrations, of *Homo erectus*, for example. 'Out of Africa' because the dominant model, especially after the decisive paper by Rebecca Cann, Mark Stoneking and Allan Wilson (1987). In that paper, they argued on the basis of mitochondrial DNA samples from 147 widely dispersed people that, except for Africa, each part of the world was colonized repeatedly. All living humanity is descended matrilineally from a single woman who lived in Africa about 200,000 years ago.

The twenty-first century

The most intriguing discovery thus far in the twenty-first century must be the diminutive 'Hobbit', *Homo floresiensis*, found in 2003 on the island of Flores in eastern Indonesia (Brown *et al.* 2004). Later finds indicate that this hominin lived as recently as 12,000 years ago. Given that *H. sapiens* arrived in Flores between 35,000 and 55,000 years ago, this means that the two species must have had contact or at least have been aware of each other's presence.

Even more important from a social anthropological point of view are new discoveries from southern Africa which hint at an early origin of art, body decoration, symbolism and broadly of symbolic behaviour. Particularly important is Blombos Cave, on the Indian Ocean coast of South Africa. That site boasts several pieces of incised red ochre which were not only decorated, but also apparently stored and brought from elsewhere. The original announcement (Henshilwood *et al.* 2002) was of two pieces dating from 77,000 years ago, but several recent finds are similar and some are dated to around 100,000 years ago. This suggests a continuous artistic tradition lasting at least 23,000 years. Blombos has also yielded the earliest beadwork: forty-one perforated shells with wear patterns indicating they were in contact with string or clothing. These date from about 75,000 years ago (Henshilwood *et al.* 2004).

Social and cultural anthropology

The discipline from which I come is generally called 'cultural anthropology' in North America, South America, Japan, etc. It is called 'social anthropology', or sometimes 'social and cultural anthropology', in Europe, Australia, Africa and elsewhere. In the United States and Canada, and occasionally elsewhere, cultural anthropology coexists with physical or biological anthropology, prehistoric archaeology and anthropological linguistics in 'four-field' departments. Yet the four subdisciplines actually operate as separate disciplines. There are few true 'general anthropologists', and very, very few who can claim competence in more than two of the subdisciplines.

In the 1980s and 1990s, the concept of society came in for criticism among politicians and social scientists alike – nowhere more than in Britain. Marilyn Strathern (1996), undoubtedly one of the two most prominent of all British anthropologists of her generation, was among those who argued that society does not exist. A few years later, Adam Kuper (1999), the other most prominent British anthropologist of that generation, set loose his critique of the concept of 'culture'. His criticism was directed especially at usage in American anthropology, where ever since the late nineteenth century 'culture' in its plural form held sway as the dominant topic of the discipline. In the relativist vision of American anthropology, peoples had 'cultures', and these exhibited almost endless variety and variation. The problem, for Kuper, was that 'culture' as a concept was too constraining, too powerful, in determining the action of individuals. We return to this issue in chapter 5.

I consider myself essentially a social anthropologist in the European sense, and I believe in society. In America I am happy to call myself a cultural anthropologist. Yet I agree with Kuper that 'cultures' are at best problematic abstractions. At worst, in Kuper's understanding, 'culture' is a euphemism for race, and it is no accident that the term was used in this way in the 'old' South Africa of racism and apartheid. That is what Kuper aims to avoid. However, in my usage here, there are no cultures. Rather, 'culture' is that which embraces the whole of humanity – that entity beyond biology which embodies human thought, arts and sciences and understanding. In other words, I prefer to think only of 'Culture' with a capital 'C', or if you like, of symbolic culture – that entity that underlies verbal, musical and pictorial expression, religion and science and the moral values shared by humanity as a whole. In this book, culture will be used only in that sense, and not as a count noun (a culture, this culture or that, French culture or Aboriginal culture), except very occasionally, when referring to the ideas of others. Cultural anthropology is the discipline or subdiscipline beyond the biological, and its subject is humanity's shared, created symbolic world. Of course, this world differs 'culturally' from people to people, but the shared is more important than what is different.

How can social anthropology contribute to the study of human origins, given that our ethnographic data can only show results of present-day, and not past, societies? There are two answers. In the first instance, it is important that social anthropology does not just include ethnographic data: the discipline also provides ways of thinking about data from other subjects, and it includes a wealth of theoretical ideas and understandings built up through the last century and a half of practice.

The second reason is that social anthropology is no different from any other subject in its application of inference. An archaeologist does not directly observe the past any more than we do. A fossilized bone must be interpreted, and ideas from social anthropology are just as relevant as any other ideas: I would say often more relevant. A psychologist who observes communication by chimpanzees or human children and makes inferences about early hominins based on the comparison is in no better position than we are, using our pre-existing cross-cultural comparative focus or our theories. Of course, contemporary hunter-gatherers are not necessarily like some form of pre-human and should not be used uncritically as models, but then neither are chimps or children. Inference is just that. I believe it is best used to specific ends, for example when attempting to think about practices like sharing. It is not that early hunter-gatherers did anything exactly like what contemporary hunter-gatherers do, but rather that having a knowledge of sharing among hunter-gatherers gets us closer to a theory of sharing. Comparing hunter-gatherers to non-hunter-gatherers advances that theory. However distant present-day hunter-gatherers may be from past ones, present-day non-hunter-gatherers are more distant – not in mentality or abilities, but specifically in economic activities, and in those forms of social organization, and sometimes cultural values too, which are directly related to these.

I argue throughout this book for the use of social anthropological ideas in the study of human origins. Not only does social anthropology have something to say to archaeology and biological anthropology on that important topic, but the exploration of the topic could be of benefit to other concerns within social anthropology. A greater interest in human origins among social anthropologists could focus our attention on boundaries between egalitarian and non-egalitarian societies, for example, and give us insights into egalitarianism, sharing, morality, social hierarchy and exchange.

It is worth considering why there is yet no subdiscipline of the social anthropology of human origins. Actually, although I am disappointed that there is none, the absence of such a field does not really surprise me. Let me suggest three interrelated reasons. First, the existence of such a field would require individual anthropologists to acquire specialist knowledge in some branch of the field and not simply the ability to have an overview of the kind I enjoy in this book. But how can one have such a specialized knowledge? No social anthropologist could reasonably claim to be a specialist in, say, the social organization of *Homo erectus* societies. Nor could one easily claim, say, to specialize in prehistoric kinship systems without also having worked ethnographically with one or more living kinship systems.

Secondly, there can be no expertise in human origins without considerable dependence on geneticists, evolutionary psychologists, linguists, archaeologists, anatomists, primatologists, and so on, for the data set (and even to some extent the interpretation of that data) that underlies the field. In other words, the field could not be an autonomous branch of social anthropology; it would have to depend too much on other subjects. That said, the potential might exist for social anthropologists to do their own field research alongside practitioners in other fields. I see this as a likely possibility in conjunction with primatology or possibly linguistics, but less likely with the other subjects. Still, how would a young Ph.D. student, with no ethnographic experience among humans, justify taking a purely theoretical social anthropological training off to a troop of chimps to study grooming, sharing, exchange or some other form of social interaction?

Thirdly, there is no obvious career trajectory for an expertise in the social anthropology of human origins. If we are dependent on our biological or primatological colleagues for data, then we cannot reasonably do a Ph.D. in the field. If one is not permitted the specialization until an advanced stage of one's career, then the field is not really self-replicating. If ethnography is required first, then what kind of ethnography would it have to be? If hunter-gatherer ethnography is required, then the field would in fact be a subfield of hunter-gatherer studies and possibly be dependent on more general findings and even debates within hunter-gatherer studies. And hunter-gatherer studies is today dependent on the existence of a reasonable degree of 'hunter-gatherer' behaviour or ideology in the wake of varying subsistence activities on the part of so-called 'hunter-gatherer' peoples, who only very, very rarely today subsist by hunting or gathering activities alone.

This book is an attempt to apply ideas from social or cultural anthropology to answer questions on the cultural and social life of our ancestors. It is not only ethnographic data that are relevant here, but also, and very importantly, the theoretical insights gained through the study of contemporary and recent past societies. I believe that these can help us understand the distant past. Chapter 2 and chapter 3 concern mainly the basics of human origins studies: what other disciplines tell us about higher primates and about fossil hominins and stone tools. Chapter 4 concerns the relationship between brain size and group size, and also ideas and data from social anthropology about migration and the settlement patterns of hunter-gatherer groups. Chapter 5 deals with classic themes in economic anthropology, especially of the economic anthropology of hunter-gatherers, and aims to put these together with data from primate studies and material from archaeology. Chapter 6 explores the origin of language in light of social anthropological ideas on symbolism, mythology and ritual; and chapter 7 takes up relevant ideas from kinship theory. Chapter 8 deals with my own synthesis, especially of my thoughts on the origin and prehistory of communication and kinship. I offer this not as *the* theory of everything, but as an example of the way ideas from social anthropology can be brought to bear in studies of human origins.

2 If chimps could talk

Social anthropology is, by definition, the study of human society. But what if we were to broaden the definition to take in chimpanzee society as well? And what if we could extrapolate from studies that have been made of chimpanzee society (by primatologists, not by social anthropologists) and compare these to studies of human society, with a view to understanding the evolution of the human species from the time of our common ancestor with the chimpanzee? After all, social anthropology is by nature comparative. We understand the lifestyles of any given part of humanity through comparison to the lifestyles of other peoples or ethnic groups. Why not do the same for humanity as a whole, through comparison to the ways of hominid cousins? And what if we consider also insights from the last 150 years of social anthropological theory, and bring these in along with theoretical perspectives from primatology, psychology and other fields, to inform our understandings? Anthropological theory has hardly ever been used in the study of chimpanzees, and is still very little used in any coherent way in studies of human evolution.

For many biological anthropologists, studies of bonobos and common chimpanzees, both in the wild and experimentally, are the key to hominin or hominid evolution (that of humans and our ancestors). It has been known since the 1960s that chimps make tools for activities such as extracting termites from their nests, and there is compelling new evidence that chimps even make spears which they use to hunt other primates. Thus 'culture', particularly material culture, is not confined to humans. There are indeed cultural differences between groups; chimps in the harsh environment of Gombe seem to have more tool-making skills than those of the easier environment of Budongo. This might suggest environmental (as opposed to genetic) influence in the evolution of culture. Also, experiments with Kanzi and other bonobos have revealed a great deal about thought processes and language skills of these creatures. Again, what we once assumed were characteristics unique to humans turn out to be common too to our closest 'animal' cousins.

But what is a hominin? A hominid? The question has no clear, agreed answer. The different viewpoints are shown in figures 2.1 (a), (b) and (c). With molecular studies and re-classifications in taxonomy, at least some biologists since the 1990s now consider chimps as well as humans as among the hominins. Mann and Weiss (1996), for example, suggested a classification for living great apes like that illustrated in figure 2.1 (b). This not only includes chimps (*Pan*) among the hominins, but gorillas (the genus *Gorilla*) and orang-utans (*Pongo*) among the hominids. In the same year, Maurice Goodman (1996) suggested a more radical classification, putting chimpanzees and humans in the same subtribe: Hominina, as shown in figure 2.1 (c). Traditionally, at least before the 1980s and 1990s, only humans and our ancestors were classified as hominids (the family Hominidae), with the great apes distinguished as pongids (the family Pongidae) within the superfamily Homonoidea. This is the scheme illustrated in figure 2.1 (a). Some prehistorians prefer an in-between classification, more inclusive than the traditional one but less inclusive than that of modern biologists, with only humans and human ancestors back to the australopithecines among the hominins. The differences stem in part from the significance each faction attaches to the great adaptational and behavioural changes in the *Homo* line since its divergence from the *Pan* line less than 7,000,000 years ago, and especially since what is sometimes known as the 'human revolution' or 'symbolic revolution'. Basically, no matter how close chimpanzees and humans may be at the level of molecular biology, only humans have (full) language, symbolism, mythology and ritual. Chimps do not.

Reflections on shared ancestors and cousins

Humans are, of course, not descended from chimpanzees, any more than chimpanzees are descended from humans. Rather, we share common ancestors, the most recent example of which could be *Sahelanthropus tchadensis*, known from the fossilized remains of a single cranium and some fragments of a lower jaw and teeth discovered in 2001 and 2002 in northern Chad. The fossil has not been precisely dated, but estimates based on comparative dates of associated deposits suggest that the creature lived between 7,400,000 and 6,500,000 years ago (Sarmiento 2007: 29–33).

More interestingly, an early ancestor of humans, but not of chimpanzees, helps us to understand the striking differences between our line of descent and that of the chimps. These differences imply that chimps have evolved and adapted to their habitats, just as we have to ours. This ancestor is *Ardipithecus ramidus* (4,400,000 years old), discovered in

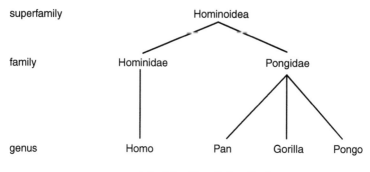

(a) A 'traditional' classification

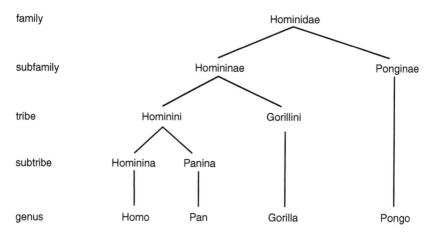

(b) A re-classification (Mann and Weiss 1996)

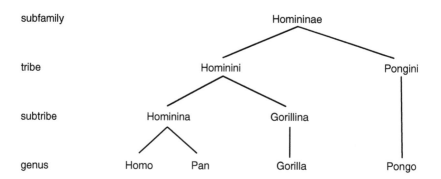

(c) A more radical re-classification (Goodman 1996)

Figure 2.1 Classifications of living human and great ape species

1992, described and named *Australopithecus ramidus* in 1994, renamed *Ardipithecus ramidus* in 1995. Further fossils of another *Ardipithecus* species were found in the late 1990s. Definitive research articles on the original find were only published in 2009 in a special issue of *Science* (e.g. White *et al.* 2009). There, Tim White and his colleagues compare the anatomy of 'Ardi' to that of *Sahelanthropus tchadensis*, which may in fact belong in the same genus, and to that of australopithecines and chimpanzees. They conclude that 'Ardi' walked upright in a woodland environment, but was partly arboreal, unlike fully terrestrial australopithecines. It had already lost the dental characteristic known as the sectoral canine complex (SCC) of mainly herbivorous hominids, and was fully omnivorous. Details of the fossilized skull suggest it had greater mental capacities than its ancestors, but was small-brained – with a skull about the size of that of a bonobo or female common chimp (300–50 centimetres), smaller than that of the smallest australopithecines (e.g. from 375 in the case of 'Lucy').

C. Owen Lovejoy (2009) goes further and notes that the loss of SCC meant that male aggressive displays of the kind found in chimps and gorillas would have been impossible for *Ardipithecus*. He also notes the implications of bipedalism, and speculates, by analogy with modern humans, on supposed concealed ovulation in *Ardipithecus*. Together, these three factors should favour monogamy, a lower rate of reproduction, longer intervals between births, with shorter intervals later as a result of reproductive success, increased parental care for offspring, increased food-for-sex exchanges (of the kind recently observed among chimps), reduced competition for mates among males, the development of multi-male groups for long-distance scavenging. This culminates later in evolutionary time with lithic technology, eventually hunting, increased meat intake, increased brain size, and so on, among *Homo*.

Whatever the truth in the detail of these speculations, there is no doubt that the combination of fossil, living primate and human data can get us closer to understanding human (and primate) evolution. In the case of both primate and human data, comparison of the diverse forms of behaviour within each species should be able to get us much closer still.

Cultural attributes of orangs, gorillas and chimps

Orang-utans

Orang-utans include the species *Pongo pygmaeus* (living on Borneo), and the rarer *P. abelii* or *P. pygmaeus abelii* (living on Sumatra). Other species of Ponginae, now extinct, were once widespread in Southeast

Asia. Orang-utans are the most arboreal of the great apes. They are also the most solitary: except when mating, males and females largely stay apart. They can live to about fifty years in the wild, and reach sexual maturity around twelve. Each evening they build nests in trees. They eat mainly fruit, but also subsist on other plant parts, insects, bird eggs and honey.

Recently, researchers have documented what they cautiously call 'putative cultural variants' among orang-utans (van Schaik et al. 2003). The researchers tried to factor out environmental influence (accounting for possibly five of their variants) and looked specifically for cultural variants whose presence is determined simply by teaching and learning (accounting for nineteen variants). The latter include 'kiss-squeaks' with leaves and with hands (putting leaves or hands on the mouth to amplify squeaking sounds), building nests for social play, erecting covers above nests to keep out rain or sun, using branches to shoo away wasps, making 'gloves' out of leaves to handle spiny fruits, and so on. The researchers further distinguish four kinds of variants, of which orang-utans and chimpanzees have the first three, and humans have all four: 'labels' (e.g. socially induced food preferences or predator recognition), 'signals' (socially transmitted arbitrary innovations such as kiss-squeaks), 'skills' such as tool use and for humans only, 'symbols'. They suggest that symbols are likely to have come into being as 'membership badges' of social units. Apart from this last causative suggestion, for which there is no evidence, van Schaik and his colleagues ably demonstrate their points.

Equally intriguing is the yet more recent study (Dufour et al. 2009) which shows that orang-utans can practise 'calculated reciprocity': the weighing of costs and benefits and keeping track of transactions. In this case, two orang-utans at Leipzig Zoo were given tokens. Each could exchange *the other* orang-utan's tokens (but not their own) for food, and thus had to give tokens to the other for the purpose. This, among a number of other experiments with orang-utans, suggests a high degree of communication skills, other-awareness and natural reciprocity in orangs which may be greater than in chimps.

In sexual behaviour, along with gorillas and chimpanzees (though not gibbons and siamangs, which are monogamous), orang-utans are polygynous. Indeed, orang polygyny is sometimes characterized as 'exploded polygyny' (e.g. Lewin and Foley 2004: 165–6), meaning that individual males maintain defence over the territory of a group of females and their offspring, and these territories are often larger than those of other primates. Still, variation seems to exist, and there are two models to represent the essence of male–female interaction among orangs. These are the 'community model', which sees social organization in terms of exploded polygyny and of residents and transients, and a 'roving male promiscuity model', which is based on male wanderings and a lack of territorial organization (van Schaik and van Hooff 1996).

Gorillas

Gorillas include two species, the western gorilla (*Gorilla gorilla*) found in several countries on the west coast of central Africa, and the eastern gorilla (*G. beringei*), including the mountain subspecies, found in Uganda, Rwanda and the eastern Democratic Republic of Congo. They eat fruit, shoots and leaves. They reach sexual maturity about ten or twelve and can live to be about fifty. Group sizes vary from two to twenty, or according to some sources from five to thirty, and gorillas are polygynous – the 'silverback' male having exclusive control over mature females in a group.

Gorillas were unknown to Western naturalists until 1847, and are still perhaps less studied than other primate species, even since Dian Fossey's pioneering work in Rwanda from the 1960s to the 1980s. There are differences between mountain and lowland gorillas and between eastern and western lowland gorillas in terms of a number of ecological factors. Ecological studies, including comparative ones (e.g. Watts 1996), have shown variability not only in diet but also in foraging effort, seasonal use of foods and territories, overlap versus separation of the territorial use of foraging areas, relations between kinship and group membership, relations among females and mating patterns. Some of these differences are biological, but others are ecological with no necessary genetic component, and others may be, at least in part, defined as cultural. While it is difficult to see how social anthropologists might improve on the collection of the statistical data that go into such findings, nevertheless it seems there may be scope for the exploration of cultural as well as ecological reasons for diversity, and fieldwork input from, for example, ecological anthropologists with a qualitative, culturalist bent may in the future yield a few new insights.

Common chimpanzees and bonobos

Chimpanzees include *Pan troglodytes* (the 'common chimpanzee', found in west, central and east Africa) and the smaller and more gracile *P. paniscus* (the bonobo, found south of the River Congo, in the Democratic Republic of Congo). Research of fossil chimpanzees is in its infancy, but there is a suggestion that they evolved in the Middle Pleistocene along with *Homo* in parts of the Rift Valley (McBrearty and Jablonski 2005).

Common chimpanzees tend to be more aggressive than other higher primates and perhaps therefore less inclined to share or reciprocate, except after grooming (de Waal 1989). Nevertheless, they are apparently capable of understanding the principles of reciprocity and do develop relations of exchange of various kinds, including skills in understanding human communication. While other primates have been taught signs in human sign languages, chimpanzees, and especially bonobos, have an extraordinary ability in this regard. Behaviourally, bonobos differ from common chimps in a number of ways. Bonobos tend to be much less aggressive. They engage in sexual activity, including homosexual activity, to a greater extent. Bonobo society, while possessing alpha-male dominance among males, is nevertheless female-focused in that much in social life revolves around specific females and groups of females. De Waal has suggested that bonobos are emotionally sensitive and have the capacity for empathy and altruism.

Chimpanzees not only use tools; they also make them. Christophe and Hedwige Boesch (1990) reported extensive tool use in the Taï National Park in Côte d'Ivoire, and compared their findings to earlier ones in the Mahale Mountains National Park and at the Gombe Stream National Park, both in Tanzania. Tool-use activities included inserting, probing, cleaning, displaying, pounding and combined activities. Although these activities were dissimilar in each case, the Taï chimps showed greater diversity in tool use in terms of technique, goals, and so on. Genetic and ecological reasons for the diversity were ruled out, and the researchers concluded that the diversity seemed to be largely cultural (see also McGrew 1991).

Yet while chimps may make tools, and show cultural diversity in the ways that they do so and in how they use them, there are crucial differences between chimp tool use and human. What is more, these differences seem to be very ancient – going back to the earliest archaeological record. Thomas Wynn and William McGrew (1989) compared tool use in the east African Oldowan complex, the oldest in the hominin record (2,500,000 BP), with chimpanzee tool culture. They found that while Oldowan tool use falls within the range of capability for chimps, apparently only the Oldowans could carry tools and food for thousands of metres, and only the Oldowans competed for their prey with large carnivores.

Studies among bonobos in the wild are in their infancy, but it does not appear that bonobos are as keen to make tools as other chimps – no doubt for ecological reasons. Of course, Kanzi is quite capable and his skills have shown improvement with time (Schick et al. 1999), but neither he nor his wild cousins have reason to develop techniques for the purpose of acquiring food.

Sharing and reciprocity among chimpanzees

Sharing is the giving of material support, often in the form of subsistence goods, from one human or animal to another. It can generally be distinguished from the more complex idea of exchange. Exchange involves calculated giving and taking of goods or services, not necessarily in equal portion, in equal value or at the same time, but with the expectation of return in some form at some time. Commonly though, researchers among chimpanzees prefer to speak of reciprocity rather than exchange or sharing. And at least in social anthropology (Sahlins 1974: 185–275), 'reciprocity' carries a degree of ambiguity in that it can be either 'generalized' (implying sharing, in humans) or 'balanced' (implying exchange). There is also the potential for 'negative' reciprocity, defined by Sahlins (1974: 195) as 'the unsociable extreme [form of reciprocity]' or 'the attempt to get something for nothing with impunity'. His examples include, presumably in a scale towards the most extreme, actions defined ethnographically under such terms as haggling, barter, gambling, chicanery, theft and other forms of seizure. For humans at least, generalized reciprocity is characteristic of reciprocal relations within the family, especially older towards younger; balanced reciprocity is typical of that within the community; and negative reciprocity is the norm only with enemies (or among gangsters).

When chimpanzee researchers speak of 'reciprocity', often, but not always, they mean a form that can be considered, in Sahlins's terms, 'balanced reciprocity'. The idea of balanced reciprocity implies, if not exchange of things exactly equal in value, then at least exchange of things that are comparable. It may be the act of reciprocity which invites the comparison, rather than the specific worth of the exchange items. Let me take some examples from chimpanzee research in the 2000s.

John Mitani and David Watts (2001) found that wild chimpanzees at Ngogo, in Uganda's Kibali National Park, hunt and share meat, and that they do this frequently. They cite three hypotheses that had been suggested to explain hunting and sharing and set about to test them. The first hypothesis is that chimps hunt so that they can overcome seasonal shortages of food. The second is that male chimps hunt in order to exchange, with females, meat for sex. The third is that they hunt in order to create and keep alliances with other males. The third hypothesis was confirmed: most commonly, the male chimps shared with each other and did this, apparently, strategically and as an aid to 'male bonding'. The first hypothesis failed to be sustained, in that the chimps hunted more in times of abundance than in times of scarcity. The second was not sustained either, in that meat-for-sex exchanges were found to be uncommon and the presence of females in oestrus did not seem to favour hunting activity.

On the other hand, data collected by Cristina Gomes and Christophe Boesch (2009) in the Taï National Park, Côte d'Ivoire, showed that the meat-for-sex hypothesis did predict chimpanzee behaviour, although not quite in the way envisaged by previous researchers. The exchanges were not immediate. Rather, over the twenty-two-month period of their research, the scientists observed that those chimpanzees who shared meat with specific females copulated with them more than with others. The study was rigorous and complex, in that factors such as male and female rank, female gregariousness and female begging behaviour were statistically controlled. In human studies, that is, those by social anthropologists among human populations, this level of control is not generally required. Rather, qualitative controls are used instead, and particularly the subjective experiences of informants. The data may lack quantitative rigour, but nevertheless add through more direct access to the thought and social norms of groups under study. The trick for social anthropologists undertaking work with chimpanzees would be to work out methodologically a way of introducing entry into normative behaviour through observational means.

In an ingenious pair of experiments, Alicia Melis and her colleagues (Melis, Hare and Tomasello 2008) tried to determine whether or not chimps have the capability to remember and make use of the memory of past collaborative efforts in what they call 'contingency-based reciprocity'. The experiments, though, were carried out not of course in a wild population, but among orphaned chimps at the Ngamba Island Chimpanzee Sanctuary on Lake Victoria, in Uganda. They involved locked rooms, a wooden key, empty food bowls, carefully selected 'nice' and 'mean' collaborators, and so on. The conclusions were perhaps not surprising: chimps apparently do have the capability of contingency-based reciprocity, in sometimes deliberately choosing collaborators who had been of help before, but such choices are not of overwhelming significance in their decisions. There are diverse forms of co-operative behaviour among primates, and human co-operative behaviour differs from the others (see van Schaik and Kappeler 2006; Noë 2006). Human behaviour alone would seem to be subject to the problem known as the 'tragedy of the commons'. This supposed problem stems from the theory proposed by biologist Garrett Hardin (1968) that what is good for the individual is not necessarily what is good for society.

When I first proposed my theory of the co-evolution of language and kinship, I had concerns over which came first: sharing or exchange. It seemed to me that sharing had to come first, for a number of reasons – not least the fact that generalized reciprocity within the family is found in nature. All mammal species, by definition, suckle their young. Mammals also share what they kill, and what they scavenge. Non-mammals, birds for example, do this too. Recently, Brian Hare and Suzy Kwetuenda (2010) have reported pro-active acts of sharing with non-kin among bonobos. A hungry, captive bonobo will open a cage door for another bonobo when food is given, so that he or she does not have to dine alone. In their experiments, this was the case even where individuals were from different groups. The findings are particularly interesting, because bonobos are, in fact, normally averse to food loss. There is no apparent reward apart from sharing itself – unless of course the expectation of reciprocation in the future comes in. And even then, sharing would pre-cede exchange.

Chimpanzee culture and cultural diversity

For a social anthropologist, what is really interesting about chimps is not that they are so similar to humans; nor is it that they possess culture. What is really interesting is that chimps possess cultural diversity.

Richard Byrne (2007) expresses an interesting point of view on the matter. He suggests that by cataloguing traits geographically, primatologists are following the methods of 'human ethnography'. He argues further that where examples of technically complex feeding behaviour are widespread in a population, they are likely to be learned and therefore 'cultural'. In contrast, according to his analysis, purely stylistic differences in such behaviour are more likely to be the result of ecological adaptation to specific environments. This separation of environmental influence from learned behaviour has long been sought as a means to identify the latter, in order to consider its implications for human evolution. Complexity of behaviour in the form of a large number of steps required for a task (for example, extracting termites from a nest) is the key.

On the other hand, conventional studies of chimps in the wild (Byrne was concerned with primates more generally) often do attempt the isolation of cultural from environmentally induced traits by other means, and aim to explain cultural differences, even with regard to specific categories of individuals: old and young, or male and female, for example. An example of this is a paper by Boesch and Tomasello (1998), essentially on chimpanzees but with human comparisons, and which looks not only at foraging and tool use, but also at body-oriented behaviour (e.g. building a ground nest or using a fly whisk) and communicative behaviour (e.g. slapping the ground or clapping hands). They attribute human evolution largely to the 'ratchet effect' of advances upon advances in cultural evolution, and some of their critics among the commentators in this article accuse them of overemphasizing the uniqueness of humans in this regard. Chimps, apparently, can also advance through the accumulation of culture traits on top of other culture traits.

There is no doubt that some chimpanzee communities are more culturally advanced than others. Tool use among this species was first discovered by Jane Goodall in the Gombe Stream National Park, in what is now Tanzania, in 1960. She observed chimps there using pieces of grass to remove edible termites from termite mounds. When Louis Leakey heard of the discovery, he famously telegraphed her: 'We must now redefine man, redefine tool, or accept chimpanzees as human!' (see, e.g., Byrne 2001: 162–4).

My only experience of chimpanzees in the wild was a brief stay at the chimpanzee research station in the Budongo Forest of Uganda. In contrast to Gombe chimps, Budongo chimps are uninventive and not terribly culturally evolved. Arguably, they do not need to be. Food is much more plentiful in Budongo than in Gombe. The lazy chimps of Budongo lack the necessity or impetus to develop more sophisticated foraging techniques. They do not need them, because their resources are better, and neither skill nor competition are factors in their social behaviour.

In their 1996 paper 'Why culture is common, but cultural evolution is rare', Boyd and Richerson (2005: 52–65) argue that both the transmission of mental representations of an activity from experienced to inexperienced individuals, and the persistence of these mental representations until such time as they can be passed down to others, are required for cultural evolution. Transmission without persistence, or persistence without transmission, is not enough. Some species (especially *Homo sapiens*), they say, are better than others at effecting this necessary combination. In this and other essays in their collection *The origin and evolution of cultures*, Boyd and Richerson (2005) explain culture as a fundamentally human attribute, and one which is rooted in human biology. Humans alone, at least among living species, possess the psychological capacity to acquire and transmit culture to the extent we do. Chimpanzees may be 'cultural', but they do not come close in this regard.

Reflections on a short visit to Budongo

My visit to Budongo was in 1996, and two years later I wrote a brief commentary on it, and in particular on differences between the methodology of primate studies and social anthropology. The following words are adapted from that account (Barnard 1998).

One thing that struck me was the relatively formal methodology used by primatologists, as compared to that employed in social anthropological studies of human populations. Of course, many anthropologists do use quite sophisticated quantitative methods, but most rely much more on intuition, and are either ignorant or very sceptical (or both) of statistical methods. It seems to me that *intuition* (although it is there with those who design questionnaires, is implicit in predicting which way chimps will go, what they are up to and perhaps even how they think) nevertheless takes a back seat in primatology.

A second factor is intensity of coverage. While some anthropologists involved in human hunter-gatherer studies have tried 'follows' as in primatology, the majority have not. James Woodburn (pers. comm.) once followed an elderly Hadza woman in Tanzania for two weeks – getting up before she did, going to bed after she did; and it exhausted him. Richard Lee (1969) in his famous 'input–output' analysis of what people eat and what work they do, tried to make observations of both activities and calorie intake for an entire Ju/'hoan (!Kung) band, non-stop over an eleven-day period in 1964. Researchers among chimps do this kind of work all the time. It is the basis of their record. The basis of the anthropological record tends to be much more on special events, such as rituals, and on results of question-and-answer sessions, for example, in order to understand ideology and the nature of indigenous knowledge. Lee later did expand his period of observation, perhaps at least partly in order to combat potential criticism that eleven days is rather few. Yet two weeks' or eleven days' work of this kind is far better than the alternative: no days at all. Lee (1968) did also study ritual, for example, and very perceptively, and the combination of fieldwork in both these realms does give an ethnographer a far deeper understanding than many realize. Nevertheless, there was no way that Lee could keep up with a primatologist, just as there was no way a primatologist could aim for the kind of insight into the symbolism of ritual behaviour that Lee gained through qualitative ethnographic fieldwork.

Another thing that struck me in Budongo was the teamwork basis of fieldwork there. Several researchers would chase after or follow together. Even though they knew where the chimps were likely to be, and even though they focused on different chimpanzee individuals, they did their work as a group. The same is true, in a sense, of palaeontologists and archaeologists: they also often work as teams, their funding is provided on the assumption of collaboration among individuals, even if each researcher has a different specialization, and ultimately their publications will be multi-authored. Even their sense of having belonged to the team, in primatology, palaeontology or (though possibly to a lesser extent) archaeology continues beyond the project. Most social anthropologists are not used to this. In social anthropology the essence of fieldwork is one anthropologist alone (or perhaps one anthropologist and his or her family) working with one group of subjects.

Fourthly, a related difference, researchers with chimpanzees do not as a rule live with the chimps. There may, of course, be odd exceptions: Jane Goodall at Gombe may have come close to this, and I would also except laboratory studies of chimps and language. Anthropologists do tend to live as much as they can both *with* and *like* their subjects. There is a hidden similarity here: both researchers at stations like Budongo and social anthropologists in the field work with their groups in what we might call the groups' 'natural' surroundings. Yet they *do* it differently: primatologists with methods based heavily on observation, if with some intuition, and social anthropologists with methods based on a complex combination of intuition, interaction (especially linguistic) and observation.

The 'bread and butter' of both disciplines – social anthropology almost as much as primate studies – is in the record of the group. Generalization is from the individual to the level of group, and perhaps in the case of chimps, to generalization for the species as a whole. Questions which confront both disciplines simultaneously also tend to be at the level of the species, and they tend to be the grander questions. One basic area of discussion, common in Western discourse from time to time ever since Aristotle, is the notion of the human species as being at once both solitary and gregarious – an idea picked up by seventeenth- and particularly eighteenth-century writers on human and 'ape' (whether monkey or baboon) society. These fundamentals remain with us. Chimpanzee studies can help social anthropologists, but only if we want to indulge in this very grand level of social theory.

Therefore, one way that I can see that primatologists can help social anthropologists, and indeed such anthropologists can help primatologists, is to share our conjectures and rekindle our dying flame of interest in the grander issues of human and animal relations. This interest was there at the beginning of our disciplines, and undoubtedly it was there in many of us when we began our university careers. In other words, I think both disciplines would benefit from some collective reflection on older, grander and altogether simpler issues of the kind that led us to look at anthropology or primatology in the first place – fascination with the richness of the human species, fascination with the diversity of cultures and what it is to be human or to be nearly human. The time may be right for the ninetenth- and twentieth-century notion that humans are apes to give way again to the notion, well known in the eighteenth century, that apes *are* (similar to) humans – at least enough like humans to deserve both social anthropological methodology and, more importantly, human compassion. The latter is already present among all the researchers I know who have worked at Budongo.

So what of the chimps as objects of research? Unfortunately, I was not present at Budongo at a time of intense social activity among them, or at a time when they were on the ground for very long (during my stay, they were mostly in the trees). However, I spent several days closely observing them with binoculars, talking with Budongo's expert staff, both Ugandan and foreign, and applying my social and cultural anthropological background to the understanding of these fascinating creatures. It may sound grand, but I was looking for the roots of human behaviour, and at the same time, for ways in which chimps are different from humans.

My interest in hunter-gatherer studies poses one fundamental question which is worth addressing here. Are chimps in any sense more like hunter-gatherers than they are like other human beings? The answer is both 'no' and 'yes'. 'No', because the possession of very high intelligence, the richness of linguistic expression and the sophistication of symbolic thought, are attributes of *all* humans. There is no difference whatsoever here between hunter-gatherers and any other human beings. However, the answer must be 'yes' in certain other regards. Hunter-gatherer group sizes and structures, for example, are more similar to those of non-human primates than are those of non-hunter-gatherers. Notwithstanding the notion that there are universals of human group size and association, chimp troops do look more like hunter-gatherer bands than they do like agricultural villages or industrial cities. Political relations are another matter. Among the chimps, one senses Westminster politics more than the consensus politics of hunter-gatherer bands.

My own specializations within hunter-gatherer studies are in kinship and settlement patterns. While 'settlement' is not quite the right word to describe what we observe among chimps, nevertheless there are similarities in seasonal activity, daily wanderings in search of food and water, hunting activities on the part of males, interaction with other groups, etc. Kinship is different. Sexual advances, birth and nurturing, and relations between infants and parents and among siblings, are all aspects of kinship. Of course, chimps live in 'one-parent families', but they do not classify their distant kin with culture-specific appellations or remember their ancestors. Still, I was struck by the vividness of kin relations I observed. Kin relations among chimps have a kind of 'purity', stripped as they are of the cultural complexities of African Bushman or Australian Aboriginal kinship systems, for example. Indeed, as with politics, it is Western kinship which comes to mind on the comparative front, as much as hunter-gatherer kinship. Hunter-gatherers tend to classify the entire social sphere as belonging to categories of kin. For them, genealogical distance takes second place to kinship category; and in some hunting-and-gathering societies, kin categorization is associated with the classi-fication of the land and the cosmos. Britons, Ugandans, Japanese, etc., have none of this. Perhaps, as Lévi-Strauss (1968: 351) once said, early human and modern hunter-gatherer societies alike produced minds of the calibre of Plato and Einstein, but these hunter-gatherer 'Platos' and 'Einsteins' were preoccupied with kinship. From a hunter-gatherer point of view, agricultural and industrialized peoples have partly returned to the simplicity of chimpanzee kinship, leaving their great minds to ponder other problems.

There may be things we can compare by observation between human hunter-gatherers, non-hunter-gatherers and chimps: time spent with the young, grooming behaviour, learning behaviour, sibling rivalry and fam-ily and group variations in all of these. Some of the findings of primatolo-gists may be useful to anthropologists in looking for human universals. Likewise, some of the classic findings and questions in the anthropol-ogy of kinship may be useful to primatologists. For example, relations between grandparents and grandchildren are in a great many societies (but less so those which anthropologists tend to come from) ones of 'joking' and licence, whereas parent–child relations are stricter. Are there parallels among chimpanzees? Would a primatologist not trained also in social anthropology be able to recognize a 'joking' or an 'avoid-ance' relationship? Would they know how to look for one? What of other classics of anthropological kinship study: lineage theory, alliance theory, uncle–nephew relations, mother-in-law avoidance? Quiatt and Reynolds (1993: 212–41) pioneered the application of anthropological models of kinship to primate data, but I cannot help feeling there is room for much more dialogue – not just in papers and conferences, but in the field at research stations like Budongo.

3   Fossils and what they tell us

I once had the privilege of holding in my hands the femur of the type find of *Homo erectus*. I say 'femur', but of course there is no organic matter in it: the bone has long since turned to stone. It had a strange but nevertheless indefinable quality. I am not sure whether the magic I felt was derived, in my mind, from its historical significance, or from its evolutionary significance. Historically, it was the 'original' *Pithecanthropus* or *Homo erectus*, the object Eugène Dubois kept under his bed. Evolutionarily, it is no different from any other *H. erectus* fossil, but it was the first one I ever held. It was my 'ancestor', but not literally of course, because my early *Homo* ancestors and those of all human beings alive today lived in eastern Africa, not on the island of Java.

Fossils can tell us a great deal. Indeed, it is right that they lead the way in the study of human origins. However, they cannot in themselves say much about the societies their owners lived in. For this we have to look to social anthropology. Some ask: how can you use social anthropology to work out how things were? I say: how can you not? Consider the alternative. Some archaeologists speculate about how primitive peoples might have done this or that *because primitive peoples were primitive*. Some subscribe to ritual explanation, because primitive life is supposed to be dominated by ritual. Much 'ethnographic analogy' is in fact not that much better, because it is less of an analogy and more of a search for precise correspondence between past action and the present. Rather, it is better to look to true analogy.

Let me ask the question again. How can you use social anthropology? The answer is to look to analogies with, for example, the science of cosmology. How do we know that the universe is expanding and not contracting? How can we tell whether its expansion is increasing in velocity or decreasing? Cosmologists can answer such questions through the construction of clever, testable and falsifiable hypotheses. That is, where direct proof is unavailable, hypotheses that explain what is known can be employed, and models can be build on these. When hypotheses lead to the wrong conclusion, they can be jettisoned and replaced with other ones. That, of course, is a great simplification, but in broad terms it describes methodology applicable through most sciences. Social anthropology's contribution to studies of human origins could work in a similar manner, as indeed the use of social anthropological findings already does in the hands of some in archaeology.

A proper methodology of the social anthropology of human origins also has to include comparison. Ethnographic analogy of a kind which assumed that living societies have close resemblances to any pre-*sapiens* societies would, of course, be not only politically incorrect but scientifically unsound as well. Yet a methodology which takes into account the full range of present-day human variation, analogies with known prehistoric contexts, geographical ranges and ecology, and appropriate ethnographic comparisons as well as anthropological theory, is significantly different. As Robert Foley (1992: 338) once put it: 'it is the patterns, processes and principles derived from contemporary studies, not the events themselves, that should be extrapolated back in time'. In other words, both the ethnographic record and the anthropological theories which explain it ought to be seen as interrelated sources for ideas with which to interpret the archaeological record.

Australopithecines all had much smaller brains than we do, walked upright but could not walk far or run fast. They lacked the capability of speech; and they lacked fire, and probably never developed the ability to make tools. Yet they mark a baseline for human evolutionary studies, and therefore are potentially important for understanding the basis of social relations among hominins more generally. But what kind of society did they live in? How big were their groups? How did these groups get along with other groups? How did individuals within them get along with each other?

This chapter uses theories and methods of social or cultural anthropology, combined with what we know from other disciplines, including primatology, comparative anatomy, evolutionary psychology and prehistoric archaeology, to propose, very briefly, reconstructions of australopithecine social organization, habits and customs. Then we explore the genus *Homo*, very broadly, in a similar vein. How did anatomy affect technology? How did advancing tool technology impinge on migration, on communication or on the organization of society? These are the kinds of questions social anthropology should be able to help answer, and here I try to give a small sample of what might be done in this regard. I do think that our best chance, though, comes in working out the intricacies of human life at the time of the symbolic revolution, rather than in worrying too much about skulls or femurs. I will turn to this later.

Three different kinds of evolution

Evolution is not one single thing, but at least two: *biological evolution* and *social evolution*. I believe there is a middle form as well: *technological evolution*. Like biological evolution it is material, but like social or cultural evolution it is driven by culture. It is indeed part of what is known as 'material culture' (as opposed to symbolic culture, expressive culture, or whatever – although these concepts may, of course, overlap). The fields of human palaeontology, comparative anatomy, archaeology and prehistory have all concentrated on either biological evolution or technological evolution, with, in the case of archaeology and prehistory, a nod to non-technological social evolution now and again. In these cases, as much as with palaeontology and anatomy, the driving force is biological evolution. While I do not deny the biological as broadly the best starting point, I often look backwards on the question – with thoughts on how modern human ethnography and anthropological theory might help to bridge the gaps between biological, technological and social evolution.

One way to bridge such gaps is through theories from outside social anthropology that might lead to social anthropological questions. This may sound obtuse, but let me give a simple and important example. In the early 1990s, Leslie Aiello and Robin Dunbar (1993) noticed a correlation between neocortex size and group size in primates. In later work Dunbar (e.g. 2003) has developed the idea further, and has noted that the correlation can be made not just with neocortex size but between brain size more generally and group size. We shall explore these ideas in the next chapter and beyond, but for now the important thing to note is that if the correlations work for *all* primates, then we should be able to calculate the group sizes for fossil hominins and even for *Homo sapiens*. The 'natural' group size for *H. sapiens* should by these means be about 150, with other hominins lower: 65 or 70 for australopithecines up to 150 for fossil *H. sapiens*. The relation between brain size and group size can tell us a good deal about social organization and communication, and again the specifics will be covered later.

The relation between biological and technological evolution can be seen in the development of tool use and tool-making skills. These require not only manual dexterity but also the cognitive abilities to plan, before it is made, how a tool will be formed. Since the 1970s, cognitive archaeologists have written much on this subject. Recent work has focused even on language and its relation to memory and tool-making (e.g. Ambrose 2010) in the Middle Stone Age or Upper Palaeolithic. It is not for nothing that Steven Mithen (2010: 481) has recently dubbed Palaeolithic archaeology 'the most theoretically advanced area of the discipline'. Yet, ironically, Mithen's own *Prehistory of the mind* (1996) stands out as a brilliant attempt to explore relations between biological evolution and culture, but is nevertheless largely silent on the mental capacity required for creating and transmitting ideas on material culture.

Nor have arguments on mind, memory and invention been entirely absent in social anthropology. In Kroeber's (1917) article on 'the superorganic', the individual was pushed to the side in favour of cultural forces which drive human invention. Kroeber points to the fact that the telescope, the telephone, photography, the phonograph, and so on, were each simultaneously invented by two or more people; and oxygen, Neptune and the North and South Poles similarly discovered almost simultaneously by more than one individual. His article brought immediate criticism though, from Edward Sapir (1917), who attacked Kroeber for overemphasizing material aspects of culture. Sapir attributed invention in philosophical, religious and aesthetic activities to autonomous individual activity, albeit activity by culture-bearing individuals in social contexts.

Earliest hominins and australopithecines

It helps to have a sense of timescale. As Bo Gräslund has put it: 'Only about 60 generations have passed since the time of Jesus Christ, but 6000 generations have gone by since the dawn of anatomically modern humankind. Yet even that is little compared to the 250,000 generations since our ancestors first walked upright' (Gräslund 2005: 2). That is a very long time.

Early hominins

We met *Sahelanthropus tchadensis* and *Ardipithecus ramidus* in chapter 2. Another early hominin was the creature dubbed *Orrorin tugenensis* (literally, in the Tugen language, 'Original man of the Tugen Hills'). There are four sites, all in Kenya, and a number of finds, the earliest being a molar found in 1974. It is not clear whether *Orrorin* was in the human lineage, but the species seems to have walked upright in a forested environment about 6,000,000 years ago (Sarmiento 2007: 34–8). Of course, far too little is known of these species even to speculate on their ways of life. They all lived between 7,400,000 years ago (the earliest *Sahelanthropus*) and 3,900,000 years ago (the most recent *Ardipithecus*). *Sahelanthropus*, *Orrorin* and *Ardipithecus* were, arguably, early australopithecines. *Ardipithecus* includes not only *A. ramidus*, but also the earlier *A. kadabba*, though the latter is known only through a few teeth. Today, most authorities presume that all these species, and all other australopithecines, walked upright or at least partially and usually upright. This is what characterizes them as proto-human, rather than ape. Bipedalism enabled hominins to escape midday heat: an upright stance allows the body to absorb some 60 per cent less heat at the hottest time of day (Lewin and Foley 2004: 250–1). This is important because it means that bipedal hominins will have required much less water than their predecessors, and therefore will have been able to forage throughout the day and to range considerably farther. Among baboons, stressed ecological conditions mean having to spend more time in food-gathering activities and less time in social interaction (Dunbar 1992). Terrestrial foraging, as opposed to arboreal foraging, gave new opportunities. There was little incentive for two-legged creatures to stay in forest environments, and the use of grassy areas enabled greater propensity for meat-eating (if they could catch the game). It also made the gathering of vegetables somewhat less reliable, since broadly forests are better for vegetable foods and grasslands better for game, especially large game. Without tools though, large game could only be procured easily by scavenging.

Australopithecines

With later fossils, we are on firmer ground, if only because of the greater diversity of species and much larger number of finds. Let me draw here on the many recent summaries of work in australopithecine palaeoanthropology, especially Klein (2009: 131–278), Lewin and Foley (2004: 228–83), and Sarmiento (2007: 46–112). Australopithecines (or australopiths) include those usually classified today as members of the genera *Ardipithecus*, *Australopithecus*, *Kenyapithecus* and *Paranthropus*. Most show considerable differences between males and females in presumed stature and particularly in body weight. For example, the average stature of *Australopithecus afarensis* was 151 cm for males and 105 cm for females, with body weights of 45 kg and 29 kg respectively. The comparable figures for *Australopithecus africanus* are 138 cm and 115 cm, and 41 kg and 30 kg (Klein 2009: 197). What exactly this means for social organization is of course impossible to tell. However, the suggestion that might be read from these data is that australopithecines might have had more differentiation than later species or indeed modern humans in activities such as hunting and in control over other individuals. Competition among males for sexual (and reproductive) access to females would seem likely, and this could imply a social organization based more on male belligerence than is found among later hominins. The bones, including hip orientation and relative length of arms and legs, of both species certainly suggest that they could climb trees to feed, but moved primarily on the ground. This in turn suggests a greater range than previous species. Thus, we could envisage a semi-migratory species with both intra-group and inter-group male competition.

The locations of the species were throughout eastern and southern Africa, but not beyond that. Some species may have used tools, as the evidence of tool use among modern chimpanzees may suggest. The earliest flaked stone tools are those of the Oldowan tradition of eastern Africa. These tools were possibly made by *Australopithecus garhi*, dated to 2,600,000 BP, but are more commonly assumed to be made by *Homo habilis*, a species which dates from 2,500,000 BP. By comparison, the Acheulean tradition (*Homo* spp.) of Africa, Europe and Asia is commonly dated to around 1,650,000 BP, with the African Middle Stone Age and Middle Palaeolithic (*Homo sapiens*) beginning around 250,000 BP, and the Later Stone Age and Upper Palaeolithic (*Homo sapiens*) around 50,000 BP. It is worth noting here that both *Australopithecus afarensis* and *A. africanus* apparently had the manual dexterity to fashion stone tools. Their hand bones were much more like those of modern humans than like those, for example, of chimpanzees. Raymond Dart, who discovered *A. africanus*, once argued that antelope bones found in association with australopithecines were in fact bone tools, although it now seems unlikely that they were anything more than accumulations collected by hyenas (Klein 2009: 251).

Clive Gamble (2008: 35), following earlier work by Aiello and Dunbar, describes well the sequence of communication systems from the australopithecines to the present. He suggests that australopithecines lived in communities of about 70 and were likely to have had 'primate grooming' as the main means of communication. *Homo ergaster* communities numbered about 100, and with the time constraints that would have been involved in maintaining communication through grooming were likely to have developed words, and vocal chorusing, as means of communication. Neanderthals, he suggests, had a typical group size of 120, and developed a form of socially focused gossip. Modern humans, in turn, have a natural community size of 150 and with full language, including capabilities in metaphor and technical description. Gamble's view is broadly gradualist. His scenario has no revolutions, but rather a slow evolution from *Paranthropus* and *Australopithcus* to *Homo*. Gamble does not speculate on whether words and ultimately language involved purely vocal mechanisms or gestural ones, although he perhaps implies the former. However, current opinion in linguistics and allied fields, and in particular in cognitive neuroscience, seems to me to be favouring gesture as the means of articulation in early forms of language (e.g. Corballis 2003, 2010). Vocalization took over later, perhaps 100,000 years ago, or as little as 50,000 years ago. It proved better in a number of ways: not least in that it enabled humans to use their hands for other activities, while communicating. This may be obvious to deaf people, if not to the

Table 3.1 *Average cranial capacity in cubic centimetres*

A. afarensis	414
A. africanus	444
A. boisei	516
A. robustus	530
H. habilis	661
H. ergaster (Dmanisi)	685
H. ergaster (early African)	795
H. ergaster (later African)	873
H. erectus (Java)	933
H. erectus (Zhoukoudian)	1,043
H. heidelbergensis/sapiens (early African)	1,201
H. neanderthalensis (early)	1,248
H. sapiens (modern)	1,345
H. neanderthalensis (classic)	1,435

Source: data from Campbell 1996: 45; Klein 2009: 307–8.

hearing: studies of modern sign languages show us that it is perfectly possible to communicate effectively through sign, but it is not as efficient.

Earliest *Homo*

The earliest members of the genus *Homo* were not necessarily, in every respect, of great evolutionary advancement over australopithecines. Anatomically, they differed, but both australopithecines and early *Homo* walked upright, and, as suggested above, possibly both used and made tools. Average cranial capacity was different in degree, but not exponentially so (see table 3.1). These data, in any case, should be taken with a pinch of salt: they are averages, and ultimately derived from a variety of sources.

The two earliest species of *Homo* are *H. habilis* (2,300,000 to 1,400,000 BP) and *H. rudolfensis* (Skull 1470, dated at 1,900,000 BP), both found in eastern Africa. Some classify the latter as a species of *Kenyapithecus*. *H. habilis* and its successors (though not necessarily its descendants) *H. ergaster* and *H. erectus* had a long evolutionary span for hominins, with the latter two dating roughly from 1,900,000 to 1,400,000 and 1,800,000 to 1,300,000 years ago respectively. Again, my main sources are Klein (2009: 279–434), Lewin and Foley (2004: 284–361) and Sarmiento (2007: 113–81), and the dates refer to Africa.

Sexual dimorphism among early *Homo* was about 20 per cent less than among australopithecines. This might suggest greater gender egalitarianism, as well as less sexual competiveness among males. Wynn and McGrew (1989) enlisted the help of a bonobo to make Oldowan-style tools, and concluded that Oldowan tool-makers, more concerned with the edges than with the overall shape of their artefacts, had perhaps more the cognitive capacity of apes than of humans. Yet there is no doubt that *H. erectus* and *H. ergaster* were well ahead of *H. habilis*, best regarded as a transitional form, and certainly the australopithecines, in efficiency. Robust australopithecines (e.g. *Paranthropus robustus*) depended much more on low-quality plant foods, and Homo gravitated towards high-quality foods such as storage roots and meat from vertebrates (Lewin and Foley 2004: 324–5).

Modern humanity is descended from *H. ergaster*, who lived in eastern and southern Africa – near Lake Turkana and at Swartkraans. The name *Homo ergaster* ('working man') dates from the 1970s, and many still prefer the designation 'African *Homo erectus*' to the separate species name. Those who make the distinction use *H. ergaster* for the African species and *H. erectus* for the Asian and European one (and finds once known as 'Java Man', 'Peking Man', possibly 'Swanscombe Man', etc.). *H. erectus* is presumed to be the first species to have made fire, although it is possible that *H. ergaster* had this ability too. Reduced sexual dimorphism, increased brain size, the shape of the cervical vertebrae, in the neck, in some specimens (possibly implying a form of speech), all suggest considerable advances over previous species. The fact of the first Out of Africa migrations suggest also *H. erectus* had greater cognitive skills than its ancestors, and it is assumed that *H. ergaster*, from whom we are all descended, had acquired these too.

The two main Out of Africa migrations are of *H. erectus*, about 1,800,000 BP, and *H. sapiens sapiens*, which some experts date to around 130,000 BP but most agree to a date about 60,000 BP (for a recent summary, see Willoughby 2007: 113–26). Evidence of the *H. erectus* migration includes skeletal and other archaeological material from Dmanisi in Georgia and from the Nihewan Basin in China, both dated at about 1,700,000 BP. In between, there were other migrations, including probably a second *H. erectus* migration about 1,000,000 BP and the replacement, before 500,000 BP, of *H. erectus* by *H. heidelbergensis* who had evolved in Africa (Gowlett and Dunbar 2008: 24).

Homo sapiens and later global migrations

There are broadly two views of the *H. sapiens* migration or migrations. One view is of a single migration across the southern end of the Red Sea before the volcanic eruption at what is now Lake Toba, on Sumatra, about 74,000 years ago. That explosion left a layer of ash around the world, and is thus associated with archaeological deposits before and since. Some say too that it caused massive problems for *H. sapiens* and other species and that this resulted in a bottleneck in human population size. The foremost proponent the idea a single pre-Toba migration is Stephen Oppenheimer, who proposed it in his book *The real Eve* (2004) (published in the United Kingdom under the title *Out of Eden*). According to Oppenheimer (2004: 73–4), a land bridge was available across the Red Sea as early as 170,000 years ago, and a population of Africans crossed to the Arabian peninsula, and on to India, from there eventually populating the rest of the non-sub-Saharan world, including North Africa.

The other view is that of Marta Lahr and Robert Foley (1994). They argue for two migrations, both later than the Toba eruption, perhaps the first being only 60,000 years ago. One possible migration was through Ethiopia and the Arabian peninsula, and the other was through North Africa to the Middle East and on to Eurasia. This implies dispersal from two (or more) points, at different times, and in a sense represents a 'soft' version of the Out of Africa hypothesis. Whatever the details, *Homo antecessor* and *H. heidelbergensis* or early *H. sapiens* (ancestor of both *H. sapiens sapiens* and the Neanderthals) spread through Africa and into Europe. *H. sapiens* expanded extensively into Neanderthal territories between 50,000 and 25,000 years ago (Gowlett and Dunbar 2008: 24). Figure 3.1 shows the major migrations of *H. sapiens*, with approximate dates indicated very roughly.

Biological, technological and cultural developments

I noted earlier that australopithecines had small brains, lacked speech, had not harnessed fire and probably never made tools. These abilities are unquestioned, though, for any species of *Homo*. Although *Homo habilis* was also small-brained, this creature did mark a turning point in evolution. Neanderthals, once assumed to be not fully human, are now seen as close to early *H. sapiens* in cultural development. *Homo habilis* may have been the first to make tools, and his cousin *H. ergaster* (African *H. erectus*) is ancestor to us all. European Neanderthals have been the subject of speculation and debate since the 1860s. In more recent times it is not only the fossils, but their location in ancient environments that were quite different from those today, and their association with tools and with ritual activity, that has attracted interest.

H. floresiensis, supposedly a new species of *Homo* living as recently as 18,000 years ago (or even more recently), was discovered in 2003 on the island of Flores in Indonesia. And in 2004, a paper in *PLoS Biology* suggested, on the basis of the divergence of two lineages of head lice (*Pediculus humanus*), direct contact between 'ancient' and 'modern' humans. It would seem that the head louse split into two lineages (or clades) about 1,180,000 years ago, about the time of the major *Homo erectus* Out of Africa migration. One clade is found today among humans

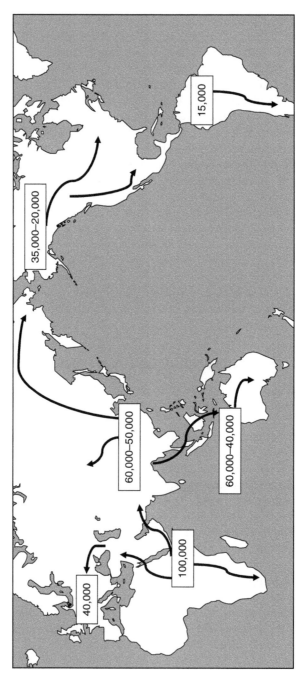

Figure 3.1 Major prehistoric human migrations, with approximate dates BP

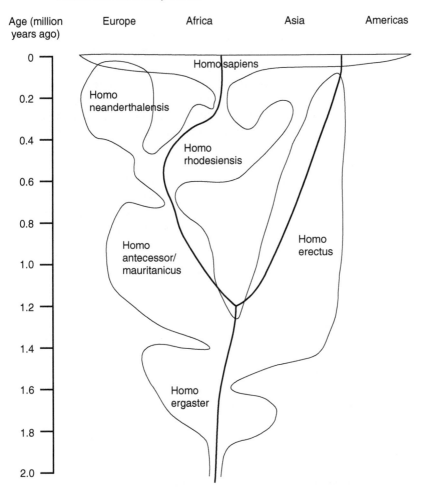

Figure 3.2 The evolution of *Homo* and *Pediculus humanus*
Source: Reed *et al.* 2004: doi:10.1371/journal.pbio.0020340.g005.

worldwide, while the other is found only in North America (specifically in the United States and in Honduras). There is no mention of *H.
floresiensis* in the article (Reed *et al.* 2004), but it seems an obvious possibility for the relatively recent 'archaic' contact required to account for the
existence of the other clade of louse. Reed and his colleagues have been
looking instead towards Neanderthals, whose divergence from modern
humans would seem, in their view, to be far too recent.

Figure 3.2 shows an interpretation of fossil evidence of *Homo*. It also
shows the geographical and, by implication, demographic bottlenecks
through which *Homo* passed in its speciation. The divergence and lineage

of *Pediculus humanus* is indicated by the lines through *H. antecessor*, *H. rhodesiensis* and *H. sapiens* and through *H. erectus*.

A significant technological development that has long been recognized is the use of fire. Fire offered warmth, greater visibility at night, protection from predators and, of course, the possibility of cooking food. Fire was certainly in use in *Homo erectus* times, and current earliest estimates of evidence of cooking date from 790,000 years ago (Goren-Inbar *et al.* 2004). Fire also allowed the ability to control the environment through burning off unwanted vegetation in order to make tuber-gathering easier. This technique is found among hunter-gatherers today in several parts of the world, but evidence of it in the archaeological record is difficult to find. At the other end of the time-spectrum, fire enabled European Mesolithic and Neolithic peoples to produce pottery – yet there may be an in-between phase of fire as a facilitator in the production of stone tools. Evidence has recently been found of heat-treated silcrete tools at the eastern coast site Pinnacle Point, in South Africa, as early as 164,000 BP, and by 71,000 BP the majority of tools at that site bear marks of heat treatment (Brown *et al.* 2009). This treatment makes tools easier to work. Thus we can envisage several stages in the development of fire use: first a *Homo ergaster* or *H. erectus* control of fire or invention of fire-making for purposes perhaps of warmth and protection, the invention of cooking at that time or later, at an unknown time the use of fire in environmental control, probably later the use of fire in tool-making among early *H. sapiens*, and later still the use of fire in pottery-making in the Mesolithic.

Colin Renfrew (2007: 139) argues that boat-building required co-operation and planning ahead, and suggests that the first (circumstantial) evidence of such activity can be dated at 500,000 years ago. Middle Palaeolithic stone tools found on the island of Flores date from that time, and were made by *Homo erectus* who, in spite of low sea levels, must have sailed at least part of the way there. Flores was an island at that time. If *H. erectus* had the ability, the foresight and the wish to sail from island to island, they would seem to have been more 'delayed return' than we sometimes give credit for in our descriptions of modern, *H. sapiens sapiens*, hunter-gatherers. In case it is needed, let me add here the simple disclaimer that of course I do not imagine that contemporary hunter-gatherers are in any way more like prehistoric hunter-gatherers than the rest of us are – except in terms of subsistence, subsistence-related technology and social organization, and with reference to very specific, related aspects of ideology contingent on that subsistence base. I have spent too long among contemporary (part-time) hunter-gatherers to see them as anything but completely modern, albeit modern with a difference. That difference is precisely in those ecological and ideological relations which these peoples, in spite of, in most cases, centuries or even millennia of contact with non-hunter-gatherers, have chosen to preserve. But, for that very reason, they are good models through which to think about possibilities with regard to social organization and ideologies that do relate to subsistence (see, e.g., Barnard 2002).

Ian Tattersall (2009: 16020) argues that 'becoming human' took place in two stages. The first involved the acquisition of the anatomical characteristics of fully modern *Homo sapiens*, in Africa shortly after 200,000 years ago. The second was cognitive and behavioural: the form of cognition marked by 'symbolic reasoning' and language (which to my mind did not necessarily appear at the same time). Tattersall dates symbolic reasoning at about 100,000 years later. The evidence we have of the earliest *Homo sapiens sapiens* beyond Africa is the Qafzeh 9 skeleton in the Levant (93,000 years ago), with symbolic behaviour (depending on how we define it) by 77,000 years ago in South Africa. Both populations seem to have died out, but happily we inherit both aspects of humanity from their east African counterparts.

Science, myth and theory

I will return to contemporary hunter-gatherers many times throughout this book, and I will consider the basics of human evolution and the argument for using ethnography and anthropological theory in the study of human origins later in this chapter. First though, let us have a look at the place of human origins in the history of anthropological thought.

Wiktor Stoczkowski (2002 [1994]), trained as a palaeo-anthropologist but later a student of the history of science, has argued that the theories of human origins devised by prehistorians and archaeologists reflect those of the popular imagination. This is as true today as in the past. Even research agendas are not immune, and Piltdown is hardly the only example. Ever since the Ancient Greeks, popular imagination has had it that early humans, monsters and animals dwelt in caves, and the prehistorians of the nineteenth and twentieth centuries looked first for their proto-humans in those environments. If they found more fossils in such places, it is partly due to that fact. Stoczkowski (2002 [1994]: 68–130) notes that hypothesized causal relations, for example between hunting and food-sharing or hunting and co-operation, or between bipedalism, having hands free and tool-making, affect what prehistorians look for and therefore what they find. These concerns, rather than empirical evidence, are the driving force of prehistoric science.

Palaeo-anthropologist-turned-science-writer Misia Landau (1991) goes further, in suggesting that theories of scientists subconsciously replicate the motifs of European folklore. The four main evolutionary events postulated by human palaeontologists occur in different orders in the differing accounts: terrestriality (moving from the trees to the ground), bipedalism (the acquisition of upright posture), encephalization (increasing brain size, leading to higher intelligence or to language) and civilization (the development of material culture, of morals and of sociality). Darwin's scheme followed that order: terrestriality to bipedalism to encephalization to civilization; whereas, for example, Sir Arthur Keith's was bipedalism to terrestriality to civilization to encephalization. The narratives of prehistorians, in turn, follow nine basic functions from the initial state of equilibrium to the 'triumph' of evolutionary change, with the 'hero' (the evolving hominin form) departing the past, being transformed through new ways, given gifts of intelligence, bipedalism or whatever, and being 'tested' by the environment (Landau 1991: 1–16), just as mythical heros are given gifts of charms tested by witches or dragons.

Quite apart from the arguments of commentators like Stoczkowski and Landau, who in spite of their training are essentially speaking from the sidelines, there are also debates from within, by practitioners of palaeoanthropology. The historical and theoretical accounts of Ian Tattersall (2000) and Robert Foley (2001) represent the most intriguing of such debates. Tattersall attempts to account for the development of palaeoanthropology over the fifty years from 1950 to 2000, while Foley offers a gentle critique and an alternative perspective, including a rejection of the long-implied idea in palaeo-anthropology of 'human uniqueness', that is, that we humans are different from other species in our evolution.

According to Foley:

While it is obvious that the notion of human uniqueness lies deep in Western philosophy, it must also have been buttressed by anthropological theory, which emphasized the all-embracing nature of human culture as humans' mode of adaptation. Rather than the modern synthesis shaping anthropology, it may have been the other way around, with anthropologists persuading biologists that the unique cultural capacities of humans meant that speciation would be inhibited, so that the course of human evolution would differ from that of other species. (Foley 2001: 7)

Foley goes on to point out that two leading American cultural anthropologists, Kroeber and Kluckhohn, were present at the Cold Spring Harbor Conference on the Origin and Evolution of Man, in 1950, which fostered the 'anthropological' thinking of evolutionary anthropology from that time onwards. He remarks that their influence may have been at work in the minds of biological anthropologists, who presumably should have known better.

In other words, anthropologists undoubtedly read the modern synthesis as suggesting that there can be no cladogenesis, but rather than seeing the true nature of Darwinian theory they merely saw their own theoretical reflection. Tattersall's wish that the anthropologists of the last half century had known more about evolutionary theory can perhaps be matched by the wish that many biologists had known less anthropology. (Foley 2001: 7)

Of course, I disagree. Knowing less anthropology can be no good thing for a biologist. But nor can knowing less biology be a good thing for an anthropologist (of either biological or the social variety). The premise of this book is that, when it comes to speculation on the social and cultural life of early humans, much the same applies. Indeed, what Stoczkowski and Landau alike tell us about palaeo-anthropology perhaps applies doubly when palaeo-anthropologists venture into the territory of social and cultural anthropologists. If my own speculations are subject to similar fates, then so be it. At least mine comes from within the field of social anthropology itself.

One final thought here. The late Richard Salisbury (see 1962) used to point out that the historical understanding we have about, for example, the invention of the stone axe and that of the aeroplane is not a universal. The people he worked with in Papua New Guinea acquired a knowledge of these two items at the same time, and therefore they did not, at least initially, perceive one of these scientific advances as more advanced than the other. The Iron Age and the age of flight were much the same thing. Although fortunately the discovery of hominin fossils since 1857 has gone roughly from more recent back to older, there is an analogy here to fossil finds. We now know that Neanderthals are much more similar to Cro-Magnon than to more recently discovered *Homo erectus* or australopithecines, but in the late nineteenth century, Neanderthal was the only possible 'missing link' and therefore was perceived as more primitive. It is the accumulated knowledge, the ability to compare, and very much also our acquaintance with the sequence of discovery, which provides our sense of understanding of fossils. Additionally, even if some scholars easily recognized the anomalous nature of the Piltdown 'find', until it was unmasked as a hoax its place in the fossil record still had to be accounted for.

What transpires about the relative importance of a fossil for the evolutionary record is not necessarily an indication of its significance for anthropology at the time of its discovery. Cro-Magnon turned out to be not very significant as a fossil, since it was simply a European variety of *Homo sapiens*. Its significance at the time of discovery lay in getting people to think about their ancestors. Haeckel's *Pithecanthropus alalus* had importance, even though it was purely imaginary: the species name is not associated with any fossil at all. *Anthropithecus erectus*, renamed *Pithecantropus erectus*, renamed *Homo erectus*, was important for the changing interpretation not only of the type find, but also of humanity's place in nature and humanity's point of geographical origin. *Eoanthropus dawsoni* turned out to be of no significance whatsoever in our record, but it was important at the time of discovery, partly because the juxtaposition of skull and jaw led us down the wrong path in 1912, but partly also for stimulating interest in human origins and thinking on the location of the origin of humanity. It does seem preposterous now that archaeologists once imagined that humanity's beginnings were in southeastern England, that the brain had got bigger before the teeth got smaller and that the ancestral creature *E. dawsoni* played cricket. Yet that is precisely what early twentieth-century Englishmen did believe. At the other end of the spectrum, *Australopithecus africanus* became extremely important, although, partly due to being misled by *E. dawsoni*, partly because the specimen was juvenile and partly because it was found on what was thought to be the 'wrong' continent, some anthropologists for some time denied its significance. They preferred *E. dawsoni* and his cricket bat.

From the 1880s to the 1920s, there was much concern over the classification of stone technology in southern Africa. The problem was eventually resolved when Goodwin and Van Riet Lowe (1929) published their new classification, based on strictly African principles. This is the scheme still in use. It differentiates three stages: Early Stone Age, Middle Stone Age and Later Stone Age. There is no direct correlation with European phases, Lower, Middle and Upper Palaeolithic, and this was, after all, the point of the separate classification scheme in southern Africa. In the 1960s, Grahame Clark (1969: 24–47) proposed a five-mode scheme to unite African and European classifications, with Mode 1 represented by Oldowan chopping tools, Mode 2 by Acheulean bifaces, Mode 3 by prepared cores of the Middle Stone Age and Middle Palaeolithic, Mode 4 by blades from the Later Stone Age and Upper Palaeolithic and Mode 5 by microliths from the Later Stone Age and Mesolithic. In some cases, the time gap between European and African technology is considerable. For example, Mode 4 blades were being produced in Africa 100,000 years ago, but did not enter Europe until 40,000 years ago. Lewin and Foley (2004: 308–19) adopt this classification, and even suggest that the tool-making abilities of Kanzi were not up to Oldowan quality – although it is not clear whether this is because of his anatomical or his cognitive limitations, or indeed just because he prefers to apply his hands and mind to other things.

Biological bases of human sociality

Hominin sociality?

In an important paper, Robert Foley and Clive Gamble (2009) present an interesting speculation of the several transitions from the last common ancestor of chimps and humans to *Homo sapiens*. I am almost in full agreement with what they say. However, let me pick a few small holes in the points of detail, which do bother me. They suggest (2009: 3269) that the formation of lineages, the heritability of social status and male control of resources are all either derived hominin traits or human novelties. I see these three traits not as fundamentally human at all, but simply as Neolithic derivations. In other words, these are not typical of human hunter-gatherers but only of humans since the dawn of domestication. While there may be social anthropologists who agree with Foley and Gamble rather than with me, this example nevertheless highlights the difference between at least some social anthropologists and representatives of other disciplines in perceptions of human nature. (Foley is a biological anthropologist and Gamble an archaeologist.) They see male control of the distribution of resources as fundamentally 'human', albeit most developed in very recent (Neolithic) human societies, specifically pastoralist ones, whereas I see pastoralism and domestication in general as fundamentally a move away from what me might call 'basal humanity', by analogy with Foley and Gamble's notion of 'basal hominin sociality'.

Let me explain further. Foley and Gamble postulate what they refer to as basal hominin sociality, which include attributes of sociality found among human ancestors deduced from comparison to our closest clade, the genus *Pan*, where *Pan* and *Homo* share similar but not identical features. The basal or primitive features proposed include female dispersal and male residence in the community upon sexual maturity, weaker male–female bonding than found among humans, intercommunity hostility and both male and female hierarchy. From these they further postulate derived hominin social traits. These are either related to basal hominin or last common ancestor traits, or quantitative extensions of these. The formation of lineages is in the latter category, extended presumably from male bonding, a characteristic of the former. The heritability of social status and male control of resources are human novelties but, at least in the former case it seems to me, still related. Where I part company with these specific hypotheses is in that they do *not* represent humankind as humans have lived for 99 per cent of our existence. They represent the 1 per cent of human time on earth as non-hunter-gatherers. In contrast, the other characteristics in their list of human novelties are very much worth such consideration, as these do distinguish all human hunter-gatherers from basal hominins: strong male–female bonding and the persistence of such bonds, increased parental investment of time in bringing up offspring, the existence of affinal relationships, complex community organization and complex relations between communities, age hierarchy and the differentiation of social roles by gender. That is not an exact list, but one based on my interpretation of their selected attributes. And I fully agree with them on all these.

Foley and Gamble argue that there have been five major transitions in human evolution. To put it simply, the first, with the australopithecines, involved bipedalism, dispersal and fission and fusion of social groups. The second, with early *Homo*, gave rise to tools, meat-eating and ultimately strong male–female bonds. The third, with *H. heidelbergensis*, led to the taming of fire, cooking and the development different levels of social structure, including families within the communities. The fourth, with *H. helmei*, *H. neanderthalensis* and *H. sapiens*, produced social brains and larger social structures, including social units beyond the community. And the fifth, among *H. sapiens*, ecological intensification, and ultimately domestication, gave resource ownership and the development of intergroup relations.

All humanity is one race, and one culture

I once saw regional cultural systems (such as Khoisan) as metaphorical languages, with each 'culture' a kind of dialect, different from but often intelligible to members of other 'cultures' (Naro, G/wi, Ju/'hoan, etc.) within the regional system (Barnard 1992a: 302). The linguistic metaphor still works for me, but I no longer see 'cultures' as countable entities (Barnard 2010a, 2010b). There is *Culture*, but there are no cultures.

In a recent book, Frederick Coolidge and Thomas Wynn (2009) have synthesized much of their earlier collaborative work and the work of others on brain evolution and the archaeology of cognition. It is relevant that this brilliant pair include a psychologist (Fred Coolidge) and an archaeologist (Tom Wynn). They argue that there have been two major leaps in cognitive ability. The first was with *Homo erectus*, who moved from African woodlands into a diversity of habitats, and eventually colonized virtually the whole of the Old World. They speculate that the switch from sleeping in trees to sleeping on the ground resulted in psychological changes which in turn led directly to increased cognitive skills. Accompanying these were, they suggest, changes in spatial understanding, landscape use and social life. This was about 1,500,000 years ago.

Coolidge and Wynn's second cognitive leap was yet more dramatic, and caused by a fortuitous genetic mutation. This is what gave us advanced human culture, and more particularly the working memory required for it and other cognitive capabilities, including those required for the use of full language. This they date to between 100,000 and 40,000 years ago. This puts it into line with archaeological material related to elaborate burials, the intensive use of pigment (implying advanced symbolic behaviour), the production of 'lion-man' and similar statuettes (possibly implying shamanism), the colonization of Australia, and so on. However, they draw the line at imputing advanced symbolic culture to the people of Blombos Cave on the South African Indian Ocean coast, who more than 70,000 years ago made beads, etched red ochre and kept it in storage chambers (see, e.g., Henshilwood *et al.* 2002, 2004). Their reluctance to accept this as evidence for advanced symbolism, and therefore advanced cognition, accords with linguist Rudolf Botha's (2009) argument against the common assertion that the people of Blombos had full language. Whatever the date, it is relatively recent in humankind's history: and cognitively, and in a sense culturally too (in spite of what we might teach in introductory cultural anthropology), all humankind is one in this regard.

Genetics, demography and social anthropology

Among the most significant scientific papers ever published is Cann, Stoneking and Wilson's 'Mitochondrial DNA and human evolution' (1987). This, along with a follow-up paper by Wilson and Cann (1992), are significant not so much because they present definitive evidence that Darwin was right about Africa being the point of origin of humankind, but because they confirm the presumption of James Cowles Prichard, Thomas Fowell Buxton and Thomas Hodgkin in the early nineteenth century that all humankind is one. Modern humans have a single and localized, rather than a multi-regional, origin. In a sense, social anthropology anticipated this genetic confirmation in that since the 1860s and 1870s in Britain (though later in some other countries), social anthropology has had as its basis this monogenist premise (Barnard 2000: 23–5).

The search for matrilineal and patrilineal ancestors obscures the more interesting question of the 'most recent common ancestor' or 'universal ancestor' (i.e. the most recently living person from whom all humans living today are descended) and the 'identical ancestors' (i.e. the total population of individuals from whom all living individuals are descended). This question has given some interesting results, based on computational methods (Rohde *et al.* 2004; Hein 2004). It is of course not possible to test this genetically since the search for specific common ancestors in this way is limited by genes traced through females alone or through males alone. But by mathematical modelling, one can estimate number of generations or time to the most recent common ancestor (76 generations or 2,300 years) and to the identical ancestors (169 generations or 5,000 years). However, although both these publications note the great problem of trying to take account of migration in determining the antiquity of such ancestors, the models as envisaged do not attempt to account for them.

Social anthropology may not have much to add in the search for the date or the migration routes, but once the date is postulated and routes suggested, comparative ethnography may contribute to the interpretation. That is in part because we can narrow the range of useful ethnography to that in which subsistence and related factors of social organization are broadly similar. Although we cannot make such comparisons with australopithecines or early *Homo*, we can nevertheless assume that worldwide uniformity among living or recent hunter-gatherers would be inspiring here.

Social science comes in three forms: structural, interpretive and quantitative. Social anthropology is, in essence, composed of the first two, but quantitative studies on the relation between brain size and group size in primates have shown us clues about the size of communities of our hominin ancestors. These, in turn, have suggested the key to understanding issues in communication, and in particular the origins of language and of human kinship structures.

In this chapter, I shall concentrate primarily on the first of these correlations (community size) and its implication for proto-human and human settlement. The origins of language are the subject of chapter 6, and my own theory of the relations among all these things, including especially kinship structures, must wait until chapter 8.

The correlation between brain size and group size

In 1993, Leslie Aiello and Robin Dunbar showed that there was a correlation between neocortex size and group size, at least among primates. Following their original article (Aiello and Dunbar 1993), further work by Dunbar revealed that the correlation worked for general brain size as well as for neocortex size. Calculations revealed too that the 'natural' group size for humans should be about 150, a figure that became known as 'Dunbar's number'.

Chimps spend about 20 per cent of their time grooming; humans spend about 20 per cent of their time in social interaction, most of it in conversation (Dunbar 2001: 190–1). As group size increases, the necessity for grooming relationships to become linguistic ones also increases. Otherwise, the effort required for grooming would be dramatically increased. According to Dunbar's (2003: 173–5) calculations, with a group size of around 150 it would have to be 43 per cent. His suggested threshold by which some form of primitive language must have existed is 30 per cent. This places it among *Homo erectus*. Using predicted figures, we have australopithecine group sizes averaging 65 or 70, *Homo*

53

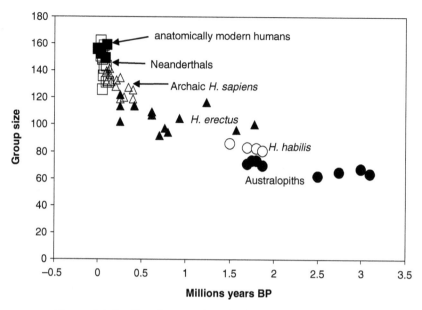

Figure 4.1 Predicted group sizes for fossil hominins
Source: © Robin Dunbar.

habilis about 75 or 80, *Homo erectus* variable, but typically at around 110, 'Archaic' *Homo sapiens* 120 or 130 and Neanderthals at 140 or slightly higher. The figure for anatomically modern humans should be 148 (commonly rounded to 150). Figure 4.1 illustrates the predicted group size for fossil hominins, based on these calculations.

According to Steven Mithen (1998: 175), at least 500,000 years ago our *Homo heidelbergensis* ancestors had developed the anatomical capability of speech, and they had already evolved communication skills. Why had they not evolved language? Or had they? Dunbar (2003) suggests that when groups became too large to make grooming the basis of society, rudimentary language took over. It became a selective advantage to develop language, because it allowed information to be shared with larger numbers. The first forms of language were essentially social, and later forms became generalized to communicate to a much greater degree beyond the merely social, with the development of art, symbolism and religion. The increase in group size thus coincided with the evolution of the brain, and with the eventual acquisition of language and therefore advanced communication. It also led to, or coincided with, increasing levels of intentionality – implied in language through recursion, and specifically embedded clauses (Dunbar 2009).

Mutual grooming is a form of sharing. It still exists as such among hunter-gatherers, especially between spouses and among the closest kin. Hunter-gatherers also generally share food, and especially meat, within this sphere. In the Kalahari, the hunting of large game is, or was until recently, quite common among Bushmen or San (I use the terms interchangeably; see Barnard 2007a: ix–x). Hunting success is spread throughout kin groups through the sharing of meat. Among virtually all Bushman groups (all except those of the Cape), parents-in-law are entitled to the best meat a man 'owns'. I use the word 'owns' rather than 'kills', because the ownership of meat is determined by ownership of the killing arrow. A hunter does not shoot his own arrow, but borrows an arrow from another hunter (see, e.g., Barnard 1992a: 54, 142–3). While meat is shared very widely, vegetable food is normally shared only within a nuclear family. A shift from mainly vegetable-gathering to large-scale hunting would involve a tendency to share meat rather than consume meat on the spot – particularly if large game is sought.

Homo ergaster or *H. erectus* lived in Africa for at least 500,000 years, migrating to Asia, the Middle East and ultimately to Europe. It was not only their ability to produce tools which made this possible, but their abilities to communicate with each other. Communication, of course, included the ability to teach tool-making skills to one's children or grandchildren. Clive Gamble (1993: 108–12) provides an imaginary ethnographic diary of two weeks in the life of a band of ancient hominins (either *Australopithecus* or early *Homo*). The band has some twenty to fifty people. This group size is quite usual for African hunter-gatherer bands today, although the size of the social unit of identity, what I have called the band cluster (a group of several bands) will be much larger. In Gamble's imagined scenario, the range of the group consists of seven habitats. In the habitat in which the group is camped, food is running out. The group moves around their habitat, and younger members, either as individuals or in small parties, scout each of the other habitats in their range. They find that one habitat is best, so the group moves there.

In Gamble's view, what is important is to find the best habitat for the females. Among more primitive primates, an alpha male might control a group of fifteen to twenty. Among australopithecines and early *Homo* species, females were much smaller than males. Alpha males were, in Gamble's view, restricted in their movements, since they needed to keep track of the females. The core group would therefore rely on the sub-adults (teenagers) for information about foraging possibilities. Males might co-operate in order to defend territory and share access to the females. In this scenario, a primary impetus for the exploration of foraging habitats would be for the formation of co-operative alliances, and these would be negotiated between core and peripheral members of the group. The sub-adult males, are peripheral here, with females and the alpha males forming the core of the group. According to Gamble, hunting would be less significant than gathering, but one could imagine an ever-increasing tendency towards hunting as communication and tool-making skills improved.

Implications for social behaviour and migration

Evolutionary psychology is a discipline with bold claims. Its premise is that there is a fundamental human nature which underlies all human behaviour, in spite of the world's social and cultural diversity (see, e.g., Pinker 1997). It does not matter within evolutionary psychology that there exist diverse notions of morality, differing cultural views on mate selection and gender equality, varieties of kinship practice, and even fundamentally unlike methods for the classification of relatives or the determination of culturally significant genealogical distance. Social anthropology tends to take the opposite approach. Dissimilarity, rather than similarity, is assumed. This is, perhaps, particularly true in (American) cultural anthropology.

Population size and migration

We have no way of knowing anything for certain about specific numbers of people involved in prehistoric migrations. However, we do have information that may provide clues to enable us to speculate on possibilities. One thing we know, because geneticists so inform us, is that all the people of the world today are probably descended from a small population of perhaps 2,000 individuals living somewhere in east Africa about 74,000 years ago (Ambrose 1998, 2003). We can envisage this population as consisting of groups numbering about 150 each: let us say thirteen groups of 150, giving a total population of 1,950. Since 1,950 or 2,000 seems an unlikely large population to be keeping in touch, we can envisage it being divided into perhaps two or more smaller ethnic units: say, one cluster with 1,200 individuals or eight macro-bands, and one of 750 individuals or five macro-bands. Each group of 150 comprises one of these macro-bands, and each macro-band is divided into several micro-bands.

A typical number of individuals per micro-band in an African hunter-gatherer population is between about twenty-five (for example, Ju/'hoan Bushmen) and thirty-five (for example, G/wi Bushmen). There are usually fewer people per band where water is plentiful, because individuals can disperse to outlying water supplies and more people per micro-band where, as in G/wi territory, water is concentrated in fewer locations. That

said, where no water is available at all, as traditionally in the dry season in G/wi country, groups may be significantly smaller, often only a
nuclear family or similar-sized unit of five or seven people in the case of
the G/wi. The reason Ju/'hoan groups aggregate in the dry season and
G/wi do not, is that Ju/'hoansi do have year-round waterholes as well
as seasonal ones. At the time of George Silberbauer's fieldwork in the
early 1960s, G/wi had to rely for water at some times of the year simply
on water-bearing tsama melons, which they exploited melon-patch by
melon-patch, the entire band moving between each, month by month.
When the melons were gone, families would each exploit their own areas
of the band's territory and live for a short time simply off of liquids in
the bodies of animals they hunted (Silberbauer 1981: 191–257; see also
Barnard 1992a: 223–36). Sadly, in spite of the introduction of boreholes,
some G/wi have had to revert to this precarious existence in these times
of intervention by politicians and mining interests. Yet except for those
who have acquired livestock, they can manage it.

The smallest level of group will be the family, typically perhaps five
individuals. I make no assumption about the exact composition of the
family. A five-person family could, for example, be two adults and three
children, two adults, one elderly person and two children, two sisters and
three children, three brothers and two children, two sisters married to
two husbands and one child, etc. In this regard, it is enlightening to look
at the rather complex patterns of family customs in India, summarized
by Pauline Kolenda (1968: 346–7). She notes no fewer than twelve different family types:

1. nuclear family (a couple with or without children)
2. supplemented nuclear family (a nuclear family with another
   relative)
3. sub-nuclear family (a fragment of a former nuclear family)
4. single-person household
5. supplemented sub-nuclear family
6. collateral joint family (two or more siblings with their spouses and
   children)
7. supplemented collateral joint family
8. lineal joint family (two couples related by descent, e.g. a mother,
   her son and their spouses)
9. supplemented lineal joint family
10. lineal–collateral joint family (three or more couples related by
    descent and collaterally)
11. supplemented lineal–collateral joint family
12. other types (random relatives living together)

I mention these only to show the potential complexity of family organization, which for humans will inevitably be more complex than for other primates, owing to the recognition of descent, either linear or cognatic. The forms of family organization observed among primates, perhaps especially among higher primates, may of course provide clues about possible family forms among australopithecines and early *Homo*. I would presume that since the dawn of combined nuclear and extended family organization, that is, since the recognition of generations, of collateral relatives, as well as pair bonding, the family types noted above will quite closely resemble the possibilities (see Chapais 2008). It need hardly be said that more than one is a possibility for any given group, and specific family forms will change for a given family.

So, we have in our total population of 1,950, let us say:

> *Total population*: 1,950 individuals
> *Ethnic cluster 1*: 1,200 individuals (eight macro-bands)
> *Ethnic cluster 2*: 750 individuals (five macro-bands)
> *Each macro-band*: 150 individuals (five micro-bands)
> *Each micro-band*: 30 individuals (six families)
> *Each family*: 5 individuals (various types of family)

Whether such a scenario represents demographic reality or not, nevertheless the bottleneck is one likely place for the social anthropology of human origins to concentrate. This bottleneck is in fact the focus in some studies of the origin of language, art and religion. In terms of fossil anatomy, we have left behind even *Homo rhodesiensis*, *H. heidelbergensis* or early *H. sapiens*, and are talking about the early *H. sapiens sapiens* who enacted the symbolic revolution. Of course, it may not have been a specific group who were responsible for language, art, religion, etc., but such a group or small set of groups in succession, related through descent or, more likely, culturally related through the diffusion of adaptive traditions, no doubt had the potential to invent and pass on these constellations of ideas and behaviour.

But what of social organization? If there is a 'natural' group size for *Homo sapiens sapiens*, in spite of enormous diversity among specific human populations, then might there be 'natural' sharing, exchange and kinship relations too? Indeed, there might be. The point at which such relations might have been most clearly observable is no doubt long past, but social relations in existence around the time of the symbolic revolution might give us a clue. The problem, though, is whether we want to define 'natural' humanity as what existed just before the symbolic revolution, or what existed just after.

Why live in a town?

While on holiday in Tunisia a few years ago, I noticed something long written about, and which I had seen many times, in southern Africa. Both Berbers in Tunisia and Khoekhoe in southern Africa often have two houses: a traditional round one, their 'real house' as Khoekhoe say, and a modern, square one. The shape matters less than the fact of maintaining tradition in such a way. People can live in either, or partly in one and partly in the other. In both cases, the traditional house is right next to or just behind the modern one, so there is no material or geographical necessity to have two separate dwellings. It is simply a cultural fact.

Tunisian settlement patterns have many other interesting features too, but I would single out one of particular relevance here. They live in small towns. I use the word 'towns' (rather than 'hamlets' or 'villages') deliberately. These are often tiny, with just a hundred or a few hundred inhabitants, but they are laid out in a street-by-street fashion, like towns throughout North Africa and the Middle East from ancient times to the present. Frequently, there will be more than one mosque, more than one shopping area, and so on, even if there is but one source of water. I would say that this is true urbanization, but, significantly, it is urbanization on a miniature scale.

Recent research in genetics (Cox *et al.* 2009) has suggested that population expansion, to ten times its previous size, occurred in sub-Saharan Africa about 40,000 years ago. That is long before the Neolithic (which began in the Middle East about 12,000 years ago or shortly before). This would imply that changes in hunter-gatherer lifestyles (either technological or socio-cultural), rather than the invention of agriculture, gave rise to large population groups. Clearly, humans have the ability to live in groups with sizes well beyond predictions based on comparative primate studies of the relation between group size and neocortex size. There may certainly be ecological reasons why it is better, with a hunter-gatherer lifestyle, to favour small groups. Yet it would seem that communication through language can enable 'unnatural' group behaviour and patterns of settlement, even among hunter-gatherers. One area in which social anthropologists might help in understanding such phenomena is through the ethnographic study of social control in communities, whether hunter-gatherer or other, that appear too large for Dunbar's predictions. Dunbar himself (e.g. 1998: 187) is fond of noting that contemporary intentional and traditional communities (like North American Hutterites, or a Tennessee mountain neighbourhood once investigated by a cultural anthropologist) limit group size to around 150 in order to avoid the necessity of alien forms of social control, such as a police force.

He suggests too, on the basis of ethnographic surveys, that human groups typically fall into three categories: small overnight camps, medium-sized lineages or villages and large tribes. These number respectively 30 to 50 people, 100 to 200 people, and 500 to 2,500 people.

Julian Steward and cultural ecology

Julian Steward (1955: 30–42) introduced to anthropology the idea of 'cultural ecology': human adaptation to the environment by cultural means. The social history of his influence is interesting. His early work, in the 1930s, was published mainly in fairly obscure places or in journals whose 1930s issues were not available to new anthropology departments established after the Second World War. A friend in the publishing business suggested he bring his various papers, from the 1930s to the 1950s, together in a single volume. That effort required him to think about the general theory he was trying to develop. It also required him to order his papers and revise some of them. The result, *Theory of culture change*, was an academic best-seller which encouraged many young anthropologists to go into hunter-gather studies and to develop evolutionist and ecological frameworks for their field research. Although he had introduced the notion of cultural ecology earlier, publication of his papers in book form was crucial to the development of ecological anthropology as a sub-discipline (Kerns 2003: 272).

Central to Steward's work (e.g. 1955: 36–9) is his distinction between the *cultural core* and the *peripheral or secondary elements* of a culture. The former, in his view, comprise those elements of culture that are associated especially with subsistence pursuits and related, economic features. The Stewardian cultural core also includes political and religious traits that are closely connected with subsistence, economics or the environment. All these elements of culture are acted upon by evolution, and they are the subject matter of cultural ecology. In contrast, the peripheral or secondary elements comprise anything else, and these are acted upon more by diffusion and culture history. I do not doubt Steward's importance or the basic truth of his propositions. Yet, I think his labels are backwards in that truly core elements of culture are those *not* susceptible to environmental influence, or closely related to subsistence or economics, but nonetheless surviving through evolutionary change and, for example, changes in subsistence from hunting to herding.

Importantly, Steward (1955: 11–29) distinguishes his own multilinear evolutionism from the unilinear and universal evolutionsim of his predecessors and opponents. *Unilinear evolutionism* is that of Maine, Morgan and McLenann in the nineteenth century. It posits a complex of stages through which all humankind passes. They believed that there was one dominant line of social or cultural evolution for the whole world, and interrelated cultural elements act on each other to drive change. Unilinear evolutionists look for the detail, for example, in the evolution of religion from animism to fetishism to totemism to shamanism; or in the evolution of kinship from matriliny to patriliny. McLennan (1865) believed that an ancient struggle for food led to female infanticide, which led in turn to women each taking more than one husband, which led to ignorance of paternity, which led to the reckoning of descent through women. McLennan contended that later men captured wives from other groups, and later still exchanged their own daughters and sisters, as wives for men in other groups, and that patrilineal descent emerged as logical consequence. *Universal evolutionism* was simply a watered-down version of this, whereby the details, rendered difficult to establish or ethnographically too complex to assure the same pattern in all societies, were removed in favour of very broad trends: from savagery to barbarism to civilization. V. Gordon Childe and Leslie White were key figures in Steward's own time. Steward's *multilinear evolutionism*, in contrast, allowed for regional diversity, including both the vagaries of culture history and environmental influence. It fitted well with the common American view that saw culture areas, like the Great Plains of North America, or the Eastern Woodlands or the Northwest Coast, as relevant units of analysis. Each culture area would have its own, distinct, line of evolution, played upon by its environment and the technology developed to exploit it.

Some of Steward's ideas, such as the notion that Bushmen lived in patrilineal bands, were overthrown by the first generation of Stewardian ethnographers. Bushmen or San, like many other small-scale hunter-gatherers, live in bilateral communities, or what Steward called composite bands – although he envisaged composite bands to be characteristic of more 'advanced' hunter-gatherers such as North American Subarctic peoples. Other ideas, such as that of levels of socio-cultural integration, failed to inspire, and the posthumous book of his further collected essays, *Evolution and ecology* (Steward 1978), has never had the influence of *Theory of culture change*.

Settlement patterns

Steward's own ideas on Bushman ethnography, and indeed the ethnography of other hunter-gatherer societies, were tainted by the inaccurate details of nineteenth- and early twentieth-century records. However, the very idea of cultural ecology spurred a generation or two of young ethnographers into action. Among Kalahari ethnographers, Richard Lee, in particular, owes a debt to Steward; and it was Lee's collaboration with primatologist Irven DeVore that led to the 'Man the Hunter' conference, held in Chicago in 1966 (Lee and DeVore 1968).

Among the major interests of the ecological anthropologists was hunter-gatherer settlement, and a concomitant concern with territoriality. We know that chimps defend territories. John Mitani and David Watts (2005) looked at variations in this behaviour, and even found that the tendency to patrol in large groups at Ngogo (in Uganda) tended to reduce the danger of aggression from members of other groups. Humans defend territory with aggression too, most obviously in the form of territorial defence and boundary maintenance by tribes and nation states. Yet this behaviour may indeed be deep rooted in hominin nature, and is common too among hunter-gatherers, and famously so in the cases of many groups from North America to Australia to the Andaman Islands. Yet equally it is worth considering the relation between ecological factors and territoriality. Both Elizabeth Cashdan (1983) and I (Barnard 1979) independently came to the same conclusions with regard to relative territoriality among several diverse Kalahari hunter-gatherer groups. Kalahari Bushmen tend to be more territorial when they have fewer resources to defend, at least beyond a certain threshold, where the reverse is true (see also Barnard 1991).

One of the most important developments in social anthropology in the last twenty years or so has been in the anthropology of landscape. The study of landscape was developed earlier in archaeology, but has come into its own in social anthropology through such works as the appropriately titled *The anthropology of landscape* (Hirsch and O'Hanlon 1995). People, land and landscape go together, and in a certain sense the idea of landscape encapsulates both people and land, and in particular captures the way people see the lands in which they dwell. 'Landscape' came into English only in the late sixteenth century (from the Dutch, and specifically with reference to painting), and notions of landscape, as the contributors to Hirsch and O'Hanlon's volume testify, are highly culturally specific. There is diversity, for example, among different Australian Aboriginal peoples, and lands have diverse historical, mythological and symbolic meanings to those who inhabit, hunt and gather on them. Landscapes may be 'read' at different levels, and there is no doubt to me that this kind of understanding must have been in practice since early *Homo sapiens sapiens* migrations and habitations of diverse habitable, and symbolizable, environments. Another consideration is the seemingly commonplace notion of identity, and in particular ethnic identity, which is often rooted in territory. So-called 'indigenous peoples' are often said

Table 4.1 *Possible upland/lowland settlement patterns*

summer aggregation upland / **winter aggregation upland**	summer dispersal upland / winter dispersal upland	**summer aggregation upland** / **winter dispersal upland**	summer dispersal upland / winter aggregation upland
summer aggregation lowland / winter aggregation lowland	**summer dispersal lowland** / **winter dispersal lowland**	summer aggregation lowland / winter dispersal lowland	**summer dispersal lowland** / **winter aggregation lowland**
summer aggregation upland / **winter aggregation lowland**	summer dispersal upland / winter dispersal lowland	**summer aggregation upland** / **winter dispersal lowland**	summer dispersal upland / winter aggregation lowland
summer aggregation lowland / winter aggregation upland	**summer dispersal lowland** / **winter dispersal upland**	summer aggregation lowland / winter dispersal upland	**summer dispersal lowland** / **winter aggregation upland**

to be autochthonous, and there is some debate about which is the better term, 'indigenous' or 'autochthonous'.

Most human hunter-gatherers are transhumant. They are not nomadic, in the sense of moving randomly from place to place, as is often supposed. Typically, and especially in savannah or semi-desert environments where many hunter-gatherers live today, they move between just two styles of settlement: aggregated and dispersed. Each style of settlement will be taken up according to season, normally wet versus dry in tropical and semi-tropical zones, and summer versus winter in temperate and arctic zones. For some groups, there is also the possibility of inland and coastal, or simply upland and lowland. An environment of upland/lowland, with summer and winter seasons and the potential for permanent aggregation or dispersal as well as seasonal aggregation, gives no fewer than sixteen possible settlement patterns (see table 4.1). Some of these will be very unlikely, but it is worth keeping them in mind as logical possibilities that humans understand, but choose not to take up. The most likely one,

Table 4.2 *San (Bushman) patterns of aggregation and dispersal*

Wet season	Dry season	Ethnographic example
dispersal	dispersal	!Xóõ
aggregation	dispersal	G/wi and G//ana
dispersal	aggregation	Ju/'hoansi (!Kung)
aggregation	aggregation	Naro (Nharo)

perhaps, is summer dispersal in the uplands, and winter aggregation in the lowlands, which is the pattern suggested by Grahame Clark (1954) in his interpretation of the *winter-aggregation-lowland* Mesolithic archaeological site of Star Carr, in North Yorkshire.

In the Kalahari, there are no uplands or lowlands, and thus just seasonality. This means only four logical possibilities. In a relative sense, all four are realized ethnographically, and this is shown in table 4.2. Relatively speaking, the !Xóõ (who live in a very inhospitable desert area) are permanently dispersed, and the Naro (who live mainly along a relatively well-watered limestone ridge) are permanently aggregated. The Naro (Nharo) are the main group with whom I have done fieldwork, in the 1970s and since. Those G/wi and G//ana who live in their traditional, waterless environments, aggregate as band units in the dry season, when they migrate in search of water and water-bearing plants. The Ju/'hoansi, who live in an environment with more water resources, aggregate, two or more bands together, at their permanent waterholes in the dry season, and disperse to outlying, seasonal water resources in the wet season (Barnard 1986). Thus each ethnic group makes the best use of its resources, especially water, although the four settlement patterns are very diverse. To simplify: !Xóõ are permanently dispersed, Naro permanently aggregated, G/wi and G//ana aggregate in the dry season and Ju/'hoansi aggregate in the wet season. Interestingly, the same diversity, and similar reasons for it, occurs in the Western Desert of Australia (cf. Peterson 1979).

Further models from hunter-gatherer studies

In 10000 BC, the world's population consisted solely of hunters, gatherers and fishermen. By AD 1500, with the spread of pastoralism and agriculture, only 1 per cent of the world's population subsisted entirely by hunting and gathering. By AD 1900 it was a mere 0.001 per cent (Lee and DeVore 1968: ii). The figures are significant. They are also slightly misleading because over the last decade or two it has become common to include part-time hunter-gatherers (i.e. those who perform other subsistence activities) within the category 'hunter-gatherers'. Full-time hunting and gathering is dying out, though many modern members of these groups, as well as South American horticulturists and African pastoralists, do engage in part-time hunting and gathering and retain a foraging mode of thought which governs their economic activities as well as other aspects of culture.

In a recent book, Russian anthropologist Olga Artemova (2009: 533–58) brilliantly argues that evolutionist anthropology tends to see the world backwards. The implication is rather like that of the old communist slogan 'Our goal is communism', except in this case anthropologists say implicitly 'Our goal is the state' or 'Our goal is civilization.' She suggests that hunter-gatherers have not 'advanced slowly', as other evolutionists would have it, but instead have travelled in a different direction, away from civilization or the state. Modern hunter-gatherers have survived, and some survive still, not because they could not transform their social surroundings, but because they have not wanted to. They continue to value autonomy, avoid outsiders and resist capitalist and imperialist pressures. Artemova notes too that Marxists and non-Marxists alike find the 'origins of inequality' in property relations, whereas she finds them rather in ideologies, often with status marked symbolically, through social class or through institutionalized secrecy. These are things that distinguish non-hunter-gatherers from modern, highly evolved hunter-gatherers.

Learned behaviour is now known to exist among monkeys as well as the great apes. *Homo habilis*, hailed in the 1960s as the first tool-making creature, may well have competitors among yet more ancient ancestors. Chimps in captivity certainly exchange, and those in the wild exhibit sharing practices. Yet there is something different about human forms of sharing and exchange. In anthropology, theories of exchange from Marcel Mauss to the present, theories of sharing and giving from Marshall Sahlins to Nurit Bird-David, and attempts to understand complex features of social interaction in such terms, have come to form a major part of the theoretical repertoire with which to analyse contemporary societies. These too may be useful for speculation on, and even in the reconstruction of, earlier forms of human social structure. Through such models we can explain likely connections between group size, power relations within and between bands and communication and exchange. Since sharing is practised by chimpanzees, it was probably not, for early human ancestors, revolutionary in itself. What was revolutionary was the establishment of the practice of sharing as the very basis of social life. This might well have occurred early in the evolution of *Homo* if not before, and it was undoubtedly followed by practices of learned behaviour, of exchange over distances and of the co-operation necessary for early migrations, including that of *Homo erectus* across most of the globe.

It is a truism that the social life of 'early man' has more in common with present-day hunter-gatherer society than it does to present-day agrarian or industrial society. Yet it is a fallacy to suppose that everything about modern hunter-gatherers is necessarily useful for analogy about human origins. Look again at Artemova's argument. The usual analogy should be inverted: it is not that hunter-gatherers today are particularly like early humans at all, but rather that early humans were more like hunter-gatherers today, in some respects, than they were like pastoralists, cultivators or factory or office workers today. No useful analogy is to be made to modern hunter-gatherers, just because they are hunter-gatherers, except in those specific areas where mode of subsistence, or ideology or group structure closely related to mode of subsistence, is in question. But actually, quite a lot in terms of ideology and group structure, including kinship structures, differs between hunter-gatherers and non-hunter-gatherers. Therefore the analogy is very useful, *in such areas*. The definition of 'hunter-gatherers' has long been a matter of debate, and I include here those groups who today retain hunter-gatherer ideology in spite of recent adoption of other modes of subsistence, and also some cultivators, particularly in South America and Southeast Asia, who do some hunting and gathering and resemble 'pure' hunter-gatherers in many relevant ways.

A number of relevant issues are dealt with by Tim Ingold in two collections of his own papers, *The appropriation of nature* (1986a) and *The perception of the environment* (2000). Ingold begins the former volume (1986a: 1–9) with a look at the idea of a 'hunter as his spear' as encompassing all four of the components he sees as the requirements for system-building in anthropology: the environment, society, technology and culture. The idea of 'the environment', says Ingold, presupposes the existence of someone there to dwell within it and to use it. For an animal, the environment is in general something to exploit as it is. For a human (and, I would add, for hominins at least since the earliest tool-makers), the environment is a resource for tool-making as well as for hunting, food-gathering, etc. Society, for a sociobiologist, is entirely instrumental – made up simply of the fellow species members within one's environment (see chapter 8). However, Ingold reminds us that for the social anthropologist this cannot be the case. I would add that it should not be true for a biologist either. While it may be true that one relies on other people for all sorts of things, it is also true that sharing, learning, communicating and living together in an environmental space that people recognize as their own all make up something rather different than just a part of the environment. The same is true for many species of animal. Notwithstanding the complications mentioned above, of defining 'a society', animals and humans alike live in societies as well as in environments. Human technology, to Ingold (1986a: 6), is 'a systematic, symbolically-encoded body of knowledge that may be applied in practice and transmitted through teaching'. Animals, or at least most animals, do not have such a body of knowledge. This implies social mechanisms for transmission, for example from parent to child, and in the case of much technology, poisoned darts and arrows for hunting for example, a reasonably sophisticated system of communication, and thus culture, and according to Ingold a cultural and not merely a biological ecology.

In another paper in the same volume, Ingold (1986a: 40–78) considers intentionality and the relation between technology (implying symbolic intelligence) and technique (i.e. practical adaptability) in the creation of tools. He makes the point that nineteenth-century writers, with their 'Lamarckian' assumption that inherited characteristics could be passed on to one's offspring, had a quite different understanding of the relation between tool-making and biological evolution than we have today. This was true even after Darwin's ideas had become commonplace. It is not, as they supposed, that the hand, the brain and technology all evolved as a result of generations learning better techniques for the production of tools, but that any improvement in the hand for the production of tools must be the result of natural selection. However, if we turn to what tools do, there are interesting complications. Social anthropology has long been torn between two radically different ideologies: relativism and evolutionism. Both are, in a way, 'evolutionist', except that relativists deny the material in their search for complexity (see Ingold 2000: 312–13). Those who argue that evolution is about maintaining greater and greater control over the environment ignore the fact that it can be about greater and greater complexity in matters such as kinship, or ritual, or symbolic elaboration, such as are found in Australian Aboriginal cultural constructions. Tools and machines help us to save time and effort and to do things we could not otherwise do, but in general (before the computer) they do not help us solve abstract problems. Kinship, ritual, and so on, are practical and non-tool-requiring matters, but they are also abstractions. Ingold's work goes a long way towards enlightening us in matters such as this, although it stops short of asking questions of the evolution of culture *sui generis*, and explicitly so in the case of language origins (see Ingold 2000: 392–405).

Hunter-gatherers, of course, exhibit a variety of different forms of social organization. However, there are a number of attributes which are common to most hunter-gatherer societies. In essence there are some ten of these (Barnard 1999: 55–9): (1) large territories for the size of population, and notions of territorial exclusivity; (2) a socio-territorial organization based on the band as the primary unit, with further units both within and beyond the band; (3) a lack of social stratification except with regard to sex and age; (4) sexual differentiation in subsistence activities and in rituals; (5) mechanisms, such as widespread sharing, for the redistribution of accumulated resources; (6) the recognition of kin relationships to the very limits of social interaction; (7) beliefs which relate humans either to individual animals or to animal species; (8) a world order based on even numbers; (9) a world order founded on symbolic relations within and between levels (such as land, society and the cosmos); and (10) extreme flexibility. In many hunter-gatherer societies, there are also religious beliefs that might seem unusual to many of us, notably the coupling of monotheistic and animist ideas, and some sort of reverence for the moon (not the sun), with the moon characterized in gender terms as male (not female). The last attribute is common especially across the southern hemisphere, and is found in some small-scale horticultural societies too, such as those of South America (see also chapter 6).

The tragedy of the commons

In an important paper for many fields, Garrett Hardin (1968) considers the theoretical example of herders in common grazing land. In Hardin's allegorical example, individual herders have an advantage in maximizing their use of common grazing land. However, common land, not regulated in its use, would become overgrazed. Each individual gains by putting as many animals as possible on grazing land, but society loses because individual maximization leads to poorer and poorer grazing. Hardin's article is often assumed to be an argument in favour of privatization, but the socialist alternative of collective regulation of communal property is a solution equally viable. And in practice, the situation he describes is not really a problem, since the use of common land in real societies is invariably regulated by custom. Significantly, Hardin invariably speaks of 'society', when in fact the relevant units, it seems to me, would be smaller ones: communities, often with chiefs or elders, that in virtually every herding society have control over grazing rights.

As his herding example is essentially allegorical, we should perhaps not take him too literally anyway, but in the absence of an example at least from hunter-gatherer society, it is difficult to imagine how Hardin's theory is applicable in the study of human origins. What strikes me as odd is that biologists, including not only Hardin himself but some of the authors in Kappeler and van Schaik's edited volume, *Cooperation in primates and humans* (see van Schaik and Kappeler 1960), seem to think that herders are relevant here as 'natural' human beings. My point is not that herding livestock is unnatural, but that any other mode of subsistence has analogies to hunting and gathering as these are practised in real hunter-gatherer societies. There will always be constraints on land used. The same is true for fishing waters used by hunter-gatherer-fishers, contrary to Hardin's idea that fishing is similar to herding in this regard. It is like his imagined 'tragedy of the commons' in the case of the Grand Banks or the North Sea, but not in the case of the traditionally fished Northwest Coast or Hokkaido.

The lesson to be learned here is that, although speculation is fine, it is best to employ it with due regard to consideration of what kind of ethnography is relevant, and to an understanding of the limits of ethnographic analogy.

A classic sociology textbook begins with these words: 'A former professor of mine ... was fond of saying, "There are not facts in sociology, there are only concepts"' (Sagarin 1978: vii). As difficult as it may be for people in some of the natural sciences to imagine, much the same can be said for social anthropology and indeed some other social sciences. Our world is built on concepts and themes as well as theories, and virtually everything is a matter of debate. What disciplines such as social anthropology or sociology can add to the study of human origins comes in the form of rigorous and debatable ideas, at least as much as in primary data.

Sagarin's book goes on to analyse these concepts, among others: society, culture, community, communication, socialization, self, values, choice, power, equality, leadership, compliance, anarchism, status, goals, roles, norms, deviance, alienation, collective behaviour, social groups, race, ethnicity, social structure and social theory. While not all the concepts discussed in that book are relevant to anthropology, all in this list are, and relevant too to the study of human origins from a social anthropological perspective. In this chapter I will explore some of the concepts from social anthropology that could be relevant. There are others, of course, but those touched on here are those that define key aspects of society that have evolutionary implications.

Problems in 'society' and 'culture'

Both society and culture are problematic concepts. Not only did Prime Minister Margaret Thatcher once say that 'There is no such thing as society; there are individual men and women, and there are families', but even social anthropologists have asserted something like this as well. In a debate on whether the concept of society is obsolete, Marilyn Strathern (1996) rejected the concept, but accepted sociality as an alternative. By rejecting the outdated opposition between society and individual, she argued, we can envisage the social as something that is internal to human existence. The counter argument is that society is neither a clearly definable thing nor something to be seen in opposition to the individual, but simply as an abstraction defining a range of social action or identity. This is all the more true for early humanity, where we need a term to make sense of a 'group' that might never aggregate and is larger and more amorphous than anything we might call a 'community'.

To some extent, we are all slaves to our words in such matters. We, speaking English, may assert that sociality is logically prior to society, and may therefore want to envisage sociality without society. We might be able to do this, if we see 'the social' in both these layers of abstraction, and the three layers of abstraction as social – sociality – society. In Japanese, however, the word *shakaisei* (sociality) is constructed from *shakai* (society), and not merely from a weaker notion of 'the social'. Perhaps it would have been more difficult for a Japanese Margaret Thatcher to claim that society does not exist? Indeed, the distinction between 'sociality' and 'society' was not always clear in earlier English usage. Note, for example, from the year 1581: 'They have neede one of anothers helpe, and thereby love and societie … growe among all men the more' (quoted in Williams 1983: 291).

In the seventeenth century Samuel Pufendorf (1991 [1673]: 35–6), writing in Latin, argued that humankind's nature was to be sociable (*sociabilis*), and that the laws of sociality or indeed sociability (the Latin for both is *socialitās*), are laws of nature. 'Society' is today the mainstay of most British and Commonwealth anthropology, and to some extent too anthropology in France, other Continental countries, and parts of Latin America. My point here is not that it does not exist, but that its definition and its relation to similar notions, like sociality, should not be taken for granted. Hobbes (e.g. 1996 [1651]: 117–21) in effect equated 'society' with 'the state' when he subsumed both under the designation *Commonwealth*. His usage of 'Society' is not as a count noun. When he says that 'certain creatures [ants and bees] without reason, or speech, do nevertheless live in Society', he means not *society* as we understand the term, but something more like what we call *sociality*.

The original meaning of 'culture' and related words in English, French and German was to do with cultivation, but from the German Romantics to American cultural anthropology the term has come to refer commonly to shared beliefs, practices and artefacts of a people (see Williams 1983: 87–93). Since Jane Goodall's discovery of tool-making and tool use by Gombe chimps, it is now used too beyond the confines of human culture. The latter usage implies that culture is cumulative (since humans have more of it than chimps), and this hints at the evolutionary trajectory and at the cultural revolutions which have occurred in hominin history.

At a more mundane level, culture is the mainstay of American and Canadian anthropology – and to some extent anthropology in parts of Latin America, China, Japan, and so on, as well as pre-war anthropology in Germany, Austria and countries influenced by the German-Austrian tradition. Indeed, American and Canadian anthropology are products of that tradition and retain the emphasis on culture over society as the primary object of interest in their socio-cultural anthropology. Yet the classic definition of 'culture', as every American anthropology student learns, is in fact not one by an American (or an Austrian), but one by an Englishman. And it is a characterization of 'culture' that has 'society' embedded within it. Edward Burnett Tylor (1871: 1) famously defined 'culture, or civilization' as: 'that complex whole which includes knowledge, belief, art, law, morals, custom, and any other capabilities and habits acquired by man as a member of society'. Thus, culture comprises pretty much everything, and North American cultural anthropology sometimes subsumes a narrowly defined 'social anthropology' within itself. In this case, 'social anthropology' is not a synonym for 'cultural', but refers specifically to the anthropology of social relations through kinship, political and sometimes economic relations.

George Peter Murdock (1940: 364–68) usefully elaborated. He wrote nearly a page each on seven attributes of culture:

1. *Culture Is Learned.* Culture is not instinctive, or innate, or transmitted biologically, but is composed of habits ...
2. *Culture Is Inculcated.* All animals are capable of learning, but man alone seems able, in any considerable measure, to pass on his acquired habits to his offspring ...
3. *Culture Is Social* ...
4. *Culture Is Ideational.* To a considerable extent, the group habits of which culture consists are conceptualized (or verbalized) as ideal norms ...
5. *Culture Is Gratifying.* Culture always, and necessarily, satisfies basic biological needs ...
6. *Culture Is Adaptive* ...
7. *Culture Is Integrative* ...

Interestingly, these attributes entail both *sui generis* and pre-determined aspects. The latter are both biologically determined ('gratifying') and environmentally determined ('adaptive'). Some of his attributes relate to individual acquisition (e.g. 'learned'), and some to the nature of culture itself (e.g. 'integrative'). For the next thirty-three years, until his retirement in 1973, Murdock went on to examine social and cultural variation throughout the world's existing societies. He also sought to explain evolutionary relations between elements of culture, such as kin terms, kin groups and incest taboos, most notably in his early synthesis *Social structure* (1949).

The British understanding of 'social anthropology' usually subsumes culture or cultural traditions. In his essay on 'Social structure', A. R. Radcliffe-Brown (1952 [1940]: 202) rejected what he saw as the Malinowskian view that different South African cultures, 'Bantu', 'Afrikaner', and so on, interact on South African soil, and argued instead that what one finds there is 'the interaction of individuals and groups within an established social structure which is itself in process of change'. Radcliffe-Brown (1952: 2–3) was quite happy to speak of 'cultural traditions' and 'cultural processes', but not of 'cultures'. Radcliffe-Brown's functionalist or structural-functionalist tradition came to view society as comprised of *systems*, each of which contained *institutions*. Classically, there are four systems in any society: economics, politics, kinship and religion. While institutions may primarily be a part of one particular system, they may also play a part in other systems. For example, marriage is an institution within a kinship system, but it also might have economic aspects, political aspects or religious aspects. Although hardly profound or nuanced, this simple functionalist paradigm is still useful as a first step in ethnographic fieldwork. It is also useful to think of it as a theoretical foundation with which to organize data on, or speculate about, earlier hominin society and culture.

Over the last two decades, there has been a challenge to culture, both from the postmodernist wing of American cultural anthropology and from the British tradition. An important example of the former is Lila Abu-Lughod's 'Writing against culture' (1991). She argues that challenges to the ideal of distinct and coherent cultures comes from feminist critiques of cultural hegemony, and also through the existence of marginalized people, including anthropologists, who do not fit neatly into one 'culture' or another. She prefers to speak of 'discourses' rather than 'cultures' in this paper and in her ethnographic studies of the Egyptian Bedouin community in which she worked. The focus of her work is on individuals and the way they see the world.

The best-known example of the latter, the challenge from the British tradition, is Adam Kuper's *Culture: the anthropologists' account* (1999). He traces the history of the culture concept in American anthropology, and he argues on the basis of ethnographic studies within that tradition that the idea of cultural determinism makes no sense. Instead, social and political forces, and even biological processes, explain why people behave in the way that they do. His own background in South Africa comes through – where culture was reified and, in a sense, equated with the concept of 'race' as understood under the apartheid government. Like Abu-Lughod, he sees culture as unduly constraining, and his vision of the individual is of a person with much in common with others, and with an ability to communicate across ethnic and national boundaries.

For these reasons, it is wise to take heed of such relatively new directions in social anthropology. Although most of us still cling to some extent to our traditional usage, nevertheless through critiques such as Strathern's, Abu-Lughod's and Kuper's we have come to see the pitfalls of oversimplification. The social anthropology of early humanity and pre-*Homo* beings would have to make allowances for an even more ill-defined idea of 'society' or 'culture'. That said, it should also recognize the difference that must have existed between social life before and after 'symbolic culture', and those before and after language, those before and after marital alliance, and before and after other forms of social communication and exchange.

Finally, consider this provocative statement from Robert Foley and Marta Lahr:

Culture is the jam in the sandwich of anthropology. It is all-pervasive ... It is often both the explanation of what it is that has made human evolution different and what it is that it is necessary to explain. It is at once part of our biology and the thing that sets the limits on biological approaches and explanations. Just to add further confusion to the subject, it is also that which is universally shared by all humans and, at the same time, the word used to demarcate differences between human societies and groups. (Foley and Lahr 2003: 109)

Much of what they say here is true. As Murdock taught us, culture is everything. Yet for this reason, it is wise to avoid reading too much into it. I prefer to differentiate *symbolic culture*, that which is truly human and truly pervasive for humanity, from mere cultural tradition of the sort that distinguishes one 'culture' from another, or to which apes as well as humans may lay claim.

Social systems

Central to structural-functionalist anthropology in the Radcliffe-Brownian mould was the organic analogy, 'Society is like an organism'. Like an organism, it was made up of 'systems': the nervous system, the digestive system, the reproductive, and so on, in the case of an organism; and the kinship system, the religious system, and so on, in the case of a society. Before Radcliffe-Brown, the organic analogy had formed a major part of the theoretical views of evolutionist Herbert Spencer and of Emile Durkheim, who bridged the divide between evolutionism and functionalism. Spencer himself was decidedly a Darwinian, and indeed a Social Darwinist: he was the person who invented the phrase 'survival of the fittest'. Spencer's (1898: 449–62) notion of society as an organism was an evolutionary one: his main concern was with what he called 'social growth'. Radcliffe-Brown (1952: 178–87) discussed this too, but he was more concerned with the workings and interrelations of social systems and the continuities in social structure that lie beyond the lives of individuals. He also remarks that societies differ from organisms in that, unlike an organism, a society can in fact change its 'type' without a break in continuity. 'A pig does not become a hippopotamus' (1952: 181), as he puts it, but an egalitarian society could become hierarchical, or a matrilineal one could become patrilineal.

The structural-functionalist idea of 'society' was essentially an anarchist one. Contrary to Hobbes, for Peter Kropotkin (e.g. 1987 [1902]) and other anarchists, society and the state were not the same at all. If anything, Kropotkin's vision of society stood in opposition to the very idea of a state (cf. Clastres 1977 [1974]). In Kropotkin's evolutionary scheme, *mutual aid* was a practice embedded deep in nature, and Kropotkin replaced the idea of *mutual struggle* with this Russian notion. Mutual aid formed the basis of animal sociability and of human society in all its forms: savage, barbarian, medieval and modern. Kropotkin (1987: 74–7) rejected the notion that humankind in its primitive form was composed of loose aggregations, or of isolated families. He argued that families were a late invention, and that bands, tribes and societies came first. Although in a sense all social anthropology from Maine (1913 [1861]) to the present would take issue with such an idea of the family as a late invention, the structural-functionalist tradition very much accepted the anarchist separation of society and the state. The vision of 'primitive society' they held was influenced both by their ethnographies of stateless societies such as Andaman, Aboriginal and Nuer, and, through Radcliffe-Brown, their touchstone to Kropotkin. Radcliffe-Brown had known Kropotkin in childhood, and at Cambridge in the early 1900s was called 'Anarchy Brown' (see Kuper 1973: 52–6). Radcliffe-Brown's understanding of society, as presented in his ethnographies and lectures and especially in the collection *Structure and function in primitive society* (Radcliffe-Brown 1952), marked not so much a break with evolutionism, as is often said, but an emphasis on synchronic analysis and on the systematic nature of society.

In the time of structural-functionalist anthropology, roughly from the 1920s to the 1960s, there was a fairly clear, agreed notion among anthropologists in Britain and elsewhere within the British tradition of what society was all about. From the 1970s the discipline did move on;

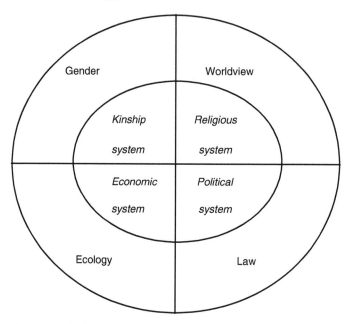

Figure 5.1 Social systems

more specific interests took over from concentration on systems, and the notion of the systematic nature of society came to be rejected by many. However, the structural-functionalist paradigm still largely dominated our teaching structures, and it still has utility for those who seek the bigger picture. It remains very much in hunter-gatherer studies, where hunter-gatherers continue to represent the anarchist vision of society without the state.

Society, it was said, consisted of four systems (see Barnard 2000: 62–3). We might think of this as an inner circle of systems as conceived by the functionalists: kinship, politics, economics and religion, with an outer circle of related social realms (figure 5.1). Kinship comprises descent, alliance, relationship terminology and symbolism. Politics comprises decision-making, the relation between individuals and groups and the idea of a social contract. Economics includes both subsistence and exchange. Religion includes both ritual and belief, and touches on aspects of expressive culture too, such as music and dance. We might also imagine an outer circle of systems, these being mainly those related to interest in anthropology that developed after the structural-functionalist era: gender, law, ecology and worldview. Each of these touched on each other, and each is tied specifically to one of the four of the inner circle: gender to kinship, law to politics, ecology to economics and worldview to religion. In another representation (Evans-Pritchard *et al*. 1963), 'the institutions of primitive society' were grouped into eight frameworks, each the subject of discussion in broadcast talks by eminent British anthropologists. E. E. Evans-Pritchard and his colleagues discuss these under the headings: religion, orientations in economic life, aesthetics, law, the family and kinship, political institutions, mind and modes of thought.

Sharing

On the biological side, Christopher Boehm (1999, 2004) has argued that it was the hunting of large game animals that led to the evolution of both egalitarian ideology and food-sharing practices. In seeking animal fat, species of the genus *Homo* developed means of co-operation in hunting in order to take larger game. Large game cannot be consumed by lone, individual hunters or by their nuclear families, and indeed co-operation in hunting makes the taking of large game easier. As human ancestors co-operated, they also shared the spoils of the hunt, as large antelope or other beasts were divided and meat spread widely across social groups. We see this today in numerous hunting-and-gathering and semi-hunting-and-gathering societies. Some present-day hunter-gatherers have developed complex social conventions to enable the distribution of such resources, while at the same time enshrining principles of relative hierarchy (where one person may be above another in some respects, but not in absolute terms).

Among Ju/'hoan, !Xóõ, G/wi and Naro Bushmen, for example, arrows are loaned to others, and the owner of the killing arrow is recognized as the primary owner of the meat – even though he did not shoot it. Others who participated in the hunt also share in the meat, and the owner's parents-in-law received the best cuts from the hindquarters. This enables the wide distribution of meat, equalizes access to it, notably where it is abundant and in quantities that are too large for one individual or family; and it also equalizes access by both good hunters and bad, thereby encouraging egalitarianism in the abstract (see, e.g., Marshall 1976: 295–301). The practice of arrow-sharing, along with the rules for distribution of meat, are thoroughly functional not only economically but also in maintaining social relations. Notwithstanding reputed dysfunctional aspects of San society, such as reported sexual jealousy, fighting and a high murder rate, particularly among Ju/'hoansi (Lee 1979: 370–400), the very fact that San society survives and in such harsh environments as parts of the Kalahari is an indication that it works.

At a theoretical level, sharing is a consequence of the abolition of property, or of the absence of property. In his *Ethnological notebooks*, Marx (1974 [1880–2]) recorded his views on his readings of Lewis Henry Morgan, Henry Sumner Maine, John Budd Phear and John Lubbock. Of the four, Morgan was always the favoured one because his views on the earliest human societies were closest to Marx's own. He may have been a railway and mining tycoon, a lawyer and a Republican politician, but Morgan was also a naturalist, an ethnographer and an anthropological theorist. As a theorist, Morgan maintained that, originally, property was held in common by the kin group. In contrast, Maine saw the larger kin group as an extension of the family, with collective ownership being derived from the expansion of the family. Marx rejected Maine because of this and bought into Morgan's theory: collective ownership came first and reflected the 'natural' condition of humankind (Bloch 1983: 45–7).

One question that comes to mind is whether ownership could exist prior to a word for 'to own'. A related question is whether the existence of such a word necessarily implies a concept of ownership which one can compare cross-culturally. The Naro language has two basic words for the transitive verb 'to own', *kào* ('to own') and *!' òò* ('to own', and especially 'to acquire ownership of'). Yet ownership takes different forms, as does giving. Territories are owned collectively, by those believed to be descended from earlier owners. They cannot be given away. Huts are owned by those who build and occupy them, such as a husband, wife and children. They are not exchanged or given away either. Movable objects are owned individually, and they may be given to others through //'àè ('to give in delayed balanced reciprocity') exchange – what is known in anthropological literature by the Ju/'hoan word *hxaro*. They may also be given in more direct exchange (//xám) or, at a more commercial level, bought, sold or bartered (//'ámá). Finally, one is said, metaphorically, 'to own' (*kào*) one's grandchildren. One cannot own one's spouse or one's children, at least in this sense. The concept of 'ownership' is specifically one associated with kin relations of a grandparent over grandchild kind.

An intriguing, though in my view rather unlikely, conclusion might be that this last usage ties in with the 'grandmothering hypothesis', that menopause, found only among humans, is evolutionarily adaptive (see, e.g., O'Connell, Hawkes and Blurton Jones 1999). It has been suggested that even in *Homo erectus* times, females must have been dependent on female kin living in matrifocal residential units, and further that matrilineal descent emerged from this as the earliest form group structure as early as *H. erectus* (Opie and Power 2008).

Exchange

Models of exchange differ from models of sharing in various ways. Fundamentally, though, sharing involves mainly members of the family, and exchange involves strangers, enemies and affines.

Formalism and substantivism

The major debate in the history of economic anthropology was that between the formalists and the substantivists. In the 1960s, a challenge to 'formalism' arose among young economic anthropologists. They argued that economic anthropology had been altogether too close to economics, and that what was needed was a more relativistic perspective. At its most extreme, the new 'substantivist' approach argued that economics held no universals, and its workings were embedded in culture, and embedded quite differently in different cultures. Proponents included a number of the contributors to George Dalton's (1967) *Tribal and peasant economies*, most notably Dalton himself. His interest was in west African market economies and 'primitive money'. The substantivists followed the political economist Karl Polanyi in rejecting the model of Western market economies as explanations for other economic systems. Those who retained the older perspective became known as formalists, and there was a formalist backlash – represented for example by several papers in LeClair and Schneider's (1968) edited volume, *Economic anthropology*. Although Harold Schneider did not like the distinction, he and his mentor Melville Herskovits were labelled formalists in opposition to what had become the dominant, substantivist, view.

In prehistory, it is difficult to imagine how a substantivist perspective might work. However, if one believes essentially in a substantivist perspective ethnographically, then arguably one should look for embedded economic structures in the archaeological record too, or try to work out how those principles might play in an archaeological context. There is a parallel here too with Darwinism, or more particularly neo-Darwinism (or sociobiology) which in these terms is basically a formalist ideology. However, one could perhaps envisage a more substantivist Darwinism that might take account of cultural practices as being of benefit in natural selection, and suitable for preservation in their own right.

The distinction, though, is not as obvious as it may seem. Formalism supposes something like economic optimization: people the world over want to have more, rather than less, capital. But capitalism too is part of culture. Formalism failed in part due to the onslaught of Marxism, which hit French anthropology in the 1960s and the English-speaking world a decade later. Marxist anthropology occurred in diverse forms, but essentially it distinguished 'base' from 'superstructure' and often gave prominence to the former – represented by those aspects of society that were seen as most related to subsistence pursuits. Superstructure included those, such as religion and worldview, which were perceived as more distant. However, things were never simple. Leading French Marxist Maurice Godelier (e.g. 1977 [1973]) then saw superstructure as fundamental to society and drew on Lévi-Straussian structuralism and implicitly too on structural-functionalism in his work, which saw things like religion and kinship as embedded in economic relations. Thus from a synchronic point of view this brand of Marxism was substantivist, while from a diachronic point of view it was, at least arguably, formalist in its presumption of a sequence of modes of production through which societies passed.

Paris, 1978: universal kinship and hxaro

I first spoke publicly on the idea of universal kin categorization (Barnard 1978) at the Paris hunter-gatherers conference of 1978. Lévi-Strauss was there, and it was really Lévi-Strauss who invented the concept when he wrote in 1949 (1969: xxiii) that elementary structures are those which, while defining all members of society as kin, class them into two categories: namely possible spouses and prohibited spouses. I simply introduced the label for the idea, and argued that it was fundamental to hunter-gatherer social organization. The idea is that in a society that possesses universal kinship, every member stands in a kin relationship to every other and can address each individual by a kinship term. It stands to reason that the distinction between close and distant kin, characteristic of large-scale Western or East Asian societies, is irrelevant for kin classification and often quite irrelevant for correct behaviour as well. There will usually be some mechanisms for extending kin classification universally throughout society, such as treating close friends or namesakes as kin, or working though moiety or section membership. Universal kinship determines things like how closely one may sit next to someone, and, of course, who is marriageable and who is not.

Polly Wiessner was also at the conference. She had discovered *hxaro* among the Ju'/hoansi (or !Kung) a few years earlier. As it happens, she had visited me in the field shortly after and told me what she had discovered. I looked for *hxaro*, and found it, among the Naro too. As I have mentioned, they call it //'ãè, or slightly more abstractly, //'ãèkù ('to give to each other'), where //'ãè means specifically not just any giving, but giving in this relationship. In Wiessner's words (from the subtitle of her

Ph.D. thesis), *hxaro* is 'a regional system of reciprocity for reducing risk'. The Ju/'hoansi use the word //'*ãè* as well, as the verb for such an exchange: '//'*ãè* me that book', '//'*ãè* me your pencil', and so on. But *hxaro* is the relationship or the abstract noun. It is obvious that Naro and Ju/'hoan *hxaro* practices are related. As far as we know, neither the word //'*ãè* nor the custom occurs among any Central Khoisan group except Naro and the small closely related groups who live adjacent to the Naro. It does not occur, for example, among the well-known G/wi or G//ana. Nor does the custom occur among any of the twenty or so Southern groups. It is found only among Naro and their neighbours and among the Northern groups – Ju/'hoansi, ≠Au//eisi and !Xũ.

So, exactly what is *hxaro*? *Hxaro* is a mechanism which is adaptive and effective at redistributing property and keeping those who have it egalitarian (Wiessner 1982). Any non-consumable material property may be given in *hxaro*. Goods are requested by the intended recipient, and may be either given or not given. One may give in *hxaro*, for example, knitted caps or other clothing, digging sticks or other tools, or trade goods. Wiessner found that on average, Ju/'hoansi have about nine *hxaro* partners. *Hxaro* partners can be of either gender, of any age, close kin or distant, Naro or Ju/'hoansi, or foreigners. Goods may be of equal value, or may be quite unequal, but exchanges can never be immediate. They must be delayed: the reciprocal *hxaro* gift may be made a week, a month or a year later. Then the other person may ask for a return gift, a month or a year after that. *Hxaro* is also tremendously useful for maintaining environmental equilibrium. The reason, as Wiessner discovered, is that the *hxaro* system overlies and defines another sphere of exchange, namely rights to utilize a *hxaro* partner's territory for hunting, gathering, and so on. Land is owned by core band members, but *hxaro* partners who do not have ownership rights nevertheless, by virtue of *hxaro*, have the right to take consumables: that is, water, wood, plants and animals.

Maurice Godelier was also at the 1978 conference. In his comments, he put my paper together with Wiessner's and suggested that where everyone is classified as kin, no one is kin. What *hxaro* also does, he was quite correct, is to allow individuals to choose their own quasi-kin relationships. *Hxaro* is 'kinship' by choice.

All social systems have two axes: competition and co-operation. *Hxaro* has both elements, though by virtue of the land and subsistence sphere that underlies *hxaro*, co-operation would seem to be the stronger. It is worth thinking about *hxaro* as a kind of *socialist* alternative to its individualist and competitive counterpart: the potlatch (see, e.g., Barnett 1938). If *hxaro* is a figment of 'primitive communism', then the potlatch is a figment of proto-capitalism. The workings of the two systems are really quite similar, only one occurs in an egalitarian society and the other in a stratified society. On the Northwest Coast of North America, chiefly hunter-gatherer-fishermen would hold feasts and ceremonies, and give away the wealth they acquired through environmental exploitation or trade. Status was defined not by the amount of wealth one possessed, but by the amount of wealth one gave away. Or at some points in the history of the potlatch, it came to be defined by the amount of wealth one destroyed. Their environment, like the Kalahari, has resources that vary from year to year. If this year I have wealth, then I will hold a potlatch and give it away in order to gain prestige. Next year, if your territory produces more berries or more salmon, enabling you to acquire more wealth, then you can hold the potlatch and put me to shame.

I do not believe that either *hxaro* or the potlatch are literally at the point of origin of property, or even of post-symbolic culture property relations. But they are indicative of highly evolved hunter-gatherer social relations, respectively in egalitarian and hierarchical societies. And as in many other such social contexts, they are threatened in their traditional forms by the transition, even the long transition, to the Neolithic. They are, not Tylorian, but Kropotkinist survivals of the mutual aid principle, and they still exist in some form, with the same labels, today in the Kalahari and on the Northwest Coast.

We take for granted our non-universal kinship systems, in the West and in the East, however defined. For most hunter-gatherers, they take for granted universal kinship, because *kinship is society*. Here I part company with Peter Kropotkin (1987). He believed that society comes first, and that kinship was a late, and a human (or we might say, hominin), invention. He stresses the fact that, with the exception of some carnivores and a few supposedly 'decaying' species of apes, higher mammals all live in societies. The first human societies, in his view, were a further development of these. This is a 'social contract' theory of society, although of course very different from that of Hobbes or even of Locke or Rousseau. Hunter-gatherers do not share just because they are 'good people' (though they might be). They share because they have deep-seated, and possibly evolutionarily early, customs that require sharing. *Homo habilis* was, by definition, a tool-maker. That meant he or she had property. The sharing of food, and no doubt of at least some manufactured goods, and knowledge of how to make them, lies deep in human nature. Yet with the Neolithic, accumulation takes over as what is valued. It is social, but in a different sense. For hunter-gatherers, immediate consumption (and therefore fewer working hours, sharing, and so on) are aspects of a quite different mode of thought.

Paris, 1968: original affluence

One of the most famous articles in hunter-gatherer studies is Marshall Sahlins's 'The original affluent society', published within his book on *Stone Age economics* (1974). Sahlins wrote the article during a stay in Paris in 1968. He argues that hunter-gatherers spend less, not more, time in subsistence-related activities than do non-hunter-gatherers. The article is important in the present context because it highlights the abilities hunter-gatherers have in obtaining subsistence, even from meagre environments, and also because it suggests that hunter-gatherers have surprisingly large amounts of free time. On the former point, others before and since have commented and provided data. For example, Richard Lee (1979: 464–88) found that Ju/'hoansi in Botswana know the names, uses and locations of some 220 plants and 58 mammals found in their territory. Most of these are used in food, some in medicine and some for other purposes – for tools, clothing or building materials. Knowledge is common to a large majority of the population, and Ju/'hoansi typically spend (according to two separate estimates) between 2.2 and 2.4 days of work per week per resident adult, and less for numerous visitors present in any Ju/'hoan camp (Lee 1979: 256, 259). On the latter point, more free time means more time for ritual, story-telling, conversation, play, and so on. It is certainly worth considering the degree to which this may be more than simply a Mesolithic/Neolithic or Later Stone Age/Iron Age difference. Did work effort go significantly down (or free time up) at some threshold, as Sahlins implies with the Neolithic? In other words, did agriculture bring with it not only surplus, diversification, division of labour and social hierarchy, but also constraints on free time? What was life like before the Mesolithic or Later Stone Age? Were *Homo hiedelbergensis* capable of finding free time? Indeed, were Palaeolithic people like their immediate successors in the, arguably symbolic, Middle Stone Age, or were they more like later Neolithic peoples, in that they needed to work long hours?

Sahlins (1974: 1–39) articulated the theoretical position which really lay beneath the hard data being uncovered in the 1960s: if hunter-gatherers maximize, they maximize their free time, not their wealth. This realization, which became apparent in the Chicago 'Man the Hunter' conference in 1966, was to transform hunter-gatherer studies into perhaps the most theoretically challenging branch of anthropology of that time. Among questions raised since then: if hunter-gatherers are affluent, do they lose their affluence as they adapt to the modern world? Resolutions to the controversy have begun to appear, following synthetic approaches like that of Nurit Bird-David (1990). In 'The giving environment', she emphasized hunter-gatherers' perceptions of their environments as rich and kind to their inhabitants. She also emphasized sharing between people, rather than environmental exploitation or the work effort exploitation requires. This is the way hunter-gatherers themselves often see the world: the environment as containing the necessities of life in sufficient amounts, provided that one's lifestyle remains based on the principles of mutual aid and communal good will. In another paper, Bird-David (1992) has gone on to reformulate Sahlins's notion of 'original affluence' to correct some of its inherent flaws. Sahlins, she argues, confused ecological and cultural perspectives. The key distinctions he drew were insightful, but he remained too much a formalist in his emphasis on labour time. What Sahlins failed to realize is that, to hunter-gatherers, what matters most is one's relationship to other people and to the environment. Ecology, in other words, is cosmological, symbolic and relational: it is not strictly economic, and not to be described strictly in terms of exploitation.

In the last few decades, property, a concern of seventeenth- and eighteenth-century social theories, has returned as a central focus in hunter-gatherer studies. It has been a major interest of James Woodburn in his Hadza ethnography and his comparative studies (e.g. Woodburn 1980, 1982). A conference on Woodburn's contribution to the study of property in hunting-and-gathering and other societies was held in Halle, Germany, in 2001, and the first volume of the two from this conference emphasized his more traditional concerns with sharing and egalitarianism (Widlok and Tadesse 2005). From the late 1970s, Woodburn had begun to talk of two types of economic system: 'immediate return' and 'delayed return'. Economies based on an immediate-return principle reject the accumulation of surplus; people either consume or share. Economies based on a delayed-return principle allow for planning ahead. Only *some* hunter-gatherers fit the immediate-return category; those who invest time in keeping bees, raising horses or making boats or large traps are, like non-hunter-gatherers, consigned to the residual, delayed-return category. In his paper for the London hunter-gatherer studies symposium of 1986, Woodburn (1988) argued that delayed-return economies are adapted to pastoralism and agriculture, whereas immediate-return ones are not. It is not that people in immediate-return systems have any technical difficulty with food production; what keeps them from doing so is their social organization and value systems, which are based on egalitarianism and sharing.

In historical perspective, it is worth remembering that the distinction between hunter-gatherers and non-hunter-gatherers was not always obvious. It was virtually unknown in the seventeenth century, and emerged in

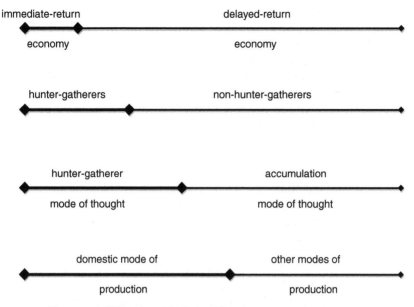

Figure 5.2 'Them' and 'us' classifications

the eighteenth only when economics (as opposed to politics) became a basis for the classification of societies, and when it was realized too that hunting and gathering were indeed legitimate activities of people in society, and not merely of pre-social human beings (Barnard 2004). Where we draw the line between 'them' and 'us' remains a matter of debate, and it depends on criteria which are judged differently by different theorists (figure 5.2).

Political order and anthropological models

In every human society, kinship is ordered and systematic. In my view, it has been this way ever since the symbolic revolution. Full kinship, like full language, can only ever be ordered, since present social relations are always dependent on pre-existing social relations, and since junior individuals within a kinship system will follow rules of reciprocal usage in the way they address and treat seniors. If someone calls me 'son-in-law', whatever that might mean, I will address and treat her as 'mother-in-law'.

It is not so with politics. While kinship structures may change with time, they nevertheless retain a continuity that depends on language and on rules of reciprocity that are grounded as much in logic as in sociality.

Political structures are simpler and much more negotiable. The degree of control one person may exert over another is contingent on personality. Loosely, political structures are of two kinds: ascribed and achieved. There is also a third logical possibility, where ascribed status is made to work through any individual's ability to negotiate power with like individuals. It is useful to think of ascribed power as typically exhibited in chiefdoms, such as those found in many African societies, and achieved power as represented at the extreme by Melanesian 'big man' systems (Godelier and Strathern 1991). The in-between form is most strongly seen in the chiefly systems of Northwest Coast North America, where they seem to contain elements of both typical chiefly and typical 'big man' forms (see, e.g., Rosman and Rubel 1971). The latter two are likely to be of more interest in prehistory, though I suspect only with reference to the times since the symbolic revolution.

Optimal foraging strategies are theoretical models of behaviour, based on the premise that humans (and animals) seek to maximize their chances of finding food with the least effort. The volume *Hunter-gatherer foraging strategies*, edited by Bruce Winterhalder and Eric Alden Smith (1981), led the way in this trend. Other examples include the work of Kirsten Hawkes, Kim Hill and James O'Connell (e.g. 1982) on the Aché or Guayaki of Paraguay. Their model is based on the idea that both hunter-gatherers and animals exhibit a kind of economic 'rationality' in their subsistence strategies, and that that 'rationality' is a product of evolutionary adaptation. For this very reason, the model has become interesting to those who *cannot* accept it. For example, Ingold (2000: 27–39) has argued that optimal foraging theory is misplaced because it confuses adaptation with rationality. It proposes *abstract models* of behaviour as though they were *explanations* for behaviour. In other words, it goes too far towards biology in seeking explanations for cultural behaviour.

In the 1990s, new trends in evolutionary theory led to great interest in the search for the origins of language, ritual and symbolic culture. Previous gradualist approaches were being challenged by new models, based loosely on recent hunter-gatherer ethnography. Among these models is that of Chris Knight (e.g. Knight 1991; Knight, Power and Watts 1995), who has overturned the post-Enlightenment concern with families and clans and the primal basis of society, with a 'social contract' view. According to Knight, all symbolic culture emerged as a result of a social contract among females of a band perhaps 60,000 or 70,000 years ago. Collectively, he says, they denied men sex and forced them to hunt between new and full moon, and then enjoyed an orgy of sex and food from the full to the new moon. Although only a small number of anthropologists accept Knight's theory, nevertheless it has sparked a surprising amount of debate and even interdisciplinary research among anthropologists, archaeologists and linguists over the last two decades. Recent archaeological data might suggest an earlier date, but his theory remains the same.

Pedagogical lessons

For teaching purposes, academic disciplines are dived into chunks. These are called 'courses', and they in turn are divided into progressive stages ordered by chronology, level of difficulty or some other organizing principle. When applying social anthropology to areas of study traditionally associated with archaeology or biological anthropology, it is often worth considering the use of social anthropological knowledge ordered in such ways, rather than randomly or on an *ad hoc* basis.

At Edinburgh, we have the following six 'core courses':

1. Anthropological Theory
2. Kinship: Structure and Process
3. Consumption, Exchange, Technology
4. Ritual and Religion
5. Belief, Thought and Language
6. Culture and Power

These in fact correspond quite closely to the classic, functionalist four systems – though with the addition of anthropological theory to provide a generalist overview, and with religion divided into two (separating ritual aspects, taught in the third year, from belief, taught in the fourth). Other universities around the world teach 'core' aspects of social anthropology in similar ways, though with course divisions often reflecting specialized interests or theoretical perspectives of a department. For example, rather than religion being divided into two courses, often the subject matter of our Consumption, Exchange, Technology is divided into two: Ecological Anthropology (environment, technology and some aspects of subsistence) being split from Economic Anthropology (subsistence and exchange).

The odd one out, it might seem, is Culture and Power (political anthropology). Yet this is a crucial aspect of any society. Certainly, modern hunter-gatherers have politics even if they have no internal social hierarchy or positions of leadership. Although such political systems may be impossible to find in the archaeological record, they will have been there in prehistoric societies: politics by consensus, decision-making through discussion and argument, intra-group or between-group violence, the dominance of one people over another, and so on. Sometimes, speculation on such things may have to take precedence over data-led archaeological exploration. It is worth remembering too that, at least since the symbolic revolution (and possibly before), humanity truly is the symbolic species, as well as the ceremonial animal.

The course title Belief, Thought and Language is to me a reminder that at the symbolic revolution we should stop talking about *behaviour* and think instead about what neuroscientists and psychologists call *cognition*. In social anthropology we call this *belief and thought*, terms which no doubt imply a more active form of cognition than we can ascribe to animals or even to pre-modern *Homo*. Coolidge and Wynn (2009: 121–7, 166–9) comment on the fact that there was a transformation in cognitive capability between *H. habilis* and *H. erectus*, and another between *H. erectus* and *H. heidelbergensis*. This is particularly true in spatial cognition and working memory, and while earlier transformations may be measured through changes in skull morphology, these ones are measured through the evidence of methods of stone tool production. There are also differences, they suggest, between Neanderthals and moderns in working-memory capacity (Coolidge and Wynn 2009: 203). I would suggest a further transformation with late *H. sapiens*, although possibly not a biologically induced one. *Belief* implies a more systematic and indeed conceptually problematic understanding of the thought processes of social anthropology's subjects. Rodney Needham taught us this in the first lines of his greatest, and highly philosophical, work, *Belief, language, and experience* (Needham 1972: 1–2), when he reflected on his own agonizing over how to translate the English sentence 'I believe in God' into his fieldwork language, Penan.

Finally, a thought on other disciplines. Social anthropology really does have at its foundation a systematic division of its subject matter that is reflected in its core teaching units (as above) and possibly too some of its supposedly more peripheral, optional ones (Medical Anthropology, Anthropology of Art, etc.). For other disciplines, the basics are less clear. For example, the Edinburgh Sociology department's only core courses are two in research methods, with no specific substantive areas of that discipline regarded as essential for a degree in the subject. And if that discipline has an overriding theme, it is methodology – regarded by many social anthropologists as prissy and hardly necessary (see Kuper 1973: 238). Mary Douglas once told me that when she asked her supervisor, Godfrey Lienhardt, about how to take fieldnotes, she was offered a cigarette. When she declined on the grounds that she did not smoke, Lienhardt said: 'I don't know what you do then; I always write my notes on the back of cigarette packs.'

If social anthropology has an equivalent to methodology, I would say that it must be *definition*. Like philosophers, social anthropologists constantly define and redefine what they are looking at. In other disciplines, this may be less crucial. I was once at a conference on 'endangered languages' and noted that none of those present had said anything about what they mean by 'an endangered language', as opposed to any other kind of language. One linguist claimed that my question was not only not important, but not relevant. To me, it was, and is in such a context, highly relevant, though this may have been not a linguistic question but a social anthropological one. If social anthropology has anything to contribute to the debates of other disciplines, we would be wise to retain the foundations and the perspectives of our own discipline, not to abandon them when we engage in cross-disciplinary discussions.

Until the 1990s, linguists tended to be very sceptical about research on the origin of languages or origins of language. They simply could not see what evidence there might be that would be relevant, especially within linguistics (Malmkjær 2004: 387). Neuroscientists and archaeologists might be doing research on the problem, but the idea that language itself might be relevant was met with disbelief. What changed things was an article in *Behavioral and Brain Sciences* (Pinker and Bloom 1990). It suggested that linguistics might actually be no different from any other field. It was just that no linguist had put together what was known that might bear on the problem.

Today, it is still the same with social and cultural anthropology. Because of this, the field of the origin of human society (as well as that of the origins of language) is still underdeveloped in anthropology in general, when compared to its potential. The problem, for reasons hinted at earlier, is simply that very few social anthropologists have made the effort to piece together the many aspects of the discipline that relate to the topic.

Thoughts and theories of the origin and purpose of language

The origins of language were central to Enlightenment debates on the nature of humanity. On the Continent it engaged a plethora of writers, including Rousseau, Condillac, Maupertuis and Herder, among others, while in Scotland, Adam Smith wrote a classic essay on the subject. Most writers of the eighteenth century assumed a gradual development of language. Today, the origin of language is more often thought of in revolutionary terms, but of course there could have been many steps – in other words, neither gradual evolution nor a single, spontaneous origin. These steps could all have involved complex physiological, psychological and social, as well as linguistic, relationships (see, e.g., Wray 2002). We must also think carefully about what we mean when we speak of 'language'. Saussure's (1974 [1916]) distinction in French between *la langue* (language, in the sense of the structure of language) and *la parole* (speech) is well known. But consider too the distinction in classical Latin between *lingua* (tongue, speech, language) and *sermō* (conversation), and Pufendorf's (1991 [1673]: 77–9) quite different usage: *lingua* when speaking of a specific language, and *sermō* for language in the abstract. The latter is language as part of human nature, which for Pufendorf is ultimately *social nature*.

But is language always social? Is human sociality always linguistic? Social anthropologist Jerome Lewis (2009) has studied the linguistic behaviour of the Mbenjele Pygmies of northern Congo-Brazzaville. He found significant differences between women and men. Women's speech is loud, especially in the forest. Men speak in a more subdued manner. Women's talk involves humour and shaming, while men's talk frequently involves mimicry. And among the Mbenjele, there are other forms of communication too: rhythmic singing and dancing, as well as talking. These can be used to 'speak' with the spirits and animals of the forest, as well as in human to human communication. Usually, talk is social, especially women's, but sometimes men will talk to themselves. Or they will sit beside each other for hours, and say nothing.

I found very similar linguistic practices among the Naro. There are differences though. In Mbenjele society (as in American or British society), it is usual for people to talk in turn. While this is common in Naro society too, Naro typically also engage in more than one conversation at a time. There may be three or four going on at once at an evening fire, with not many more speakers than that in total. At the same time, conversations are kept within the circle of those around a given fire. Even though one can hear others nearby, one does not enter the conversations of other fires any more than a Londoner or a New Yorker would speak to someone he can hear over his garden fence. In general, a domestic domain in Botswana is also defined by a fence. For Botswana's hunter-gatherers it is defined by the backs of individuals facing a fire, and hunter-gatherers make fires outside, not inside, their huts.

Another Naro ethnographer, Mathias Guenther (2006: 243), argues that Naro San talk 'is not just oral discourse, but is instead *rhetorical* discourse'. By this he means that it exists in order to persuade. Persuasion, he suggests, is central to Naro discourse in general, except in storytelling. The Naro language in fact has twenty-six words for 'talk' or 'talking' plus another seven for 'tell': 'talk' (*kx'ui*), 'talk about' (*ǀhôà-kx'am*), 'talk at the same time' (*ǃgàbàkú*), 'talk too much' (*ǃnabè sa tsi ko gone*, literally 'you are chasing a giraffe'), etc. (Guenther 2006: 242, 256–7; Visser 2001: 209–11). Naro notions of when to talk and when not to talk are often different from my or Guenther's expectations. Not only may Naro contribute to several conversations at the same time; they may repeat what someone else is saying, while they are still talking. Conversations may involve 'demand sharing', in which coveted goods are repeatedly requested, even when the general conversation or conversations are about something else. Conversation itself is a form of reciprocity, as well as a form of communication. It is also a form of mutual entertainment. Contrary to conversational styles in Guenther's German-Canadian background or my American-British one, Naro appear to talk too much, and that talking often serves different purposes than in Western, non-hunter-gatherer societies.

Over the last few years, I have developed two theories of the origin of language. On the one hand, language originates in hominin communication, which is closely tied to the development of sociality through sharing, exchange and especially kinship. The fuller theory, which is a theory of the co-evolution of language and kinship from *Homo habilis* to *H. sapiens sapiens*, will have to wait until chapter 8. On the other hand, the development of full language stems from narrative. In the former case, language is likely rooted in more gestured forms, and very definitely in communication. And in the latter it is rooted in deeply symbolic thought, and in speech, and it goes far beyond the need of ordinary conversation. My second theory (Barnard 2010c) is an attempt to explain why languages are so complicated. Depending on how one counts them, Naro has something like eighty-six person-number-gender markers. One could count many more, up to 204 I think, or rather fewer, depending on how one defines case function, whether changes in tone according to case should count and how one deals with duplicates, that is, the same form with different meanings.

The same applies, more or less, to all other Khoe (Central Khoisan) languages. Consider too this statement: 'English has no future.' By this I mean that English, like other Germanic languages, is missing a future tense. Of course, in the absence of one, 'will' or 'shall', or 'is about to', and so on, may be inserted before the verb to give future meaning. But why should English have to do this? Languages seem to be put together in ways that make no practical sense. Most languages are more complicated than they have to be. And very few of them are quite as perfect in their ability to express anything as Benjamin Lee Whorf (1956 [written *c*. 1936]: 84–5) imagined Hopi to be. And Hopi, according to Whorf (1956: 57–64), is tense-less.

In short, language is both over-determined and under-determined. This might be explainable partly with reference to the cognitive capabilities of the human mind, and if I were a neuroscientist I would certainly look there for explanations. But as a social anthropologist I require social and cultural explanations as well. It troubles me that there is no correspondence between social structure and linguistic structure. Yet I do have a tentative answer. The answer lies in the evolutionary power of myth, and in the complexity of language required to meet the semiotic and social requirements for myth-telling. My paper, cited above, analyses a single sentence, which occurs in the /Xam San language, in a myth told by a /Xam to a folklorist in 1878: '*Hé tíkẹn ē, /kuaṁmaṅ-a há /ne kúi: "Ṅ kaṅ ka, a ≠kákka !kṓïṅ, tssá ra χá ā, !kṓïṅ ta /kŭ /ê̩ //ĕ !k'é ē /χárra?"*' ('Then /kuaṁmaṅ-a said: "I desire thee to say to grandfather, Why is it that grandfather continues to go among strangers [literally people who are different]?"') (Bleek and Lloyd 1911: 32–3). The phrase *!k'é ē /χárra* (meaning 'people who are different'), is the object of a complex, and specifically narrative-form, verb *ha /kŭ /ê̩ //ĕ* (roughly, 'to continue habitually to go among'). An implied sentence describing habitually continuous action, within an interrogative sentence ('Why is it ...'), within an interrogative sentence (my translation: 'Ask Grandfather ...'), within an imperative sentence ('I say to you'), within an indicative sentence ('Then /Kuammana-a demanded'), within a myth or fable in which animals act as people, and deceive them and other animals, told to an English woman by a /Xam man, who had learned it from his mother, who had learned it from someone else, who had put it together with culturally significant social action, with metaphor and with complex syntax, for a reason well beyond the requirements of ordinary communication.

In short, linguistic complexity is not required for communication, but it is required for myth. Myths are never just stories. They always occur in the context of a mythological system, which is specific to a given 'society' or 'culture'. Myths are not only shared within a speech community. They are related to each other. The same deities, the same mythological beasts, the same themes of trickery, death, hunting, sex, kinship, and so on, will occur in many myths within the same speech community, and beyond it. Myths occur in sequence, and they are cross-referential. They impart cultural knowledge, and they also draw on prior cultural knowledge, as well as on meaning derived more directly from the words in the myths.

One of the most intriguing theories of recent years in the biological bases of language concerns a mutation in the FOXP2 gene. FOXP2 is a gene that controls brain and lung development in humans and other vertebrates (Enard *et al.* 2002). In humans it also controls movements in the larynx and mouth that govern speech, and apparently also controls the ability of the brain to formulate the complex rules of grammar found throughout the species. Wolfgang Enard and his colleagues suggest that this mutation is recent, that is, coincident with the symbolic revolution. There is little doubt that invention of language was of the highest importance in human evolution, but do we need a change in the whole human genome at all in order to account for its universal occurrence? Ian Tattersall (2000: 14) suggests another possibility. The spread of language could as easily have occurred throughout the world among populations who had the latent biological capacity to acquire it. Language spread, in other words, through cultural contact and not through biological evolution. Of course, the situation may not be simply 'either'/'or', but might well have involved both biological evolution and cultural transmission.

Full language?

Did Neanderthals have full language? Probably not. There were biological constraints (to do with speech production), and possibly cognitive constraints as well – though the former need not be affected if we grant them either sign language or some phonologically limited form of speech. The balance of opinion is that *Homo sapiens* pushed Neanderthals out of their habitats or killed them off more directly. Neanderthal genes have not, as far as can be ascertained, entered the *H. sapiens* gene pool to any great extent. Perhaps *H. sapiens* technology was superior. Perhaps *H. sapiens* communication skills were vastly superior. I think that that is likely, although it may not account for the evolution of full language.

Numerous studies hint at biological reasons for the evolution of language. Even those which are socially oriented tend to assume a Darwinian selective advantage in the communication of practical knowledge. While I would not deny that that was true in early phases of language evolution, I cannot believe it is at all likely for the development of full language, with all the absurdly complex rules of syntax for individual languages, and all its diversity worldwide. In my view, full language evolved not for mere communication of information about hunting, gathering, water resources, and so on. Nor for mere conversation. It evolved for the purpose of narrative. Stories of hunting, of love, whatever, were crucial, but as I have suggested above, even more crucial were myths that from place to place were passed on both from place to place and through the generations.

Consider this statement by Alison Jolly (1996: 167): 'As a Darwinian, I start from the assumption that language was useful to our evolving ancestor. Selection for rapid advances in linguistic capacity probably related to the advantages of efficient communication between members of social groups.' What kind of 'capacity'? The eleven classificatory verb stems of Navajo? The eighteen noun classes of Swahili? The eighty-six person-number-gender markers of Naro? Recursion in all languages (with the possible exception, famously, of Pirahã)? In fact, Jolly's concern is with social abilities such as the ability to deceive linguistically or to hide (another form of deception), and with the transmission of short vocalized messages between rhesus monkeys, with symbolic play among gorillas, and with the use of communication to develop long-term social bonds among chimpanzees. Full language is something entirely different. Recursive constructions give us an infinite capacity for enabling the invention of new sentences.

Boas noted that in every language 'certain classifications of concepts occur', and mentioned for nouns masculine/feminine, animate/inanimate, or according to grammatical function within a sentence; and for verbs, according to tense or even locality. He wrote: 'The behavior of primitive man makes it perfectly clear that all these concepts, although they are in constant use, have never risen into consciousness, and that consequently their origin must be sought, not in rational, but in entirely unconscious, we may perhaps say instinctive, processes of mind' (Boas 1911: 67). In this way linguistic behaviour, he argued, differs from all other cultural behaviour. Grammatical categories need not be (consciously) known to native speakers, but they exist in mental processing just the same. In the same decade, Emile Durkheim and Lucien Lévy-Bruhl in France, and Sigmund Freud in Austria, were talking about the unconscious too. Of these, Lévy-Bruhl held special interest in grammatical categories, and especially in *How natives think* (Lévy-Bruhl 1926 [1910]) explored the nature of complex and 'concrete' grammatical categories, which he held to be functions of 'primitive' ways of thinking. Of course, and as Boas and his student Benjamin Lee Whorf well knew, the complex morphology of languages touched on by Lévy-Bruhl were best not regarded as indicators of primitive thought, but quite the opposite.

Archaeological evidence for symbolic behaviour

Ochre and beads

Over the last decade or so, an amazing amount of archaeological material on symbolic behaviour has surfaced. While recent criticisms (e.g. Botha 2009) have dented the assertions that this material suggests the use of (full) language, they should not be taken as implying a lack of symbolic expression, through material artefacts, for communication. Art, and for that matter ritual too, may precede verbal expression as a manifestation of symbolic or 'supernatural' communication. I am hardly the first person to claim this: R. R. Marett said it in one form or another, repeatedly, in the early twentieth century. His emphasis was on ritual, and in particular on dance (e.g. Marett 1932: 6–7). The idea that music precedes words is also commonplace in theories of language origin, not least in that of Steven Mithen (2005, 2009).

Without dwelling on the details of the many splendid papers over the last decade, the publications by Christopher Henshilwood, Francesco d'Errico and their colleagues (e.g. Henshilwood *et al.* 2002, 2004; d'Errico *et al.* 2005) tell us that more than 70,000 years ago southern Africans on the Indian Ocean coast were making decorative shell beads, and presumably wearing them, etching ochre, and presumably using it to decorate themselves, and acquiring the ochre and transporting it, and placing it in receptacles in their caves. That is the evidence from Blombos Cave, with related data from other rock shelters and caves nearby. In another paper, d'Errico and his colleagues (d'Errico *et al.* 2003) reflect in an explicitly interdisciplinary way on the meaning of all this, and similar data from Europe and elsewhere, for the origins of language, music and symbolism.

Henshilwood and Curtis Marean (2003) propose that understandings of modernity be classified as belonging to four basic explanatory models, The first is the *Later Upper Pleistocene Model*, which suggests that modern behaviour has evolved in Africa since 50,000 years ago. In other words, modernity is characteristic of the Later Stone Age, and not before. The Middle Stone Age (of Blombos Cave), according to this view, is lacking in beadwork, ochre use, symbolism, trade networks, geographical or temporal variability, knowledge of seasonal variations in resources, fishing or bird-catching capabilities, sophisticated techniques for hunting large game, and so on. Henshilwood and Marean ascribe this view to a number of scholars, or at least a number of publications by Stanley Ambrose, Lewis Binford, Desmond Clark, Clive Gamble and Richard Klein. The other models are the *Earlier Upper Pleistocene Model*, *Later Middle Pleistocene Model* and the *Gradualist Model*. All these latter models assume essentially the opposite: that at some point either during or before the Middle Stone Age, modernity began, either with a 'big bang' or with a gradual evolution of technological, cognitive and symbolic capabilities.

Let me simply add that, beginning with Lawrence Barham's (1998, 2002) findings at Twin Rivers, in Zambia, evidence of ochre pigment use in south-central and eastern Africa has grown. It is now generally accepted that ochre was in use 200,000 years ago, and possibly much earlier. This implies perhaps not language (as some maintain), but certainly symbolism, maybe pre-linguistic symbolic action, and maybe art.

Rock art

The best ethnographies, and perhaps the best rock art descriptions too, have a good combination of what Gregory Bateson (1958 [1936]: 123–51, 198–256) referred to as *ethos* and *eidos*. Ethos represents the ethereal aspects of culture: the feeling of a place, the collective emotions that spring from it, its distinctive spirit. Eidos represents the configuration of culture: its form or structure. The distinction is very clear in rock art studies, not only in result but in method. Patricia Vinnicombe, for example, sought the eidos. She wrote: 'One of the most striking facts that emerges from an objective and quantitative study of the rock paintings is that they are not a realistic reflection of the daily pursuits or environment of the Bushmen' (Vinnicombe 1976: 347). 'Art for art's sake' writers such as the artist and rock art commentator Walter Battiss tended towards presentation of the ethos, and even as early as the 1940s criticized colleagues for their theoretical prejudices:

It is far better to have no pet theories seeking confirmation, for the happy research worker is he who learns from the paintings what really is, rather than he who tries to teach the paintings to be what he wants them to be. Some men go to the sites to prove their fantastic theories, other, more humble and honest, go to learn what they can. (Battiss 1948: 22)

My own ethnography, like that of many of my colleagues in Bushman studies, is undoubtedly top heavy with descriptions of the eidos. This is true in ecological studies, in discussions of kinship and politics, and even in works in ritual and religion. A better balance, I think, is that achieved by Megan Biesele (e.g. 1993) in some of her work on Bushman folklore, religious ideas and worldview. Her work is commonly cited by specialists in the rock art of southern Africa for its hints at interpretation on the art, based on the assumption that the religion of the painters of long ago and that of Ju/'hoansi living today is very similar. Indeed, they are probably right that it is, in spite of time (more than 25,000 years, from the earliest rock art of Apollo 11 Cave in southern Namibia to the present) and distance (more than 1,000 kilometres, from distant rock art in the Drakensburg to the centre of Ju/'hoan territory) (see also Barnard 2007a: 83–96).

In a paper on the reinterpretation of southern African rock art, Thomas Dowson (2007: 51–2) has argued that 'shamanism' is an intellectual construct, and, in particular, a construct of two simultaneous forms. One form is a non-Western one, based on the acceptance of mystical relations between shamanic practice and the environment. The other is a Western one, based both on a logical division between humanity and nature, and on a distinction between rational explanation on the part of Western thinkers and culturally determined irrational modes of explanation on the part of peoples practising shamanism. Of course, Western thought is culturally determined too, though Dowson's construct side-steps the issue. Rather, his more general argument in this paper is that rock art specialists, both those of the shamanic approach and those who oppose them, have given too much emphasis to discussions of the power of shamans. Dowson suggests instead that what is revealed in the art is a wider link between humanity and nature, the mundane and the ritual. In his view, humans (not just shamans) and animals all play a part in the creation of the art. Therianthropes (presumed shamanic beings, part animal and part human) figure prominently in southern Africa rock art, but not necessarily in other traditions.

Whether his rigorous analysis of the rock art proves this or not, I think Dowson is on to something. Social anthropologists as well as archaeologists should take into account part of the cosmological construction entailed in presumed 'shamanic thought': to be human is to be symbolic. Wendy James too implies this in *The ceremonial animal* (James 2003), a complex review of traditional social anthropological concerns and their relevance to contemporary problems such as new reproductive technologies and religious fundamentalism.

I will not dwell on the details of the vast literature in rock art here. Let me just mention two quite recent books by David Lewis-Williams. *The mind in the cave* (Lewis-Williams 2002), in line with his many earlier works, tackles the relation between rock art and ritual. His own field research is in southern Africa, but he couples that understanding, including not only the details gained from studies of rock art there, but also a knowledge of the rituals of living Bushman groups, with the interpretation of European rock art. Just as in earlier works he looks to the trance dances of Kalahari San to interpret Drakensberg rock art, here he looks to their essence, and the essence of shamanism broadly, for more clues to the hallucinogenic experiences of painters of the Upper Palaeolithic caves of southern France. He also employs his knowledge of general archaeology and San mythology to do the same. *Conceiving God* (Lewis-Williams 2010) adds further dimensions, including a deeper exploration of San spirituality (also dealt with in his other recent works), medieval Christian mysticism and cognitive explanations from neuroscience. The point is that religiosity and mysticism comprise not just belief in deities, or the performance of rituals, but a capacity for music, myth, and so on – and I would add language in its full state, at least since the symbolic revolution, as a function as well as a cause of the development of narrative and, in particular, mythology.

Although I have concentrated here on southern African rock art, and to a degree on European, no doubt I could equally have used other examples. Australian rock art, although possibly not as old as southern African, has an internal coherence in styles and themes across that continent. So too, to a degree, does European rock art. Rock paintings are found throughout the world, on all inhabited continents, and rock engravings are nearly as widespread. The dates are contentious, but given claims of the presence of rock art fragments, pieces of red ochre, and so on, in archaeological sites on several continents and going back more than 30,000 years, it might even be worth thinking further about rock art as a clue to migrations and to the spread of early religions – as was done for southern Africa, at least in then unpublished work, as early as the 1870s (Barnard 2007a: 34–6). A few rare objects, notably the mammoth ivory Lion Man of Hohlenstein-Stadel, are also in the region of 30,000 years old. While social anthropology may have less to say on these, the principle is the same: ethnological history need not be confined to groups that are in existence today or whose recent history can be deciphered, as the nineteenth-century rock art expert George W. Stow knew full well (see Stow 1905). We can still know people long gone though the archaeological record. The same goes for the grander field of deciphering early symbolic culture. This is all too often left in the hands of scholars with hard-line, or at least 'strong', theories that few accept. I am thinking of course of Chris Knight and the strong version of his menstruation hypothesis (Knight 1991). There is a place too for subtle speculation on life at the dawn of symbolic culture (cf. Klein and Edgar 2002), through such things as comparative analysis of the earliest art across the continents and constant reinterpretation of symbolic universals, or the subset of these that form symbolic universals among the world's hunter-gatherer peoples. Of course, often the symbolism of hunter-gatherers differs from that of non-hunter-gatherers, as I have shown in earlier work (see Barnard 1999, 2002).

Ethnographic examples of symbolic behaviour

The art of tracking: the origin of science

South African anthropologist Louis Liebenberg (1990: v) has put forward an intriguing theory of the origin of science. He claims that science originated in the tracking of game animals. What is more, this science is not merely about empirical observation and conclusion about what is 'written in the sand'. It is about being able 'to read into the sand'. It involves imagination as well as observation.

Liebenberg's book explains that hunters have empathy with the animals they kill – a fact attested in many part of the world, though in Liebenberg's case derived from his interviews with !Xóõ trackers in Botswana. To track an animal successfully, a hunter will put himself in the place of the animal, and ask what he would do if he were that animal. Liebenberg (1990: 8) implies that rock art might reflect this. It is important to remember that tracking is an essential part of hunting. Modern hunter-gathers, with bows and arrows or spear-throwers, tend initially to wound an animal. They must chase it and generally track it in order to bring it down. *Homo ergaster* or *H. erectus* had a greatly inferior tool kit. Of course, some environmental conditions favour tracking far better than others, and areas with little vegetation but with soft or wet soil or sand, or with a smooth surface, are better than other areas.

Hunters also know the terrain they hunt in and can take advantage of local knowledge, as well as of animal behaviour, to predict animal movements. Hunting is a co-operative enterprise. In the Kalahari, men hunt typically in groups of two or three, and often more. Elsewhere, such as the Canadian Subarctic, yet larger groups are found. Hunters know too not just that there is an animal ahead of them, but the species, often the age and sex, how fast the animal is moving, and so on. They will know the gait of the animal: walking, trotting, galloping, jumping, and so on. And they put this knowledge to use in order to make predictions and judgements that are required for successful hunting. *Homo erectus* may have done the same. Might science be older than religion?

The evolution of science and religion

Another theoretical perspective, with some affinity to the views of Liebenberg, is relativistic approach to religion. Although one can find relativism in Durkheimian thought and certainly in mainstream American anthropology since Boas, the example I have in mind is rather different. The key, two-part, paper is that of Robin Horton (1967a, 1967b), who argues that traditional African thought and Western thought are similar, though often represented in different idioms. African thought is represented as magical and mystical, whereas Western thought is wrongly seen as more objective and scientific. In Horton's view, these two forms of thought are much more similar than anthropologists and others would give credit for. Horton's argument has had much influence in the specialized field of philosophy of science, and in the study of modern African belief and religion, but not perhaps among those who speculate about the beginnings of religious belief. I think it could have, if we are prepared, as Horton did, to set aside assumptions of naivety on the part of our ancestors and think of them instead as proto-scientists trying to grapple with form and meaning of the universe.

In the closing pages of *The Golden Bough*, Sir James Frazer used the metaphor of three threads to explain the evolution of human thought: the black thread of magic, the red thread of religion and the white thread of science. In the earliest times, he tells us, the black and white threads were intertwined, with the red thread of religion appearing later. Its 'dark crimson stain' comes to dominate the fabric of history, but tails off into lighter hues as the white thread of science again comes to the fore (Frazer 1922: 713–14). In short, there was at first magico-scientific thought, not magico-religious thought.

Earlier thinkers, in the heyday of unilinear evolutionism, often pre-ferred more clear-cut schemes, and divided religion into different forms. Sir John Lubbock (1874 [1870]: 119), for example, stated that the order of evolution was from atheism, to fetishism, to nature-worship or totem-ism, to shamanism, to idolatry, to theism. This particular trajectory was common among Lubbock's contemporaries. However, an interesting trend later emerged when diffusionist thinkers, Catholic priests among them, argued that theism came first, and specifically monotheism. This was the view of Father Wilhelm Schmidt (e.g. 1939 [1937]), in particu-lar, who rejected the trend among his contemporaries that Tasmanian or broadly Australian Aboriginal culture was the earliest form. He saw African Pygmy culture as the most deeply primitive. He believed that monothesism had been divinely revealed to the earliest peoples, and that to this day vestiges of it remain among Pygmies, Bushmen and other non-Australian hunter-gatherers. The theological question aside, this is not as far-fetched as it may seem. Hunter-gatherers, along with herders, do tend to be monotheistic. Having a plurality of gods and goddesses would indeed appear to be a later development, characteristic of agricul-tural societies such as those of the Ancient Mediterranean and the Indian subcontinent. Whatever the specifics, social anthropological enquiry can certainly aim to unravel those intertwined threads of human thought. And it is likely that comparative anthropology's main contribution to the study of early humans will be at the time depth of the symbolic revolu-tion, which I would put at least before the Toba eruption and the habita-tion of Blombos Cave.

From religion to the person

There is a good deal of literature in social anthropology, as well as in psychology and philosophy, concerning the 'concept of the person'. An important exposition touching on the concept is Tim Ingold's

(2000: 89–110) 'A circumpolar night's dream', which draws especially on work by psychological anthropologist A. Irving Hallowell (e.g. 1955, 1960). Hallowell conducted fieldwork with Ojibwa, a Canadian Subarctic people. In Western societies, normally only humans are considered 'persons', and it follows that any attempt at classifying animals as persons is bound to render them anthropomorphic. Ojibwa, however, regard the human as only one of many forms of person. Animals, winds, thunder, heavenly bodies, stones, and so on, can also be persons. Furthermore, persons are encountered not only in waking life but also in dreams and in myths. And in the telling of a myth, the 'other-than-human' persons are not present merely in the narrative, but also in front of the audience hearing the myth. For this reason, myths can only be told by certain people, and with ritual formality.

The Ojibwa concept of the person assumes that persons have an inner soul. They have consciousness and memory; they can act and they can speak. It is this essence of soul and these attributes that makes something a 'person', not its outward form. Humans and all other persons can indeed change form, and non-human persons are far better at this than humans. Most humans only succeed in such metamorphoses at death, although shamans are said to have this power in life. The assumed abilities of Ojibwa shamans and non-human persons to metamorphose into animals or other beings is not unique. Many Arctic and South American peoples have similar beliefs about their shamans. Among Bushmen too, we find very similar notions. The Naro of Botswana also say that spirits of the dead and living medicine men can transform themselves, especially into snakes, lions and shooting stars. What we in English call a 'shooting star' is to the Naro not a star at all, but 'the eye of a lion' and the means by which sprits and medicine men travel from one point in the landscape to another. And when they land, they take the form of a lion (and the Lion Man of Hohlenstein-Stadel may be a shaman?). Ingold's (2000: 106–10) purpose in recounting Hallowell's ethnography is to show an alternative to the Darwinian view that animals and humans differ only in degree, and that humans are superior to animals. He does this not to suggest that we should adopt an Ojibwa worldview, but to propose that we be more conscious of the 'poetics of dwelling' that underlies both scientific and Ojibwa ontology. My purpose in drawing on this example here is to show *how humans think*.

Let me take another example. Gregory Bateson (1987 [1972]: 8–11) argued that the Iatmul of Papua New Guinea have a theory of order which is the opposite of that of the Book of Genesis, and says that Western scientists (theist and atheist alike) have inherited a version of the latter theory. In Genesis, God created heaven and earth, but in the beginning the earth was without form. God divided the light from the darkness, and divided the waters from the dry land. In other words, active divine intervention brings order and form. Iatmul, says Bateson, see the world in the opposite way. According to their myth, the crocodile Kavwokmali once paddled his front and back legs and thereby kept water and earth together as mud. Their culture hero Kevembuangga then killed Kavwokmali, and the land separated from the water in which it had been suspended. In other words, order would occur, and does occur, once the crocodile is removed from the picture. Western knowledge assumes that *order needs to be explained*, and Iatmul knowledge assumes *the reverse*.

My general point, and Ingold's and Bateson's too, is that we should not assume that the way 'we' think is necessarily the only way humans can think. Nor should we imagine that our way is better, or less primitive, than any other way. It is just one possibility among many. Early symbolic thought might well have been more like Judeo-Christian than like Iatmul, but it is only by understanding the possibility of such differences that we are in a position to speculate. The later work of Lucien Lévy-Bruhl, unpublished in his lifetime, is relevant here too. Earlier in his life Lévy-Bruhl (e.g. 1926 [1910]) had divided human thinking into two classes: 'primitive mentality', which is mystical and pre-logical, and 'higher mentality', which is sophisticated, complex and abstract. 'Primitives', according to this view, think logically in practical situations, but not in the abstract. However, in the private notebooks in which he jotted later ideas, Lévy-Bruhl (1975 [1949]: 100–1) revealed a gradual shift towards the view that there is 'a mystical mentality ... present in every human mind'. It may have, he said, greater presence in some societies than in others, but it is an essential aspect of all human thought.

It is worth emphasizing that the concept of the person is not the same thing as the concept of the individual. Ingold (1986a: 222–42; cf. 1986b: 222–92), for example, has also considered the latter, and considered it particularly in terms of the opposition of the individual to collective, and in terms of the opposition of hunter-gatherer to non-hunter-gatherer. According to Ingold, hunter-gatherer societies not only have sharing mechanisms; they also have collective rights to property and a lack of distinction between public and private. Ingold further suggests that the phrase 'band society' does not employ the word *society* in the same sense as 'tribal society'. The former is 'society' in the sense of individuals who act together in order to share and distribute material things, whereas the latter involves social consciousness rather than simple and practical co-operative activity. On top of this, individualism involves not co-operating individuals, as we find in hunter-gatherer or band societies, but rather the negation of this, as in Western societies.

Reflections on revolutions and human nature

Some archaeologists, such as Sally McBrearty and Alison Brooks (2000) and Clive Gamble (2007) argue for gradual evolution, while most who write on the origin of language or on the origin of symbolic thought see things in terms of a single human revolution. However, the strong possibility exists that there was not one revolution at all, but a series of revolutions. My argument (Barnard 2008, 2009) is that there were at least three revolutions in human culture (associated respectively with sharing, exchange and symbolic behaviour), and that these coincide respectively with the linguistic stages (proto-language, rudimentary language and language) proposed by neurobiologist William Calvin and linguist Derek Bickerton (2000). (*Proto-language* had only words and phrases, like 'find food'. *Rudimentary language* had simple syntax, with sentences like 'Jane find food'. *Language* has complex syntax and morphology, with sentences like 'Jane has found the food'.)

The third revolution was the most important, and this is the one described by many earlier writers. In particular, since the early 1990s work by Chris Knight has highlighted the relation between symbolic culture and language among so-called 'Archaic' *Homo sapiens* or their immediate descendants in Africa. Anthropologists and archaeologists in this school pinpoint the dawn of symbolic culture to a rapid series of events, such as females taking control over their fertility by exchanging sex for meat. In common sense terms, we might think that at one point in time, biological evolution ceased and cultural evolution took over. Such a simplification, of course, is not part of the understanding of specialists: no matter how one wants to define it, there was some considerable overlap in time between cultural and biological evolution (cf. Richerson and Boyd 2005). However, what differentiates *Homo sapiens* from all other living species is the ability to produce language, and this has had evolutionary consequences both in cultural advances and in cultural diversity. Other animals communicate, but they do not have language. Other animals exhibit cultural diversity, but not remotely to the degree that humans do. What this suggests is that in fact it may well be useful to think, not of a point at which culture took over from biology, but of a point when fully linguistic humanity achieved the capability to expand exponentially its faculty of culture. As Boyd and Richerson (e.g. 2005) have shown, biology and culture are not best seen as distinct but as interrelated entities. To me at least, that means that it should be obvious that social anthropology ought to engage in dialogue with the biological sciences, as well as with linguistics and archaeology.

In his magnificent posthumous book, *Ritual and religion in the making of humanity*, the ecological anthropologist Roy Rappaport (1999) gives priority to ritual over belief and the fundamental property of religion. However, in it he also argues (1999: 5–9) that language is a factor in adaptation. He suggests too that language not only permits thought and communication about 'the possible, the plausible, the desirable, and the valuable' (1999: 8), but also makes this kind of thought inevitable. Thus for humans, 'nature' is not definable solely in terms of organic or tectonic processes but also in terms of linguistic expression and consequent cultural meanings of 'natural' phenomena. In short, although he stops short of making such an assertion, it appears that human ecology cannot be divorced from human culture. Even more strikingly, Rappaport (1999: 7) suggests that words are similar to genes in their capacity to enable a species (specifically *Homo sapiens*) to dominate great varieties of environments, except they can do this pretty much instantaneously, without the necessity to transform this species into another one.

Since the late 1990s, linguists such as James Hurford have picked up some ideas from Knight's approach and even collaborated with Knight in conference organization and co-authored and co-edited work with him (e.g. Knight, Suddert-Kennedy and Hurford 2000). At the same time, the increasing sophistication of rock art studies and archaeological discoveries of ochre use as body decoration have pushed back the dating of symbolic culture first by tens of thousands of years (in the case of Blombos Cave), and very recently by hundreds of thousands (in the case of Twin Rivers). Through careful, analytical ethnographic comparison, it should be possible to reconstruct something of the society and the belief system of the last common culture of humankind, presumably African and related to a population bottleneck at some point in time. For social anthropologists, this population should inspire more interest than the idea of Mitochondrial Eve, Y-chromosome Adam, or the *biological* 'most recent common ancestor'. We know there are human universals, and these must presumably be part of that early common culture. Beyond that, we can look to the common culture, for example, of hunter-gatherers, since we know all living at that time were hunter-gatherers. We know that those who left Africa first did so across the Red Sea and onwards to the Indian subcontinent, the Andaman Islands, the East Indies and Australia (see, e.g., Oppenheimer 2004; Wade 2006; Roberts 2009), so that should at least tell us that these first non-Africans knew about the sea, and therefore about tides and possibly the relation between tides and the lunar cycle. This may not have been true of *Homo erectus* migrants, with limited cognitive capabilities, but it seems inconceivable to me that *H. sapiens* migrants to Southeast Asia and Australia did not know about these things.

In the West there is sometimes a supposition that the sun is masculine and the moon is feminine, as indeed the words for these are in Indo-European gender languages. However, in a world perspective the reverse is true. The notion of a masculine sun and a feminine moon is actually mainly post-hunter-gatherer, characteristic of but few hunter-gatherer societies and primarily only those of the northern hemisphere. Southern-hemisphere hunter-gatherers nearly always have a feminine or female sun and a masculine or male moon, and often deify the latter. Indeed, there are other reversals of what are commonplace notions in the West: sometimes the sun is 'cold', and sometimes the moon and sun are called by the same term. They stand in kin relationships, but these are varied as they can be: brother/sister, husband/wife or both at the same time. They can be both female or both male, and in myth, father/ son, mother's brother/sister's son, two brothers, etc. (Lévi-Strauss 1976 [1967]: 211–21). Intriguingly, even in Western fiction we have, in the mind of Tarzan of the Apes, the conflation of God and the moon and the reversal of gender, with the moon's female gender as perceived by the Apes inverted to male gender in Tarzan's mind (Burroughs 1963b [1916]: 51). Lévi-Strauss had a substantial background in Amerindian ethnography, but Edgar Rice Burroughs did not.

Let me make it clear that I am not saying that post-hunter-gatherers are either better than or biologically different from hunter-gatherers. I am saying the opposite, on both counts. Hunter-gatherers most closely represent natural humanity. We ourselves, post-hunter-gatherer peoples, are in a sense beyond 'normal' natural humanity. We have found ways of coping with our unnatural state. Instead of *groups* of 150, we have *networks* of 150. And there exist unnatural (anarchists would say 'inhuman') political structures to keep us under control. The state and the city are not part of human nature, though they may today be part of our 'natural' environments.

In the eighteenth century there was much debate over what we might think of as the human species, and also over whether the natural state of the human species is solitary or gregarious. Monboddo included the Orang Outang as an example of humanity – for him, a non-speaking but gregarious and tool-using 'Man'. Monboddo's 'Orang Outang' included both the Southeast Asian, relatively solitary orang-utan, and the quite different and much more sociable chimpanzee (see chapter 1). To me, such eighteenth-century examples are interesting and important *not* because any of these thinkers made useful empirical discoveries, anticipated nineteenth-century developments or held views that later turned out to be correct. Rather, they are interesting and important because they were debating precisely the issues which should be engaging us

today: the limits of the human species and the nature of this species –
solitary or sociable. If Monboddo, Rousseau, or even Linnaeus, turned
out to be correct in any way, it was fortuitously. They did not have the
data we now have, and their conclusions are as likely to have been made
on what we now hold as false premises as on true ones. But, as I say, this
does not matter. It is the fact of their debates on these points that is of
interest.

Where is human nature? To my mind, if there is such a thing as 'natural
humanity' we can define it as a post-symbolic-revolution (or post-social-
contract) form: with full language and full kinship recognition. If there is
a 'natural humanity' it is pre-Neolithic. Tim Ingold (2000: 372–91) has
argued that the concept of the 'anatomically modern human' is theoretically flawed because of its assumption that biological inheritance can be
separated from individual childrearing practices. A human being is not,
he argues, programmed to be able to speak or even to walk. These skills
require learning, and children must grow up in a society that teaches
these things. Otherwise, they cannot learn them. Ingold adds that a rep-
resentative of the species *Homo erectus* reared in an Upper Palaeolithic
environment could *not* have mastered language because, the common
understanding goes, he or she would have lacked the capacity for language. Yet a Cro-Magnon man (who would have been 'anatomically
modern') brought up today could, of course, be taught to read and write.
Does this suppose, he implies, a capacity for reading and writing? Of
course it does not. Yet linguists and others are happy to speak about the
'capacity for language' as a separate element from the learning environment which enables language to be acquired. I am not convinced
by Ingold's argument, which seeks to overturn the usual separation of
history from evolution. Yet his insistence that for such things learning is
as necessary as innate capacity is persuasive, and to that end it is useful
to see rather that nature and culture cannot be separated. Both are inherent in any full-developed human being. In a sense, this was known to
eighteenth-century science. That is why there was so much theoretical
debate at that time over feral children. In the absence of much ethnographic data, and in the almost complete absence of relevant and meaningful archaeological material, feral children were a key source of evidence
on the nature of humanity and human sociality.

Of interest here too is Barbara King's (2007, 2009) recent theory of the
origin of religion. She emphasizes something she calls 'belongingness',
the need to matter to another being. In her view, this operates through
families and communities and enables the development of empathy, grief
and belief in an afterlife. King is a primatologist, and she claims that her
ideas are supported by data from primatology and archaeology. Indeed

they are, but more controversial is her claim (King 2009: 7) that the reliance on cognitive 'agency-detection' theories by some scholars (e.g. Norenzayan and Shariff 2008) has led to the de-emphasis of social perspectives. In my view the cognitive emphasis is due at least in part to the domination of psychological explanations and especially of neuroscience, but even more so to the almost complete absence of social anthropology in debates on prehistoric human thought. Psychologists and neuroscientists will naturally look to their own disciplines for explanation as to how and why religious ideas emerged. And while it may be perfectly true that cognitive structures of a certain kind were necessary for the emergence of ideas on supernatural intervention, nevertheless a social anthropologist (or a social primatologist) will also require social explanation, which has within it a requirement for emotional awareness and empathy on the part of the first religious believers towards their fellow hominin beings as well as towards their incipient deity or deities.

Norenzayan and Shariff (2008: 61–2) claim that there is a correlation between belief in morally concerned deities and group size. This is true enough at one level, but it obscures the fact, well known to Father Schmidt if not to modern psychology, that belief in morally concerned deities occurs at both ends of the spectrum: in small-scale hunter-gatherer societies as well as in large-scale agricultural societies. Modern African hunter-gatherers, in particular, have such beliefs. The fact that the mainly Christian United States or Islamic Indonesia have them too is irrelevant to the evolution of the belief systems of hunter-gatherers. This is a good example of the kind of mentality which is found among non-hunter-gatherer specialists: seeing the world backwards through Neolithic spectacles. As we shall see when we turn to kinship in the chapters which follow, hunter-gatherer societies should be understood in their own terms. It is the Neolithic and all that followed that is aberrant.

Back to Tarzan, back to myth

Neither the Tarzan of the Edgar Rice Burroughs novels nor the Tarzan of the movies actually said 'Me – Tarzan! You – Jane!', although Johnny Weissmuller did jokingly utter those words to Maureen O'Sullivan on set (Fury 1994: 68). In the 1932 film *Tarzan, the ape man*, the actual words are: 'Tarzan – Jane'. And in the 1942 film *Tarzan's New York adventure* we find the following: *Jane*: 'Wouldn't it be strange if someday I became as brave as you are?' *Tarzan*: 'Jane no need to be brave – Jane beautiful.' *Jane*: 'You're my goodness, darling – my strength.' *Tarzan*: 'Jane – Tarzan. Tarzan – Jane.' This dialogue apparently put romance into Tarzan's head, for immediately afterwards he scoops Jane up and carries her away (Fury 1994: 97).

Can such a dialogue really be the origin of fully developed language? Or of a relation between language and thought of the kind implied here? I doubt it. It may well be that such a dialogue and its aftermath figured at some point in the earlier evolution of language, but for me the origin of full language is late and it is related not only to changing kinship structures but also to the development of myth. /Xam mythology comprises a system of knowledge, composed of elements of natural history, Bushman-world prehistory, ethical guidance, kinship structure, narrative composition, metaphor and, of course, language. Wilhelm Bleek and his family (including Lucy Lloyd, who recorded the /Xam sentences cited earlier) are often said to have been interested in /Xam because they believed it was close to the *Ursprache* of all humankind. Of course, I do not believe that it is, and have used /Xam as my example here simply because it is an example that I know. However, I do believe that the mythologies of the world are based on universal structural principles. I also believe that they *might* preserve elements of a very deep mythological system dating to the time of *Homo sapiens* migration. Certainly, there are enough similarities in the mythologies of the world to suggest that, along with language, myths travelled across the continents. The possibilities for language change were far greater than those for myth change. Myths changed by combining and re-combining elements, or *mythèmes* as Lévi-Strauss calls them, to create new mythological systems, but almost always within larger systems of systems recognizable from continent to continent (see, e.g., Lévi-Strauss 1978).

Mithen (2009) argues that language and music evolved from the same source. The original form of musical-linguistic communication in his view was a 'holistic' form composed of phrases of meaning, rather than a 'compositional' form based on morphemes and lexemes. He suggests a late date of within the last 200,000 years. With a subsequent divergence and co-evolution of language and music, language became compositional as it took on the function of passing on information, while music remained holistic and its purpose narrowed to form the basis of emotional communication and social bonding.

Ever since Durkheim (1915 [1912]), social anthropologists have generally distinguished the 'sacred' from the 'profane'. Most would agree that this is a cultural universal. However, it is not a universal without a beginning. Unless we admit the notion of the sacred to hominins in general, there will certainly have been a point in time when the idea of the sacred, and its distinction from the profane, came into being. To suggest otherwise, we would have to imagine a scene as in the Tarzan novels (e.g. Burroughs 1963b [1916]: 51–7), where 'apes' perform rituals in order, apparently, to make sense of what they cannot understand 'scientifically'.

I would suggest that rather than at the 'ape' end of human evolution, the sacred/profane distinction came into being towards the *Homo sapiens* end, if not precisely at the *Homo sapiens* symbolic revolution. Whether it was a precise event, as in Sigmund Freud's (1960 [1913]: 140–55) account of the origin of the incest taboo, or a gradual development is open to speculation. Freud imagined that this taboo, along with totemism, originated in the guilt felt by members of a primal horde who had killed their alpha male father and had sex with their mothers. To Freud, vestiges of this dreaded event remain in 'primitive' totemic customs and in the universal human subconscious.

Drawing on Fison and Howitt's *Kamilaroi and Kurnai* (1880), Durkheim and Mauss (1963 [1903]: 17–18) point out that 'if [Australian] totemism is, in one aspect, the grouping of men into clans according to natural objects (the associated totemic species), it is also, inversely, a grouping of natural objects in accordance with social groups.' They add (1963: 21) that the associations found in totemic thought 'are not products of a logic identical with our own', but 'governed by laws which we do not suspect'. Even new things may be fitted into totemic systems, such as, in their example, a newly introduced bullock. Such is the strength of totemic thought, and such is the value of ethnography and, by extension, ethnographic analogy as a means to explore the unfamiliar in human cognition.

One value in *Primitive classification* is its comparative framework. Durkheim and Mauss, like their followers many years later such as A. R. Radcliffe-Brown and Claude Lévi-Strauss, saw value in looking both for correspondences and for differences. Durkheim and Mauss discuss similarities and differences among Australian systems of classification, then move to Zuñi and Sioux, and to Taoist China. Their conclusion is that the first logical categories were social: nature is modelled on society, not the other way around. What is more, it is not merely the categories but the relations between them which have social origins. We see these in mythical relations between animal species that represent moieties or clans and in other perceptions of nature. And the mind which thinks up these relations is, of course, a collective mind. For Durkheim and Mauss, it was essentially the collective mind of a given society, although for their successors, including Radcliffe-Brown (1958: [1952]) late in life and Lévi-Strauss (e.g. 1978) throughout his career, it was a universal mind. In evolutionary terms, this begs the question of whether that universal mind precedes the origin of symbolic culture or whether it is the mind at the point of that origin. Intuitively, I favour the latter, but evidence has yet to be brought to the question.

7   Elementary structures of kinship

What is the basis of society: the social contract or kinship? Adam Kuper begins his classic, *The invention of primitive society* (1988: 17–41), with this problem, as seen through Henry Sumner Maine's *Ancient law* (1913 [1861]). Maine championed kinship over the social contract, and the reversal of the previous dominance of the social contract marked the beginnings of social anthropology. It also marked the rise of kinship as the key area in which much in anthropological theory – whether evolutionist, functionalist, structuralist, relativist or interpretivist – would be tried out, before being passed on into other areas: totemism, mythology, and so on.

The notion of a 'social contract', people agreeing collectively to give up their individual freedoms in exchange for mutual protection, had been central to Thomas Hobbes's argument in *Leviathan* (1996 [1651]). For Hobbes, living sociably and living under the authority of a state were much the same thing, and they were *not* natural for humans. Society is not the natural condition of humankind because it was invented. Humans are not social in what he calls 'the state of nature'. Rather, humans become sociable individually thorough training, and collectively through a social contract and submission to social and state authority. Later in the seventeenth century, Sir Robert Filmer attacked Hobbes's ideas on the social contract and argued instead that the state should be seen as a kind of family, with the king as 'father-figure'. It was Filmer's attack on Hobbes that sparked John Locke's rebuttal in *Two treatises of government* (1988 [1690]). Rousseau's version of social contract theory followed in the next century, as did Jeremy Bentham's. Maine's attack on social contract theory was, in fact, largely directed at Bentham (see Barnard 2000: 16–18, 30–3). Therefore, in a sense there is a clear line from Hobbes to Bentham which puts society before kinship. Then there is almost all of social anthropology, from Maine onwards, at least until the late twentieth century, which gives priority to kinship.

There are four broad subfields in kinship studies. Each corresponds closely to a grand theoretical point of view in social anthropology.

Debates were played out both within these larger paradigms and between them. The four are descent theory, alliance theory, relationship terminologies and the 'new kinship'. *Descent theory* is today largely associated with structural-functionalism or sometimes with evolutionism. It emphasizes the importance of kin groups and postmarital residence. *Alliance theory* is associated with structuralism and is concerned with relations between groups, specifically relations through marriage. The study of *relationship terminologies* places the emphasis on the classification of relatives. Classification has implications for kinship behaviour, such as defining whom one may joke with or marry and whom one may not. The *'new kinship'*, developed since the 1970s, with those who followed Schneider's (1968) interest in cultural configurations, and especially in the 1990s, often with kinship specialists interested in the theoretical implications of new reproductive technologies. It entails a rejection of the formalism of these earlier approaches. Proponents often talk of 'relatedness', rather than kinship, and their interest is in affective and emotional aspects of kinship. Specifically, they seek to explain cultural differences in these things, and look, for example, to the culturally specific symbolism of 'blood' or of what it means to be 'related' in a particular society or culture (e.g. Carsten 2004). Although certainly of great importance in kinship studies today, it need not involve us here because its concerns, unlike those of the other subfields, probably lie beyond utility in the study of human origins. Neverthess, they do remind us that, whatever our theoretical position, we should take for granted that the notion of what it means to be 'kin' is the same in all societies: it is culturally constructed, and must have been so for as long as 'kinship' was culturally recognized.

Descent theory

Descent theory is the oldest and has both evolutionist and functionalist forms. It began in the era of evolutionary concerns, with the publication of *Ancient law* and *Das Mutterrecht*, both in 1861, two years after Darwin's *Origin of species* and four years after the discovery of the first Neanderthal. In *Ancient law*, Maine replaced the social contract with the family. He disliked legal fictions, and the social contract, grandest legal fiction of all, could not stand against his research in jurisprudence which put Roman institutions at the heart of his search for the earliest forms of social organization. The Romans had been strongly patrilineal, and Maine's model was based on this.

In contrast, J. J. Bachofen's *Das Mutterrecht* (1967 [1861]: 67–210) postulated primeval male dominance, but with early society based on a feminist movement which put an end to this. In his model 'mother-right' was eventually itself overthrown by a resurgence of male authority. Bachofen's evidence came from ethnographic accounts of female deities and of the custom of *couvade*, whereby a husband will feign pregnancy, for example, to deflect evil spirits away from his wife. That custom is found in the Basque country, and in South and North America, and in Japan, China, India and Africa. Bachofen seems to have confused matriarchy and patriarchy with matriliny and patriliny, but nevertheless his was the first theory to give prominence to descent through females and to female authority. From then onwards, late nineteenth-century anthropologists debated the merits of patrilineal and matrilineal descent among the earliest (modern) humans, and the trajectory of advances over the supposedly earliest form. Debates centred not only on which was first, but on the evidence from ethnography, such as whether kinship terminology held the best clues, or whether clues were best found in customs such as *couvade* or exogamy, or indeed in known history.

Around 1922, functionalism took over from evolutionism as the dominant theory of British and Commonwealth social anthropology. Evolutionist-turned-diffusionist W. H. R. Rivers died in that year. Both Bronislaw Malinowski and Radcliffe-Brown, the twin pillars of the British tradition, began their teaching in earnest that year in newly founded departments, respectively at the London School of Economics and at Cape Town. And both Malinowski and Radcliffe-Brown had their most important ethnographic texts published then as well (see Barnard 2000: 61–79). While Malinowski became the godfather of the fieldwork methods, Radcliffe-Brown's specific theoretical perspective became the agreed model. Radcliffe-Brown's (1952) 'structural-functionalism' (as others labelled it) emphasized understanding society in the present. It rejected past methodological interests in conjecture, and therefore left little room for evolutionary explanations. In several of his essays, Radcliffe-Brown (1952: 32–89) paid particular attention to the organization of descent groups. His students and followers, such as E. E. Evans-Pritchard, Meyer Fortes and J. R. Goody did empirical studies of systems of descent, especially in Africa, and were concerned with the role of descent groups in dispute settlement, the relation between descent and residence, the transmission of inheritance and succession to office.

There are four basic ways in which descent groups can be organized (figure 7.1). Patrilineal is descent from father to children and is indicated in the diagrams by numbered patrilineal groups 1 and 2. Matrilineal is descent from mother to children, indicated here by lettered matrilineal groups A and B. Double descent is the system involving both patrilineal and matrilineal at the same time, and cognatic or bilateral descent is in theory the system in which neither patrilineal nor matrilineal groups are

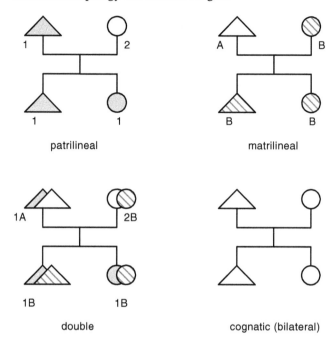

Figure 7.1 The four basic forms of descent

found. In practice, all human societies have a degree of cognatic descent in that any given relatives may either belong to one's own lineage or not. For example, the Romans distinguished two kinds of relative: *agnati* (in English, 'agnates', those of one's patrilineal group) and *cognati* ('cognates', blood relatives who belong to some other group, such as one's mother or mother's brother). In addition to these four basic forms of descent, there are also two very rare forms: parallel descent (patrilineal for men but matrilineal for women) and cross or alternating descent (where men belong to the group of their mother and women to that of their father), but these need not concern us here.

In the late twentieth-century, some in social anthropology abandoned functionalism as a complete explanation and returned to the nineteenth-century debates on origins and evolution. Debates in the late twentieth-century evolutionist circles tend to be between those who, like Bachofen, Morgan and McLennan, see matrilineal descent as prior, and those who do not. The latter need not necessarily substitute patrilineal descent, but can argue for cognatic. That is my own position (e.g. Barnard 1999: 60–6). While probably no one takes double descent as logically prior, there are theorists who look to alliance theory, and in that a kind of double descent is logically implicated – notably in the section systems of Western Australia. Double descent is also logically implicated whenever geneticists speak of Y-chromosome Adam and Mitochondrial Eve. Yet these concepts are socially irrelevant, and it is best to avoid them completely when imagining the prehistory of kin group structures.

Those today who see matrilineal descent as prior include Chris Knight (e.g. 2008). His arguments return to the classic nineteenth-century texts and take in too the twentieth-century writings of Lowie, Westermarck, Radcliffe-Brown, Murdock, Schneider and a number of others who have examined living matrilineal societies in order to understand the way they work. Knight suggests complexity in the issue, and he notes too biological arguments in favour of early matriliny, notably the requirement for children to remain in infancy close to their mothers, while fathers are free to travel and hunt. Several sources he cites take the commonly held view that matriliny when combined with monogamy also has Darwinian benefits, in favouring a man nurturing his own genetic children over others (Knight 2008: 75). Indeed, one such source imputes monogamy to *Homo erectus*: 'Females may have had difficulty providing food for themselves and their dependent young. If *H. erectus* hunted regularly, males might have been able to provide high-quality food for their mates and offspring. Monogamy would have increased the males' confidence of paternity and favoured paternal investment' (Boyd and Silk 1997: 435). While this scenario may seem plausible, it is too speculative to count for much. It also seems to me too focused on a Western assumption that the nuclear family is what is important. As we saw in chapter 4, there are many ways to organize a family. In actual matrilineal societies, men are generally as important as women in kin group stability. It is a young man's mother's brother, not either his father (a member of some other kin group) or his mother (important for tracing descent through, but, by virtue of her gender, not necessarily in a position of authority in the group), who is key to kin group stability. This is true across the world, in matrilineal societies in South Asia, the Pacific and North America, although possibly slightly less true in Africa and South America (see, e.g., Schneider and Gough 1961). It is also worth noting that in some matrilineal societies (one could cite quite diverse examples, from the Nayars of Kerela to the Hopi of Arizona) husbands are never quite incorporated into the wife's group or even into her family. They have their own kin groups to concern them: those of their sisters, who normally live elsewhere.

I take cognatic descent as prior for a number of reasons. I have argued that case particularly in my essay 'Modern hunter-gatherers and early symbolic culture' (Barnard 1999), where my concern was to find the best model for early human kinship at the time of the early *Homo sapiens* symbolic revolution. There, I rejected an Australian Aboriginal model, as this would require too much complexity, and since some of its characteristics are rare or non-existent elsewhere in the world – especially sections and subsections. The overwhelming majority of hunting societies outside of Australia are cognatic. Matrilineality is found in some Australian societies and in some small-scale Amerindian ones, but is virtually non-existent among hunter-gatherers elsewhere. In North America matriliny is associated with hierarchical, chiefly, hunter-gatherer and fishing societies (those of the Northwest Coast), not with small-scale egalitarian ones. In most parts of the world where matrilineality is found, agriculture is the dominant means of subsistence. Often too it is associated either with *avunculocal* residence (residence with a man's mother's brother, a custom which unites the men of a given matrilineal group but disperses the women through whom they are related) or with *uxorilocal* residence (postmarital residence in the wife's group, a custom which unites the women of a group and disperses the men). Avunculocal residence is characteristic of male-dominated, chiefly societies: a famous example is the Trobrianders of Papua New Guinea. Uxorilocal residence is characteristic of societies in which women own and till fields, for example the Bemba of Zambia (see Barnard and Good 1984: 78–83). Nearly the majority in a sample of the world's matrilineal peoples in the twentieth century were definitively or predominantly uxorilocal (49 per cent), and a significant minority were definitively or dominantly avunculocal (27 per cent). The rest were virilocal, duolocal, ambilocal or neolocal (Aberle 1961: 666).

One of Radcliffe-Brown's (1952 [1924]: 15–31) greatest contributions was to highlight the importance of the mother's brother, not only in matrilineal societies but in patrilineal ones as well. In a matrilineal society with property in the hands of men, inheritance is from mother's brother to sister's son. In a patrilineal society, inheritance would be from father to son, but the mother's brother quite often plays a particularly important role as a figure of indulgence. Not uncommonly in strongly patrilineal societies, a sister's son may take the mother's brother's property without asking or exchange defective goods with better ones owned by the mother's brother. Radcliffe-Brown gives several examples. In his main example, the patrilineal Tsonga of Mozambique (whom he calls BaThonga), the words for 'mother's brother' are *malume* (literally 'male mother') and *kokwana* (which also means 'grandfather'). His purpose in this paper, 'The mother's brother in South Africa', was to focus on contemporary meanings and contemporary social organization, which was then a break with prior notions, that social anthropology existed in order to decipher past social structure from evolutionary survivals in present-day ethnography. He emphasized the role of mother's brother as *malume*, although among Tsonga and neighbouring peoples, calling him *kokwana* is just as common.

It is noteworthy that among the earliest reputed kinship terms are three found throughout the world: *mama* (mother), *papa* (father) and *kaka* (Bancel and Matthey d'Etang 2002; Matthey de l'Etang and Bancel 2002). *Kaka* (or a cognate form) most commonly means 'mother's brother', but in some languages refers instead to grandparent, elder brother or father-in-law, or some other relative. Such changes in meaning are not uncommon, but in evolutionary terms it can be important to see how they occur. There is a structural similarity between mothers' brothers and grandfathers, for example, as these relationships are in each case, in those societies which make a distinction, the nearest male 'avoidance' relatives of ego's mother, and should therefore be expected to be the closest 'joking' relatives to ego. *Kokwana* is derived from Proto-World **kaka*. Although some have, even in recent years, found evidence of earlier matrilineality among Tsonga, that is a historical phenomenon specific to the region, and not a product of the evolution of humanity as a whole. Radcliffe-Brown was right to focus on Tsonga society as it existed in his own time, and not in the past, and in fact the idea of *kokwana* (or **kaka*) as 'joking' relative makes sense in any system, patrilineal, matrilineal or cognatic, in which men are distinguished as either 'fathers' (typically 'avoidance' in a strongly patrilineal society, because formal relations should exist between them due to authority within the kin group) or 'not fathers' (typically 'joking' in such a society, with informal behaviour expected).

In comparing two double-descent LoDagaa groups in Ghana, Goody (1959) notes that among those known as LoWiili, who vest property in the patriclan, relations between sister's son and mother's brother are 'joking'. Among the other group, known as Lodagaba, property is divided into two types: immovable (which is in the hands of the patriclan) and moveable (which is dealt with by the matriclan). Lodagaba have more formal relations between mother's brother and sister's son. This suggests that inheritance, as well as descent, forms the basis of social relations: more formal where inheritance is at issue, and less so where it is not.

Apart from their work on lineages, Fortes and Goody (e.g. Goody 1958) also explored what Goody called the 'developmental cycle of domestic groups'. These were homestead settlements in matrilineal and patrilineal agricultural, and generally hierarchical, societies of Ghana. However, the principles they uncovered are equally applicable to the study of hunter-gatherer bands, and, by inference, also to archaeological data. In methodological terms, the idea of the developmental cycle is to

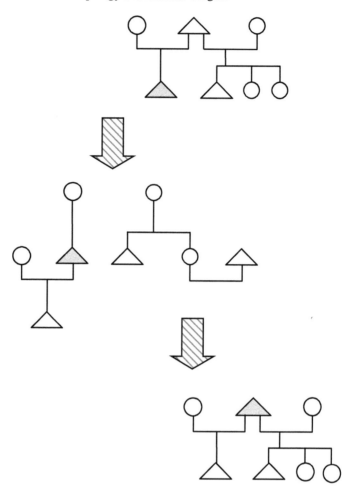

Figure 7.2 The developmental cycle of a domestic group

see diverse forms of household or band size and structure not merely in terms of diversity in a synchronic spatial context, but rather in terms of an imagined diachronic structural change. A fieldworker may be present in a field location for just a year or two. He or she will see large units and small. In terms of the Ghanaian homesteads, these could be, for example, a male-headed household, a household headed by two women, a household of two brothers and their families, and so on. At first glance, synchronically, figure 7.2 appears to show we have three households, the first and third being similar in structure. However, what may appear random when seen synchronically is in fact not random when seen diachronically.

Diachronically, figure 7.2 can be read as showing an imaginary kin group seen through, say, a forty-year period. Imaginary ego (coloured in) at the first snapshot in time is a young man, the only son of his father's first wife. In the second snapshot, he is married and has a son, his father is dead, and his late father's co-wives preside over the homestead. In the third, his mother is dead and the family of his mother's co-wife have moved away. The third is identical to the first, with ego replicating the exact position of his father, forty years later.

Alliance theory

The term 'alliance theory' and its opposition to descent theory dates from the 1950s. Its origin is in Claude Lévi-Strauss's *doctorat d'État* thesis on 'elementary structures' of kinship. Published in French in 1949 (English edition: Lévi-Strauss 1969), this work soon became the première tract of the French structuralist movement. Even so, it is difficult for most non-anthropologists to read, and its rationalist premise is hard for many anthropologists today to understand.

Alliance theory: the basics

In essence, Lévi-Strauss's position is in fact quite simple. There are two kinds of kinship system: elementary and complex. *Elementary kinship* involves a 'positive' marriage rule: one *must* marry someone of a certain category, usually a cross-cousin (a cousin related through an opposite-sex sibling link). It is divided into three types according to whether a man may marry a category that includes cross-cousins on the mother's side only, on the father's side only, or on either side. *Complex kinship* involves a 'negative' marriage rule: one *must not* marry someone of a certain category, e.g. a sister, a daughter or a member of one's own clan. (One could argue that such systems are not literally complex, but just the reverse: elementary structures are the complicated ones.)

Elementary systems in which a man may marry the category of the mother's brother's daughter (or a woman, the category of father's sister's son) are called systems of *generalized exchange*. That is because repeated marriages of this kind create 'generalized' relations between unilineal (patrilineal or matrilineal) kin groups. I (a man) belong, let us say, to kin group A. I take my wife from kin group B, or C or D. My sister, who also belongs to group A, may not marry B, C or D, but will find a husband in E, F or G. Each group stands in either a 'wife-giving' or 'wife-taking' relationship to any other given group. 'Sister-exchange' is not possible. Because entire kin groups stand in wife-giving/wife-taking relationships, these systems create, or maintain, hierarchical relations between groups. Either wife-takers are considered 'superior' (as in Hindu societies, which maintain dowry systems) or wife-givers are considered 'superior' (as in much of Southeast Asia, where goods may be passed to the bride's parents in bridewealth). These structures are found throughout much of Southeast Asia and parts of South Asia and Melanesia, and are inconsistent with the egalitarian ethos of a typical hunting-and-gathering society. Therefore, they are not sufficiently ancient to require further attention here.

Elementary systems in which a man may marry the category of the father's sister's daughter (or a woman, the category of mother's brother's son) are called systems of *delayed direct exchange*. They actually have a different pattern, since, for formal reasons, relations between kin groups are not precise but alternate in each generation. If I (group A) marry my father's sister's daughter, of group B, and my daughter marries her mother's brother's son (i.e. the groom is marrying his father's sister's daughter), then in the first generation a woman is moving from B to A (or a man from A to B), and in the second the situation is the reverse. This makes such structures extremely unstable, and of no use on the ground to regulate relations between groups. Not surprisingly, they exist pretty much only in the mind!

However, the other alternative, marriage to a cross-cousin on either side, creates a very stable relationship between two groups, and these, called *direct exchange* or *restricted exchange*, are common in Aboriginal Australia and among native peoples of South America. They typically involve moieties, literally 'halves' of society, and the rule is that a person always marries the half he or she does not belong to. If I, and my sister, belong to group A, we marry people from group B. It follows that sister-exchange is possible, and the closest relatives that would be marriageable are, in fact, one's cross-cousins. Figure 7.3 illustrates direct exchange. In the figure, there are two patrilineal moieties. In each moiety in each generation, the brother–sister pair each marry members of the brother–sister pair in the opposite moiety. Two generations are illustrated. In the following (third) generation, the same would occur, and in effect the first generation is replicated. Thus, there are but two genealogical levels: 'mine' and the other one; just as there are two moieties: 'mine' and the other one. In other words, each man and woman in the entire society is represented in one or other of the eight triangles and circles in the diagram. If, for example, I am represented in the top left triangle, then my brother is too (same sex, same moiety, and same generation as me). So too is my father's father, and my son's son. My father and my son are represented in the triangle immediately below. The system would work in the same way, and equally well, if the moieties were matrilineal.

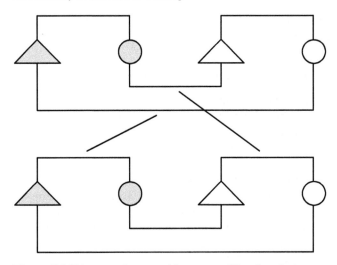

Figure 7.3 Direct exchange with two patrilineal moieties

There is an in-between type though: a Crow–Omaha system (Lévi-Strauss 1966). This is a kind of complex structure, but one with so few marriageable categories that it behaves a bit like an elementary structure. A 'Crow' kinship terminology is one in which I call any female member of a given matrilineal descent group by the same term; likewise any male member. More precisely, the defining feature is usually taken as father's sister's daughter is a 'father's sister'. From this it follows that father's sister's son is 'father'. Reciprocally, if I call my father's sister's daughter 'father's sister', she calls me 'brother's son', and if I call my father's sister's son 'father' he calls me 'son'. And so on down the generations: thus any member of my father's (matrilineal) clan is my 'father' or 'father's sister'. An 'Omaha' terminology is the patrilineal mirror-image. What Lévi-Strauss did was to note that if I cannot marry, say, a 'father's sister', then my choice of mate is limited. Just as in an elementary structure, there will be marriageable and unmarriageable clans. The system may be ideologically complex (because it has negative marriage rules), but it is empirically elementary (because the choice of spouse is so narrow).

For our purposes Crow–Omaha systems can probably be ignored. It is unlikely that they are primal, unless we wish to envisage very strong, prehistoric systems of unilineal descent. This is perhaps conceivable if Knight (2008) is right about the primacy of matriliny, although there are few exemplars among hunter-gatherers, apart from the Crow and Omaha themselves and some of their neighbours in the Great Plains of North America. Classic Crow–Omaha alliance structures are found in several parts of Africa, but typically among agricultural, and not hunter-gatherer, peoples.

Alliance theory: implications for human origins

Another way to look at alliance theory is in terms of a theory of exchange. Indeed, this is how Lévi-Strauss first envisaged it, under the inspiration of Marcel Mauss (1990 [1924]), who had argued that giving implies an obligation on the part of the recipient to reciprocate in some way. This could be repaying with a return gift, or simply owing deference to the giver. For Lévi-Strauss as for Mauss, giving (or exchange) marks the beginning of human social solidarity. In my own theory of the co-evolution of language and kinship (Barnard 2008), the mother's brother becomes important as a figure in exchange relations, as (from a child's point of view) he will be the male figure in my mother's family who is involved in such exchanges. Of course, there may be more than one mother's brother, and such exchanges could involve groups as well as individuals. The mother's brother is pivotal also in Lévi-Strauss's theory of kinship and marriage. This comes out most clearly in his first essay on language and kinship structures (Lévi-Strauss 1963 [1945]: 31–54), in what he later described as 'the atom of kinship' (1963 [1952]: 72). This is the set of relations between, on the one hand, sister and brother, and wife and husband, and, on the other hand, sister's son and mother's brother, and son and father (figure 7.4). If sister/brother is a familiar relation, then wife/husband will be, relatively speaking, more formal. And vice versa. If sister's son/mother's brother is familiar, then son/father will be more formal. And vice versa.

The 'atom of kinship' is a good place to begin in the examination of possible early forms of family and kin relationships. There is too much emphasis outside social anthropology in the nuclear family and in genea-logical proximity. The 'atom' instead places the emphasis, additionally, elsewhere – for example, in the relation between a man and his brother-in-law, which has implications for all kinds of exchange relations, includ-ing brideservice and bridewealth. Brideservice is common among hunter-gatherers, and bridewealth is the equivalent in those societies that permit accumulation of property, particularly pastoralists. Occasionally, the two are found together: both the Ju/'hoansi and the Naro prac-tise brideservice, for a number of years after each marriage, and have a sequence of marriage and childbirth prestations, which in effect are bridewealth (Barnard 1992a: 51, 145–7). The !Xóõ also sometimes have such gifts (Heinz 1994 [1966]: 181–2). The 'atom' also contains struc-tural oppositions, which are the basis of significant social relations: a

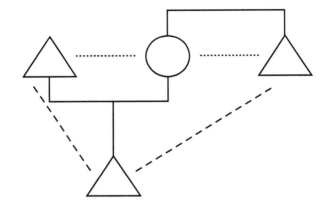

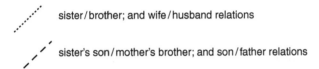

sister / brother; and wife / husband relations

sister's son / mother's brother; and son / father relations

Figure 7.4 The atom of kinship

woman's relationship with her husband in opposition to the one with her brother. Brother/sister is, as a San once told her ethnographer, 'for life', whereas a husband/wife relationship is 'only temporary'. This is in spite of the fact that brother/sister is a formal 'avoidance' relationship, whereas husband/wife is intimate and 'joking' (Heinz 1994: 165).

The consideration of the mother's brother/sister's son relationship in opposition to father/son also highlights the equal significance of mother's brothers, whose role is precisely worthy of consideration where brother/sister is important. In most societies, mother's brothers are classified differently from father's brothers. Note in this context the possible Proto-World concept represented by *kaka* (see Matthey de l'Etang and Bancel 2002).

Kinship classification

The importance of kinship classification was first recognized by Lewis Henry Morgan. He discovered that the Haudenosaunee or Iroquois, with whom he spent some years, on and off, in the 1840s and 1850s, classified cousins differently from Americans, Canadians and Europeans. They called both siblings and parallel cousins (those related through a same-sex sibling link) by one pair of terms, distinguishing older from younger, and cross-cousins (those related through an opposite-sex sibling link) by a different term. He thought at first that he had found something unique, but he later discovered the same structure, with different words, among the linguistically unrelated Ojibwa. He subsequently sent questionnaires, mainly to American consuls throughout the world, and did further research himself with Native American peoples. The result was *Systems of consanguinity and affinity of the human family* (Morgan 1871).

Basically, there are two classification schemes: one based on the *first ascending* generation (that of one's parents) and the other based on terms in the zero generation (one's own). Both were invented in the early twentieth century. The former distinguishes four types, according to the classification of parents, uncles and aunts: *generational* (all called by the same term), *lineal* (parents classified differently from uncles and aunts – as in English), *bifurcate merging* (parents' same-sex siblings classified together with parents, rather than with parents' opposite-sex siblings) and *bifurcate collateral* (all called by different terms).

The latter distinguishes six types on the basis of the classification of siblings and cousins. The labels are usually put in inverted commas or quotation marks to indicate that these are not the real ethnic groups that bear these names, but abstractions named after them. *'Hawaiian'* systems call everyone in the same generation by the same term, or with terms differing only according to gender. In other words, a cousin is called as if a sibling. *'Eskimo'* terminologies (such as English) distinguish siblings from cousins. *'Iroquois'* terminologies distinguish cross-cousins from parallel cousins and usually group parallel cousins with siblings. *'Sudanese'* terminologies classify all these relatives differently. *'Crow'* terminologies are like 'Iroquois' ones, but classify father's sister's daughter as if father's sister. *'Omaha'* terminologies are like 'Iroquois' ones, but classify mother's brother's son as if mother's brother. In 'Crow' and 'Omaha', while relatives on one side of the family are 'raised' a generation, relatives on the other side who represent the reciprocals of these are 'lowered'. (If I call my father's sister's daughter 'father's sister', logically she would be expected to call me 'brother's son'.) The reason that 'Crow' and 'Omaha' terminologies exist is that the terminology structures have embedded in them not only notions of gender, genealogical level and a parallel/cross distinction, but also implicit lineages. And, in fact, these usually coincide with explicit recognition of such lines through real lineages, clans and phratries. 'Crow' is matrilineal, and 'Omaha' is patrilineal. A full discussion of terminology structures may be found in Barnard and Good (1984: 59–66).

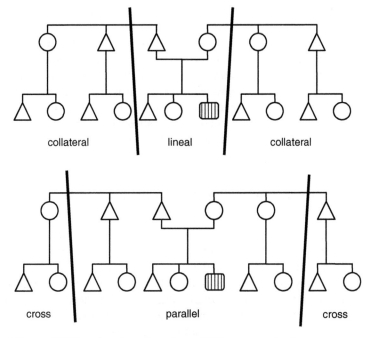

Figure 7.5 Lineal/collateral and parallel/cross terminology structures

Morgan in fact had only two types: *descriptive* (those which make lineal/collateral distinctions) and *classificatory* (those which do not). Thus, in twentieth-century terms, he would group 'Eskimo' and 'Sudanese' (descriptive) and distinguish this type from that of 'Hawaiian', 'Iroquois', 'Crow' and 'Omaha' (classificatory). I believe he was on the right track, but that the relevant distinction for the evolution of kinship structures is in fact that to be made between *parallel relatives* and *cross-relatives*. In other words, it is not lineal/collateral that is important, but parallel/cross: and it depends on where one draws the line between 'close' and 'distant' (see figure 7.5). 'Iroquois', 'Sudanese', 'Crow' and 'Omaha' (which make parallel/cross distinctions) are one larger, and earlier, type, and 'Hawaiian' and 'Eskimo' are, logically, another. ('Hawaiian' is grouped with 'Eskimo' on logical grounds, but may in fact be much earlier.) For reasons which will become clear in the next chapter, I believe that terminology structures like the French or Modern English 'Eskimo' one, or possibly even the Old English 'Sudanese' one, are post-Neolithic. They centre on genealogical distance. The 'Iroquois' is related to alliance structures like those of our pre-Neolithic ancestors. It is more complicated, though, and in fact some hunter-gatherers, including obviously

some Inuit groups and hunter-gathers in central Africa and southern
Africa (notably the Ju/'hoansi) have 'Eskimo' structures; in other words
they do not distinguish parallel from cross-relatives. Nevertheless, all terminologies may be understood as having no distinction ('Hawaiian'),
one distinction only ('Eskimo', 'Iroquois', 'Crow' and 'Omaha') or both
('Sudanese'); and it is parallel/cross which is the more significant, and
the one found in any system which allows cross-cousin marriage, including moiety systems and section and subsection systems, and systems
of generalized exchange. It is also rather more common in the world's
languages.

Other implications for the evolution of kinship systems

Are living hunter-gatherers primitive? This is not really a 'yes' or 'no'
question, but one with several possible answers. At one extreme, some
might argue that they should be considered innately primitive and less
cultural than other present-day people. This answer is unacceptable to
me, not only because it is politically incorrect but also because it is,
simply, incorrect. Others would argue that modern hunter-gatherers
are fully cultural and the same as 'us'. I would dispute their sameness
though: they are indeed the same biologically, the same (or better) in
abstract mental skills and in abilities to cope with everyday problems, but
culturally they can have very different ideological understandings of economic and political relations. They generally possess what I have called
a 'foraging mode of thought', as opposed to an 'accumulation mode of
thought' (see chapter 5). A third possibility, which is the answer I prefer,
is that they are fully cultural but without the post-cultural accumulations
of the post-Later Stone Age.

One crucial difference between most hunter-gatherers and most non-
hunter-gatherers is the presence of universal kinship among the former.
Lévi-Strauss's (1968: 351) comment that really intelligent early humans
were probably interested in kinship, rather than in philosophy or mathematics, is relevant too. Whether consciously or not, they built complicated structures of alliance, and these regulated incest prohibition and
relations between groups. Universal kinship enabled them to do this.
How ancient such systems are is open to argument, as is whether Allen
(e.g. 1982, 2004) is right that four sections are at the root of primal
kinship, whether Lévi-Strauss (1969: 69–83, 215–17) is right that it is
instead two moieties, or whether I (Barnard 1999) am right that it is
a flexible regime, with universal extension of incest avoidance through
egocentric categories.

Many of the ideas to be explored with reference to kinship were present in nineteenth-century concerns within social anthropology. Nineteenth-century thinkers, though, were almost entirely concerned with biologically modern humans. The difference in a social anthropology of human origins today is that we must look also to hominins who were not modern. This makes the task both more complicated and more interesting. Did polygny lead to patriliny, or polyandry to matrininy? Did a form of early monogamy imply cognation, as the earliest form of descent, as I think it did: based on African hunter-gatherer models (Barnard 1999)? Was group marriage an aspect of primitive communism – as envisaged by Morgan (1877)? Did group marriage lead to age sets, alternating generations and generational taboos?

Wendy James's (2008) discussion of age sets in east Africa is possibly relevant here, as is Nicholas Allen's (1989a) discussion of the assimilation of alternate generations. Certainly, the great importance of alternating generations, through much of Africa, in hunter-gatherer societies generally and especially in Australia is worthy of comment for anyone looking to generational relations as a key to evolution. In Australia, one belongs to the same section or subsection as a grandparent. Among several Bushman groups, one is named after a grandparent, and the grandparent/grandchild relationship is (unlike parent/child) 'joking' and friendly. Grandparents in these, and many other hunter-gatherer societies, are not more senior relatives, but relatives of a generation that is understood as being like one's own. To an Aboriginal or a San, a grandparent is like one's self: a parent is completely different.

8   A new synthesis

In the mid-1970s evolutionary biologist Edward O. Wilson (1975) proposed a 'new synthesis' to unite the biological and social sciences. His book was large (over 700 pages), but widely read. The abridged edition (Wilson 1980), about half the size, was even more widely read, and adherents to the overarching field, known as 'sociobiology', passed the notion on to their students. Onlookers such as cultural anthropologists picked it up too. Especially in the United States, many cultural anthropologists feared that sociobiology impinged too closely on their subject matter, and for a time they feared that it might be a serious threat to their subject itself.

Wilson's 'new synthesis' was actually less a true synthesis of anything, and more a redefinition of social science in biological terms. Wilson's background was in the study of insects. From this basis he sought to apply his knowledge and theoretical understandings to the study of vertebrate societies, such as those of amphibians, reptiles, birds and mammals. The implication for anthropology was clear in his final chapter, 'Man: from sociobiology to sociology', which because of its interest and importance was left virtually unchanged in the abridged edition (Wilson 1980: 271–301). There, Wilson considers the negative impact of some features in culture, such as slavery in the seventeenth, eighteenth and nineteenth centuries. He then boldly tackles reciprocal altruism, pair bonding, communication, ritual and religion and ethics and aesthetics. Still more controversially, he attempts to explain in his final sections not only 'early social evolution', but also 'later social evolution' and 'the future', including interrelations between genetic, demographic and cultural factors in societal change. His explanatory framework is so integrative that he marks sociology out for a transition from purely phenomenological theory to a perspective which requires the integration of both genetics and brain science. To some extent, evolutionary psychology has become that very field, but it has replaced neither sociology as we know it nor social anthropology.

Prominent figures in social and cultural anthropology, most notably Marshall Sahlins (1976), instigated a backlash to defend our discipline against the apparent biological attack. As it turned out, anthropology departments in general did not join the bandwagon, and universities did not allow their biology departments to swallow up their anthropology ones, as some perhaps had thought they would. Sahlins's short treatise was well argued, especially in areas such as kin selection and reciprocal altruism, whose cultural basis Wilson badly misinterpreted. In retrospect, though, Sahlins's defence of anthropology was probably a bit unnecessary. He attacks the implications of Wilson's theory where Wilson is, to say the least, less than explicit. In his concluding chapter, Sahlins (1976: 93–107) attacks the supposed Hobbesian basis of sociobiology, comments on Western capitalism's Hobbesian roots, examines relations between Social Darwinism and sociobiology, and touches on moral implications of Wilson's purportedly right-wing theory. Wilson in fact mentions neither Hobbes, nor Western capitalism, nor Social Darwinism, nor, at least in Sahlins's terms, morality.

Wilson's 'new synthesis' did not succeed, but it has left a legacy in biological sciences and perhaps too in the fears of social anthropologists over attempt by 'the enemy', biological sciences, to take over our territory. With that in mind, let me explain my position briefly. Unlike Wilson, I see the social and biological sciences on more equal terms, and I see each set of fields as essentially autonomous. While there are areas where biology should be seen as the driving force in human evolution, biology cannot be allowed to take over as the explanation for everything. Rather, what is sometimes required is an explanatory framework which draws on both social and biological causation and gives precedent to one or the other when and only when precedent is due.

Sociobiology: advances and failings

Let me outline some of the results of Wilson's research and that of his colleagues among the biological scientists who supported his work in its heyday. Sociobiology as a concept and as a wider discipline began even before Wilson's treatise. Sometimes it did take on a wider remit, with less specific ideological concern with Wilson's biologically determinist line. Yet one figure who did anticipate this line was W. D. (Bill) Hamilton (1964), often described as the greatest Darwinian since Darwin himself. From the standpoint of social anthropology, though, Hamilton's notion of 'kin selection' has proven to be the greatest failure of sociobiology, particularly in its prediction of altruistic behaviour with reference to 'kin' but not 'non-kin' or distant relatives (see also Sahlins 1976: 17–67).

'Kin selection' suggested that from a Darwinian point of view, individual organisms should not invest in their own reproductive fitness but rather in the fitness of their genes. This means that altruism to the point of 'group selection', meaning selection for the good of the kin group, is best. The simple equation for this is $r \times b > c$, where r is genetic relatedness, b is the benefit to the receiver of the altruistic gesture, and c is the cost to the actor. An actor could sacrifice himself and his own ability to pass on his genes in order that his brother might do so instead, or his cousin, or his nephew (with a lesser degree of commitment because of the lesser degree of genetic relatedness).

However, from a social anthropological point of view, this will not do. There are, for example, Inuit communities that regard relationships through the same sex as oneself to be 'closer' than those through the opposite sex (David Damas, pers. comm.). A man's closest cousin in such a community would be his father's brother's son, and a woman's her mother's sister's daughter. If this interesting but rare, if not unique, ethnographic case were the only one in which conventionally assumed genetic inheritance is not recognized, then that would not be too worrying for Hamilton's hypothesis. One counter-example alone would not refute the general hypothesis. Yet across the globe more languages classify people according to whether they are related through same-sex siblings or through opposite-sex siblings than do not, and the former are invariably considered closer. This means that Hamilton's hypothesis could only hold true in a minority of cases, those being typically in agricultural societies, not hunter-gatherer ones. Thus it should have little to say about humankind before the Neolithic. Hunting and gathering means of subsistence have dominated *Homo sapiens* lifestyles for rather more than 95 per cent of our existence (if we assume a time depth for *H. sapiens* of about 200,000 years, and recognize that when pastoral and agricultural lifestyles were invented, not everyone jumped to them). Indeed, in evolutionary terms we can go rather further: hunting and gathering means of subsistence have dominated the genus *Homo*'s lifestyles for some 99.5 per cent of its existence. James Hurford, drawing on theoretical ideas and ethnographic evidence from social anthropology, makes a similar point in *The origins of meaning* (Hurford 2007: 262–4): kin selection alone is not adequate, when cultural as well as biological adaptation needs to be taken into account, and when cultural classifications and practices run counter to Western notions of biological relatedness, however 'true' these may be within the biological sciences.

In most languages and in the societies which speak these languages, my aunt on my mother's side (usually called 'mother') is closer than my aunt on my father's side (which anthropologists call 'cross-aunt'); and her children (usually called 'brother' and 'sister') are closer than those of my cross-aunt (whom anthropologists call 'cross-cousins'). This parallel/cross distinction, which we met in chapter 7, cannot be accounted for by genetic relatedness. The very notion of a form of 'kinship' which follows genetic relatedness is a very Western concept, and only the West, the Far East, and a relatively small number of other societies, regard the lineal/collateral distinction as the significant one. Hamilton's hypothesis assumes this as the norm. Thus it may be useful to see Hamilton in opposition to Lewis Henry Morgan. In a sense, all social anthropology has followed Morgan's emphasis on cultural difference, as all biology has followed Hamilton's emphasis on the implicit similarity of human societies with respect to kin relations. The twentieth-century biological evolutionist assumed the significance of biological relatedness, whereas the nineteenth-century social evolutionist discovered, to his surprise, the relevance of social diversity.

All that said, there may in fact be two senses in which Hamilton's hypothesis can be salvaged with reference to social anthropology. First, we could avoid his mathematics and not take him too literally. Kin selection may work with reference to kin groups, if not with reference to siblings and cousins. This may be the best way in which to conceptualize his great idea. Secondly, as we shall see below, my own theory of the evolution of kinship systems suggests that an egocentric, Hamiltonian vision might be correct for early *Homo*, possibly until the symbolic revolution of early *Homo sapiens* times (see also Barnard 2008: 235–9).

The significance of Hamilton's hypothesis may, in any case, be largely unconscious. Yet even if it is recognized unconsciously in societies which possess instead a *linguistic* distinction between parallel and cross, it is impossible for me to accept that that unconsciousness should override their explicit recognition of the importance of same-sex sibling bonds and primary classification of kin on *that* basis. It is no use invoking models derived from the study of insects (e.g. Hamilton 1972), since insects do not have cultural mechanisms to classify their kin in defiance of genetic relatedness. For this reason, sympathetic as I am to some unconscious truths in human evolution (such as group size as predicted in Dunbar's model), I cannot accept the plausibility of Hamilton's hypothesis if taken too literally. It simply runs counter to the cultural understandings of the majority of the world's populations, and in particular of modern small-scale hunting-and-gathering and horticultural societies throughout the world.

The other key thinker prior to the publication of Wilson's *Sociobiology* was Robert Trivers. Although very active and making significant contributions to sociobiology today, Trivers is perhaps still best known for his early work on reciprocal altruism (Trivers 1971), parental investment (1972) and parent–offspring conflict (1974). Reciprocal altruism is the idea that animals help each other and thereby gain advantage for the group or set of reciprocating individuals within the group. His main examples are altruistic behaviour in symbiotic cleaning relationships between fish, warning calls among birds and human reciprocal altruism, especially among kin. He states that human reciprocal altruism includes helping in times of danger; sharing food; helping the sick, wounded, old and very young; sharing implements; and sharing knowledge (Trivers 1971: 45). Each of these, Trivers suggests, is efficient in that it involves minimal investment on the part of the giver, while conferring potentially great benefit to the receiver.

Parental investment involves the investment of effort in individual offspring by a parent in such a way as to maximize the potential for survival of the offspring and ultimately their reproductive success. Trivers's (1972) examples include dragonflies, lizards and other animals, but he also broadens the definition to include pair-bonded species protection against the stealing of one's mate. He argues that the sex which invests most in raising the offspring will be more discriminating in its mating habits, and the other sex more promiscuous. Among humans, he discusses in this regard violence towards suspected adulterers among African Bushmen or San, Australian Aborigines and Arctic Inuit (Trivers 1972: 149–5). The investment of effort in raising or simply planning for offspring (including building nests, protection of eggs, and so on, among birds) may reduce the number of offspring one may have. Ultimately, siblings compete with each other for parental care, while parents employ sex-specific strategies for maximizing reproductive success, and their older offspring compete with their parents for their own reproductive success (Trivers 1974). This theoretical notion, derived in part from Trivers's own studies on pigeons, has obvious implications for human evolutionary biology as well as for the explanation of adolescent and adult behaviours in present-day human societies (see also Fuentes 2009: 16–63).

Some of Trivers's ideas are interesting for their implications in explanations of many aspects of human behaviour. Yet they are far from as significant as 1970s sociobiologists assumed they would be for social anthropology, sociology or perhaps even psychology. Among social anthropologists very few have taken to the sociobiological paradigm. Napoleon Chagnon, author of America's most popular teaching ethnography (original edition: Chagnon 1968), is one of the few. It is worth recalling that the 1970s was a decade of several attempts to shift social anthropology into grand interdisciplinary thinking, all of which to some extent failed. The others were structuralism, post-structuralism, Marxism and (begun in the 1970s but hitting mainly in the 1980s) postmodernism.

A theory of three revolutions

My own theory of the evolution of kinship structures is very much a (true) synthesis of ideas from diverse disciplines. It is based on the

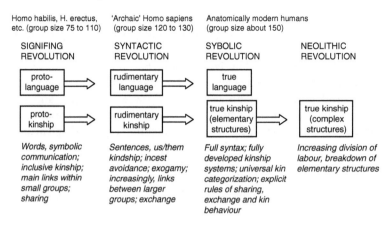

Homo habilis, H. erectus, etc. (group size 75 to 110)	'Archaic' Homo sapiens (group size 120 to 130)	Anatomically modern humans (group size about 150)	
SIGNIFING REVOLUTION	SYNTACTIC REVOLUTION	SYBOLIC REVOLUTION	NEOLITHIC REVOLUTION

Figure 8.1 A theory of three revolutions

notion of the co-evolution of kinship and language (see figure 8.1). That is built in turn on the work of the teams of Aiello and Dunbar (1993) (a palaeo-anatomist and an evolutionary psychologist) and of Calvin and Bickerton (2000). The theory of the former team, largely developed by Dunbar (e.g. 1993, 2003), is built on the idea of the co-evolution of neo-cortex size and group size. This is discussed in chapter 4. The latter team, and more specifically Bickerton in his published dialogue with Calvin (Calvin and Bickerton 2000), give us a three-stage theory of the evolu-tion of language, on to which I map a three-stage theory of the develop-ment of society and kinship. This in turn reflects the changes in cognitive structure and group size predicted by Aiello and Dunbar. All of these ideas are dependent on the work of archaeologists, and Dunbar's contri-bution on the calculation of group size is further dependent on the work of primatologists. Indeed, Dunbar himself is a primatologist, as well as an evolutionary psychologist.

Let me summarize the two papers (Barnard 2008, 2009) in which I developed this theory. With increasing neocortex size and brain size gen-erally came changes in cognitive abilities and an increase in optimal, and actual, size of social groups. According to Dunbar's (2003) calculations, we would expect australopithecines to have lived in groups of 65 or 70, *Homo habilis* in groups of 75 or 80, *H. erectus* perhaps 110, *H. heidel-bergensis* or 'Archaic' *H. sapiens* 120 or 130 and modern *H. sapiens* 150. It is not possible to associate my proposed three revolutions (based on Bickerton's three stages of language) accurately with fossil finds, but my assumption is that the first revolution might be associated with *H. habilis*, closely related or later species, the second with 'Archaics' and the third with anatomically modern humans.

In earlier books and papers, Derek Bickerton (e.g. 1998) had argued against a gradual development of language, and for a catastrophic birth of language coinciding with the 'cognitive explosion' which I refer to as the symbolic revolution. His later model has three phases: proto-language, rudimentary language and true language. Proto-language contains words and phrases but no sentences. Simple sentences, and the rudimentary language phase which characterizes their formation, are products of proto-language plus a 'social calculus' comprising specific knowledge of such things as who is grooming whom or who is in dispute with whom (see Calvin and Bickerton 2000: 129, 136–7). Full language entails complex syntax, including for example grammatical agreement between subject and verb. This is the phase Bickerton now associates with the symbolic revolution.

The signifying revolution

The signifying (or sharing) revolution marks a stage at which hominins are capable of using words and therefore classifying things. I envisage this as a phase somewhat reminiscent of Lewis Henry Morgan's (1871: 467–510) notion of the earliest human society and the developments towards the 'Malayan' (today called 'Hawaiian') classification of relatives – all cousins being classified as siblings. For Morgan, the earliest societies were characterized by promiscuous sexual intercourse, with later refinements including the cohabitation of brothers and sisters, the sharing of spouses in common and the 'Malayan' form of classification that followed from this.

I have suggested that this revolution occurred at an early time of the genus *Homo*, perhaps *Homo habilis* or some other antecedent of *H. ergaster* and *H. erectus*. There may, or may not, have been an incest taboo. There may or may not have been relationship terms to distinguish legitimate from illegitimate mates, terms to indicate generation (mothers/daughters) or collateral distance (sisters/not sisters), but the recognition of various relationships should logically follow from the earliest use of proto-language. The ability to classify is one step away from the ability to name. It would thus accompany the use of common nouns.

This stage of evolution would also be expected to be the one in which sharing becomes culturally developed. With *H. habilis*, and possibly earlier, we have a stage of biological evolution accompanied by a stage of cultural evolution marked by the production of stone tools. According to Dunbar's 'social brain' hypothesis, it is also a stage in which grooming gives way to speech or gesture, and some form of language would emerge to replace grooming as the primary means of communication. While chimpanzees share, they nevertheless do not possess rules or definitions of sharing practices. According to Morgan, the earliest phase of human evolution involves the sharing of 'spouses'. It is easy for us to imagine that early society was based on family ties, with sexual and non-sexual relations among family members, and in a linguistic milieu which for the first time would enable the transmission of knowledge across distances. Group size may be 75 or 80, but the community within which knowledge of people, of food or of tool-making or materials for tool-making was extended could, for the first time, have been much larger.

Leslie Aiello and Peter Wheeler (1995) argued that the increased brain size and decreased gut size of *H. habilis* over the australopithecines accompanied the development of a cultural practice of intensive meat-eating. This accompanied increases in group size, and also the improvement of intellectual abilities which were required in order to make tools and to teach tool-making skills (see also Mithen 1996: 95–114). Glynn Isaac (e.g. 1978a, 1978b) argued that early *Homo* consumed large amounts of meat, which led to food-sharing, to a division of labour and to the acquisition of home bases. Pre-*Homo* hominins inhabited nests, and were much more migratory. According to Isaac, early *Homo* developed pair bonding and male investment in childrearing, followed by longer dependency of infants on their parents. And finally, they acquired enhanced abilities to communicate. An opposing view, put forward by Lewis Binford (1981), was that scavenging rather than large-scale hunting was the essence of *H. habilis* subsistence. Binford's view would render Isaac's model unsustainable. In spite of the lack of archaeological evidence one way or the other, it seems to me that Isaac was broadly correct. The relation between meat-eating, brain size, group size and communication does suggest that sharing, if not necessarily pair bonding, would form the basis of *H. habilis* sociality. Still, there is counter-evidence, and there are other views. For example, Adrienne Zihlman, writing at much the same time (Zihlman 1978, 1981), argued that women as food-providers in gathering (as opposed to hunting) times must have been crucial for invention as well as for social and economic advances. Men supported their kin (with their concern for reproductive success), but hunting was a 'late' innovation.

Sharing, including possibly the sharing of mates, thus became important among early *Homo*. Pair bonding possibly came later, with increased time spent in the socialization of children. Early *Homo* had personal names. They categorized things, and possibly categorized kin. Even if fathers were unknown, mothers would be known. Even at such an early stage of human social and cultural evolution, we might see the signification of brothers and sisters, and, by implication, also of potential mates (those who were not brothers and sisters). The culture of social relations would be expected to be bound up with the culture of the transmission of knowledge, including that required for the production and employment of material culture.

The syntactic revolution

If the first phase is reminiscent of Morgan's era of primitive promiscuity, the second, following the syntactic revolution, for me resembles John F. McLennan's (1865) theory of the dawn of exogamy. McLennan was Morgan's great rival. He agreed with Morgan that matrilineal descent preceded patrilineal, but his method of arriving at this conclusion was very different. He believed that a shortage of food led to female infanticide, which in turn led to a shortage of women, and then to polyandry as the norm. Each woman would be married to more than one man, and thus the genitor of any child would be difficult to determine. Descent in such a society had to be matrilineal, but this changed when men adopted the practice of bride capture. They began to steal wives from other tribes, and thus gained control of their own wives and families. The battles which ensued led, in turn, to a desire for peace. Peace came as an exchange of women replaced the practice of bride capture, and this led in turn to patrilineality and patriarchy.

The signifying revolution brought the recognition of categories such as mother and possibly father, and of brother, sister, son, daughter and mate. The syntactic revolution (or exchange revolution) brought much more. With rudimentary syntax comes the ability to formulate complex kin descriptions, and therefore the recognition, of mothers' brothers and mothers' sisters. This would likely yield the recognition of the categories implied by Proto-World *kaka* (mother's brother, etc.) as well as *mama* (mother) and possibly *papa* (father), although not necessarily these words themselves, especially if these hominins were using gestural language (cf. Bancel and Matthey de l'Etang 2002; Matthey de l'Etang and Bancel 2002). If Aiello and Dunbar (1993) are right that *Homo heidelbergensis* group size had increased to 120, we should certainly envisage smaller bands interacting with other bands of the same group and possibly with bands of other groups.

The increase in neocortex size suggests a level of intentionality and a degree of communication enabling the transmission of knowledge about resources, populations and kinship over geographical distances. Dunbar (2004: 108–37) has suggested that the earliest 'Archaic' *Homo sapiens* or *H. heidelbergensis*, along with Neanderthals, probably filled a 'bonding gap' through the development of sophisticated communication through chorusing, and possibly dance, prior to the development of full language.

At this stage, we would anticipate too the strong possibility of at least rules governing mating exogamy, although not yet its full fruition as part of a typical hunter-gatherer social structure in which everyone is classified as 'kin'. The latter would have to wait until the 'human' or 'symbolic' revolution that marks both full language and full kinship systems such as are found today in every human society in the world.

The symbolic revolution

The third revolution was, in a sense, Lévi-Straussian. True kinship coincides with the emergence of elementary structures of kinship. For Lévi-Strauss (1969), kinship is based on reciprocity, and dual organization, with direct exchange, is logically the simplest form of social structure. The simplest elementary structure in Lévi-Straussian terms is a moiety structure. Nicholas Allen (2008) disagrees, ascribing a four-unit structure logical priority, because that makes it possible for people to eliminate the necessity of keeping track of genealogical level. My own view, as I have said, is that cognatic kinship is probably prior, and that in any case we must give recognition to one fact that is crucial for nearly all living hunter-gatherers. That is universal kinship: where everyone classifies everyone else as some kind of 'kin', and there is no such category as 'non-kin' (Barnard 1978). In universal kinship systems, any strangers who might have cause to engage in marital alliance or possibly even the trade of material goods would be fitted into kin relations, since society was definable entirely on a kinship basis. This is true today of peoples who practise direct exchange, and not only of virtually all hunting-and-gathering societies (whether of savannah, deserts, arctic wastes or rainforests) but of many other small-scale cultivating societies too (such as those of the rainforests of South and Southeast Asia and South America). Such peoples do of course know who is closely related and who is distant (or who is related merely through namesake-equivalence, through moiety and generation category membership or friendship redefined as kinship, etc.). Nevertheless, they see kinship differently from those, like most of us, whose concerns lie not in category, but rather, or much more so, in genealogical proximity and distance.

With the evolution of full kinship, several potential structures were available to our ancestors, but these are all characterized either by making a parallel/cross distinction or not making one. For a great number of reasons, not least the ease in maintaining elementary principles (positive marriage rules), I favour the idea that the earliest full kinship systems did make that distinction. Other reasons include: the necessity to differentiate opposite-sex individuals by category, the likely extension of such

categories through links to close kin in a universal system and the prob-
able association of such structures with the evolution of sexual taboos
and other aspects of symbolic culture (cf. Knight, Power and Watts 1995);
and the very widespread occurrence of elementary structures, same-sex
sibling joking and opposite-sex sibling avoidance and the related parallel/
cross distinction itself among the world's small-scale societies today. That
still leaves the problem of how the parallel/cross distinction is played out.
Lévi-Strauss maintained it was a product of moiety structures reminiscent of those of contemporary South America. Allen maintains classification distinctions through tetradic structures, which may or may not
imply moieties intersecting alternating generations. I maintain a third
possibility as the simplest: the structures can be generated purely by relations among siblings in small social groups and the distinction between
possible mates and those not possible in the next generation (see Barnard
1999). Young people 'marry' their cousins, but only their cross-cousins,
and egocentric kinship alone can do this. In short, neither moieties nor
Australian-type sections are needed – a point noted too by Allen (2004),
whose vision of tetradic structures is not dependent on the differentiation of egocentric and the sociocentric categories.

Whatever the actual earliest full kinship system, however, it was a product of the distinction between possible spouses and prohibited spouses, a
distinction which after 1949 overthrew the then-current notion of seeing
kinship primarily in terms of descent groups. My proposition is that the
earliest system was universal, but of course not all kinship systems are.
What makes a kinship system 'full' is first that it recognizes that most
crucial of distinctions, between possible and prohibited, and secondly
that it allows for classification of a set of relatives on both sides of the
family. In all such cases, the classification will be uniform, or will rapidly
become uniform in the case of a system in transition, in what we consider
a society. The situation is analogous to that in language: pidgins become
creoles; bilingual people, even children, do not mix English and French
indiscriminately; above all, no one speaks half a language. The point is
that no one lives in a society where there is half a kinship system, or where
relatives play by different rules. Kinship systems change through time,
but in order to maintain the systematic nature of kinship change has to
be rapid. Kinship systems are, or rapidly become, logical. Like languages,
they are always fully formed. Kinship terminologies are, if not always, at
least usually internally logical, as demonstrated, for example, by the fact
that if I call, say (in an 'Omaha' structure), my mother's brother's son
'(cross-)nephew', he will call me '(cross-)uncle'.

The recognition of kinship links beyond the nuclear family, the acquisition of ties to in-laws as well as to spouses and classification of society

according to kin categories would undoubtedly give early symbolic people the facility, and indeed encourage the propensity, for communication through enhanced rules for exchange and sharing. Add to this the ability, through art, linguistic metaphor and symbolic representation, for cultural elaboration, and the relation between society, culture and language becomes humanly 'complete' (cf. Knight, Power and Watts 1995).

The break-up of elementary structures

Later, there would in a sense be a fourth 'revolution': the Neolithic. In terms of kinship, the Neolithic is marked not by a stone tool tradition or by the adoption of agriculture, but by the loss of universal kin classification and the change from elementary to complex structures of alliance. These changes did not necessarily occur immediately and were not inevitable (as evidenced today by the persistence of such structures among Dravidian-speakers), but they were nevertheless perhaps a logical consequence of neolithization. It may be best to think of the true revolutionary change in mode of thought as occurring, not at the beginning, but at the end of a slow (over a thousand years) Neolithic transition. In other words, the true 'Neolithic Revolution' followed rather than accompanied the Neolithic transition (see also Barnard 2007b). It is in this period of transition that we still find remnants of direct exchange, for example in South America, where moiety systems occur along with horticulture.

The transition, of course, was preceded by the *Homo sapiens* Out of Africa migration, and it led to the creation of the variety of kinship structures found today. As shown by both Nicholas Allen (1989b) and Maurice Godelier (2004: 511–13), terminology structures eventually evolved (or broke down) from 'Dravidian' and 'Iroquois' forms to forms which do not differentiate parallel from cross-relatives or which simply make all possible distinctions, forms that include 'Hawaiian', 'Eskimo' and 'Sudanese' structures alike. The genealogical emerged again from a long age in which kinship was classificalogical, and we find the disappearance of anything like tetradic structures in most of Asia and the Americas accompanying the gradual transition from Lévi-Straussian elementary to complex structures across the globe.

Another way to see the transition is in terms of a divergence from African hunter-gatherer social organization. Hunter-gatherers in southern, eastern and central Africa all have relatively flexible forms of social organization. For example, where kinship is important as a determinant of marriageable and non-marriageable people, the mechanism for determining these is egocentric and flexible. In contrast, the kinship systems of hunter-gatherers and small-scale horticulturists in those parts of the

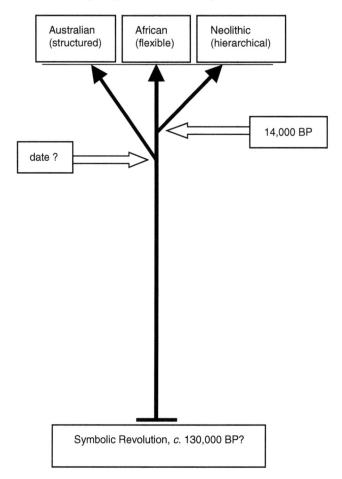

Figure 8.2 Divergence from African hunter-gatherer
culture since the symbolic revolution

world settled much later, notably in Australia and South America, are
highly structured. Additionally, Australian peoples in particular, and
many South American ones too, have cosmological structures which map
on to these. One can think of these as *structured systems* that diverged from
African-type systems long ago, perhaps early at the time of settlement in
Australia. Likewise, *hierarchical systems*, as found among throughout the
world since the Neolithic, diverged later, and distinguish the *flexible systems* of African hunter-gatherers from those of almost all other peoples of
the world (figure 8.2). To a lesser extent, even African agro-pastoralists fit
this model. Once, when speaking in a German anthropology department,

I encountered an objection, on grounds of political correctness, to my African and Australian models. Yet I favour these labels both since they are clear and since the immediate descendants of African and Australian hunter-gatherers do not object to them. Indeed, in my experience, San and Aborigines like the idea of having retained primal, or 'natural', social systems that the rest of us have deviated from. It is, after all, the Neolithic that was aberrant, not the lifestyles of hunter-gatherers.

The San worldview, in contrast to that of the Aborigines, is based on one simple principle: an extreme flexibility at all levels. San possess a belief in one or many deities; a close connection to the land but not an attachment to any sacred sites; emotional, but not totemic, relations to animals hunted; a lack of clan organization, but wide cognatic kin networks; marriage rules which follow genealogy and not sociocentric categories like moieties or sections and *a lack of fit* between all these attributes. In other words, Aboriginal culture values order, whereas San culture is much more flexible, even disordered.

Alternative syntheses

Chris Henshilwood (pers. comm.) once suggested that perhaps another revolution beyond those I have suggested might be worth considering. This additional revolution was most likely to have occurred between my signifying (sharing) revolution and my syntactic (exchange) revolution: in the time of *Homo ergaster* or *H. erectus*, or perhaps *H. antecessor*. Exactly what sort of revolution it was is no doubt open to some question. It may be related to the improved technology of Acheulean tools, or perhaps the taming of fire, or changes in diet or changes in social relations enabling ease of migration along coastlines around Asia and to the Far East and Europe. It may, of course, have involved some combination of these, and may have been a slow, rather than a rapid, revolution – but nevertheless one that was revolutionary in its long-term results for human evolution.

Another possible revolution, of course, is a Neolithic, one – which is coincident with the break-up of elementary structures. My vision of a 'Neolithic Revolution' is very different from that of Gordon Childe, although contrary to some he did seem to see the Neolithic as possibly gradual if revolutionary: 'not a catastrophe, but a process' (Childe 1941 [1936]: 99). My Neolithic Revolution lies at the end of the Neolithic transition. However, Childe's Neolithic does correspond roughly to James Woodburn's (1980, 1982) notion of a shift from immediate to delayed-return economic systems. Archaeologists in recent years have largely given up reference to a Neolithic Revolution, preferring instead

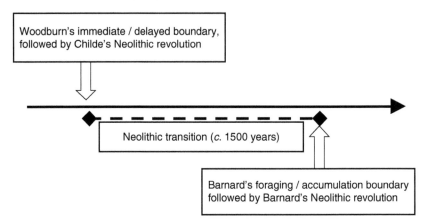

Figure 8.3 The Neolithic transition and 'Neolithic revolutions'

to speak of a Neolithic transition. With figures from Europe and southern Africa, this transition seems to have lasted 1,500 or 1,800 years (see
Barnard 2007b: 7, 17). It marks the time period between the introduction or first adoption of husbandry or horticulture, and the completion
of the shift from hunting and gathering to full husbandry or horticulture
as the basis of subsistence (figure 8.3).

Woodburn's model assumes that the adoption of any form of food production, or even of delay in achievement of a subsistence aim due to planning ahead (such as making hunting nets for use later) results in a shift
from an immediate-return to a delayed-return ideology. My assumption
is the reverse. The retention of hunting and gathering, even for a small
percentage of one's subsistence, allows the retention of values associated
with what I have called the foraging or hunter-gatherer mode of thought
(e.g. Barnard 2002). These values include favouring immediate consumption over accumulation (since consumption involves sharing, and
accumulation implies stinginess), followership over leadership (in other
words, deference to the will of the community over self-interest), and
so on. The Neolithic transition involved the eventual rejection of these
values in favour of their opposites. In these two examples, accumulation
became the 'social' option, since it meant saving for one's dependants;
and leadership came to be associated with public service rather than
self-interest. Others are more subtle or more complex. Hunter-gatherers
see land as sacrosanct (and associated with primordial possession) and
people as sovereign (free individuals operating in spite of any constraining authority). Non-hunter-gatherers see the reverse: land as implying
sovereignty (ultimately with political authority in the hands of the state)

and people as sacrosanct (as citizens, ultimately with the state as a sacred trust (see Barnard 2002, 2007b).

Of course, I am not the first person to suggest a sequence of revolutionary changes in social life or cognitive faculty. One attempt also with three revolutionary transitions is that of Merlin Donald (1991). Donald's first such transition is from what he calls episodic to mimetic culture. Episodic culture is represented by the cognitive systems of the great apes. Their memory consists of a series of concrete episodes, and it lacks any reflection beyond that on the specific. Mimetic culture, in contrast, involves either internal reflection and analysis or the communication, without language, of a deeper understanding. According to Donald, *Homo erectus* had this capability, and it enabled the teaching and learning of tool-making technology, and ultimately the ability to dance and to perform ritual. It also enables conscious collective action more generally.

His second revolutionary transition is from mimetic to mythic culture. Donald conceives of the earliest use of language as in the construction of models of the world through mythology. In his view, the first acquisition of language, through either gesture or speech, gave rise to the creation of symbolic systems relating, say, the moon, menstruation, power over animals and life and death. Mythology was a logical consequence, as are the development of arbitrary symbols such as non-onomatopoeic words, and also grammar. He hedges his bets on the association of specific fossils, but speaks broadly of 'archaic humans'.

Donald's third revolutionary transition is from mythic to theoretic culture. This involved pictorial representation, including cave art and body decoration. It is associated with the earliest forms of pictorial art, and continues through the inventions of writing and numerical representation.

Donald's thesis today seems hopelessly old-fashioned in many respects, not least because his starting premise seems to lie in the logic of an evolution of cognition, rather than in genetics or fossil discoveries. Yet, it is in another sense refreshingly pure in its attempt to work from cognitive logic and slot the fossils in afterwards. There may be a lesson here for social anthropology, but I would be wary of attempts to account for social evolution across the diversity of hominin species without embedding theory, in so far as is possible, in species difference. Speculative theories such as Donald's no doubt work best over shorter timescales, as indeed social evolutionary theory did function in the nineteenth century, with Morgan (1871), McLennan (1865) and others, when only *Homo sapiens* was assumed. I might add that although it may be methodologically old-fashioned, it accords with more recent neurological work and especially with William Calvin's (2004) semi-popular account of the 'history of the mind', based on archaeology but with neuroscience in the background. Calvin looks to climatic change around 2,500,000 years ago, and consequent speciation and, in the case of the earliest *Homo*, bigger brain size and consequent stone tool-making abilities. Then, in his account, there was a second 'brain boom' about 750,000 years ago, with *H. antecessor*. After that, we have the rise of the Neanderthals, *H. sapiens* 'without the modern mind' and finally anatomical 'moderns' around 100,000 years ago, though with language and symbolism some time later. Calvin (2004: 69) notes a long (and implicitly gradualist) sequence leading, archaeologically, to symbolism: blades, grindstones and pigments, points, mortuary practices, shellfish, long-distance trading, fishing, bone tools, barbs, mining, incised patterns, beads and images.

There remains the question of how any of these theories relate to the bigger picture of anthropology, or of the social or biological sciences. My own theory of the co-evolution of language and kinship is a theory of quite a lot, but it is not a theory of everything. Wilson, and Hamilton and Trivers before him, had a greater, and I believe more mistaken, vision. They saw a unity in the social and biological sciences which I do not. Likewise, in a recent book Marion Blute (2010: 7) argues for 'a unification of the social sciences themselves within a broadly synthetic sociocultural evolutionary framework'. Her proposed framework is socio-cultural, but not sociobological. She is right in her conclusion (2010: 206–8) that interdisciplinary studies in the origin and evolution of language offer tremendous models for others to follow. I, however, prefer not to see any such paradigm as a way forward for all of anthropology, much less the social sciences generally. It would be much better if instead a strong subdiscipline of the social anthropology of human origins were to emerge, leaving the rest of anthropology intact and as source material for this new specialization. The failure of sociobiology shows us the fallacy of trying to push an entire academic discipline, much less a set of such disciplines, in any particular direction.

9   Conclusions

Social anthropology can and should be part of the interdisciplinary study of human origins. Anthropological theory and ethnographic comparison can easily be brought into the frameworks of both primary research and intellectual debate on the subject. I would go further: the study of human origins can and should be a legitimate subdiscipline within social anthropology. I hope I have demonstrated that its inclusion among the sciences dealing with this issue is warranted and that its contribution could be considerable.

From within social anthropology the contribution of the discipline might at first seem more speculative than that of some other disciplines, but social anthropology is a qualitative social science by nature. It need not be any more speculative than, say, archaeology or human genetics – disciplines in which plausibility and likelihood are often sufficient for the construction of hypotheses and even for longstanding and widely accepted theories. No modern scientist has ever seen the origin of tool-making, the development of language, a symbolic revolution or a migration which has led to the colonization of an empty continent. In this, social anthropology is on exactly the same footing as archaeology or human genetics. The only difference is that genetics and archaeology rely on 'hard data', which are almost invariably either material (in the case of archaeology) or quantitative, or at least involving careful sampling (in the case of genetics). After that, the rest (for archaeologists and geneticists) is pure inference and deduction.

In *Before the dawn*, the eminent science writer Nicholas Wade (2006) gives numerous examples of the successful use of inference and deduction in the studies of human origins. The chance observation, in 1999, that human head lice cannot live for more than a day beyond a human body gave rise to the study of the genetic differentiation of head and body lice as a determinant of the date of the origin of clothing and as a check on the dates of the *Homo sapiens* Out of Africa migration. The size of tortoises in archaeological sites can indicate the relative size of human populations, since larger tortoises are eaten first, medium-sized ones second and small ones only once these are gone. The study of the creation of creoles from pidgins provide clues about the origin of languages. Observations of the birth of two new sign languages, one in a Nicaraguan school for the deaf and the other among Bedouin in the Negev desert, also shed light on the origins of language and languages. In the Nicaraguan case, signers developed rules of sentence syntax, and in the Bedouin case they created the signed equivalent of case endings.

In other examples suggested in Wade's book, Dunbar's social grooming hypothesis is a theory of language developed from speculation about what might happen if humans did what they were supposed to, according to predictions based on observations of primates. Inference from observations and genetic studies of two families afflicted by faulty FOXP2 genes led to studies of worldwide variations in FOXP2, and the resulting proposal of a rough date for the 'language gene' (within the last 200,000 years). Dates of the separation of species, human migration, and so on, are based on assumptions about the rates of genetic change, and are similarly inferred, with or without corroborative fossil or archaeological evidence. Likewise, deductions by geneticists have led to the assumption of a bottleneck population of perhaps 5,000 to 10,000 (some say 2,000), living in eastern Africa between 100,000 years ago and 50,000 years ago, and probably nearer the latter date. Then there is the assumption of a group of 150 as the *Homo sapiens* Out of Africa migrants who settled first across the Red Sea and whose descendants spread to all the continents.

Especially towards the end of the book, Wade (e.g. 2006: 60–73, 148–54, 177–80, 241–57) turns to ethnographic analogy as a method to produce models of human evolution. This is sometimes coupled with linguistic, archaeological, genetic or even comparative primatological evidence. Certainly, Wade's use of ethnographic analogy is *ad hoc* and fragmentary, as well as rather less developed than his arguments based on other kinds of data. But it is surely a start, and it shows that ethnography, and anthropological ideas developed with the framework of ethnographic analysis, can make contributions comparable with those from other disciplines.

Another work of relevance is Steven Kuhn and Mary Stiner's (2001) lengthy article on 'The antiquity of hunter-gatherers'. It is framed purely in archaeological terms, but it does highlight some similarities between contemporary hunter-gatherers and those, particularly, of the Late Upper Palaeolithic. They concentrate on technology and on subsistence. The exchange of goods, though on a limited scale, for example, is not something of recent origin (as Kalahari revisionists might claim), but 'virtually ubiquitous in the LUP' (2001: 115). Variation in diet among specific groups was common throughout the Palaeolithic. Maritime sources are more common in the northern hemisphere, and terrestrial resources in the southern. Shellfish were part of the diet of the Middle Palaeolithic, but a decline in stocks cause less reliance on them later. Such findings can aid in the application of ideas from social anthropology, especially in the use of hunter-gatherer ethnography, and they do show as well that there is much continuity with the past. Kuhn and Stiner remark that modern hunter-gatherer adaptations were established across the world by 20,000 years ago, and possibly by 45,000 years ago. Traps, nets and grindstones like those in use today do not receive much comment in archaeological literature, but they were there long ago too. Wooden spears have been around for 500,000 years.

Human origins from a social anthropological perspective

In spite of Adam Kuper's (1994) account of the interplay of cultural and biological anthropology and his optimistic vision, most of social anthropology has been stuck in a synchronic quagmire. This began about 1922, when Malinowski settled in at the London School of Economics and Radcliffe-Brown took on his first student at Cape Town. However, Radcliffe-Brown was not quite the anti-evolutionist he was portrayed as (see Barnard 1992b). He founded the School of African Life and Languages and in 1922 became its first director, and in it included archaeology along with African languages and social anthropology. He also declared himself an evolutionist, and wrote to the newspapers offering his interpretations of fossil finds. His unfinished textbook on social anthropology concludes with an affirmation of (social) evolution as a legitimate area for the practice of his subject (Radcliffe-Brown 1958: 178–89). The anti-evolutionist enemy, he says, was Boas – whose cultural anthropology lacked a systematic, comparative theoretical framework. It is certainly true that Radcliffe-Brown objected to the methods of the evolutionist 'conjectural historians' of the eighteenth and nineteenth centuries, but his overriding interest, and theirs, was in generalization, and ultimately in the natural laws which govern social organization, social structure and structural form.

However, along with Malinowski, Radcliffe-Brown helped to mould a new British anthropology with a methodological emphasis on field research, the ethnographic present and synchronic comparison. In the United States, the tradition of Franz Boas and his followers built departments based on the four-field model. The Boasians saw physical anthropology and not their own field as the rightful place for evolutionary studies. Then the separation of physical and cultural anthropology within departments, throughout the twentieth century, led to an assumption of diachrony only in the former and of pure synchrony in the latter. In both Britain and America, the basis of social and cultural anthropology on intensive, long-term field research, along with the regional specialization that that entailed, meant that bridging the gap between prehistory and the present was in the formative years of the discipline almost impossible in the spheres of culture and society. This was replicated throughout the world, almost everywhere social anthropology was taught.

Recent decades saw a rise in interpretive studies, where the object of social anthropology was to 'translate' alien cultures into cultural languages intelligible to other, usually Western, anthropologists. This fitted well with the American Boasian agenda, and has in recent years become common-place in the United Kingdom, Australia and Scandinavia, among other places. Along with problems of finding an appropriate use for fieldwork, this shift in theoretical bent has made it difficult for a social anthropology of human origins to come into being. Hunter-gatherer studies might have offered the opportunity, but intensive fieldwork and good description, especially of ecological relations, became the norm in the late twentieth century; and this was largely at the expense of wider comparative studies or of comparisons to life in the distant past. There have been scattered attempts and dabblings, such as Richard Lee's marvellous paper 'The hand-to-mouth existence: a note on the origin of human economy' (Lee 1979: 489–94). Yet it is a telling fact that that paper was written and presented in 1968, but not published until eleven years later and then only as an appendix to The !Kung San. Considerations of political correctness, and a genuine concern for the sensitivity of recent foraging populations and how they are viewed by often hostile outsiders, are also factors miti-gating against certain kinds of ethnographic analogy and especially of comparisons between modern foragers and Palaeolithic ones. In some circles, in the West, even using such hunter-gatherers as examples can invoke a hostile response, especially from naïve listeners who misinter-pret any talk of a hunting-and-gathering lifestyle as implying diminished humanity on the part of such people. This is a pity: although opinion is of course divided, modern foragers, or their children, are often proud of their historically deep cultural roots. In their view, it is we agricultural and industrialized people whose humanity is questionable.

There have been a few attempts by social anthropologists to enter debates on human evolution and on the origins of symbolic culture, lan-guage and kinship. The work of Knight and Power on symbolic thought, and of Allen on kinship, are obvious examples. There is also related work by W. G. Runciman (e.g. 2001, 2009), which although billed as sociology or comparative sociology, speaks by its example to social or cultural anthropology as well. Runciman is much more explicitly selectionist and Darwinian than I think is necessary. It is not that I object at all to the importance of natural section, to the analogy between biological and social theory, or even to the idea of memes as analogous to genes, but rather that I would prefer an appeal to anthropology's great thinkers rather than to W. D. Hamilton (e.g. 1972) or Richard Dawkins (e.g. 1976). Another sociologist whose work is relevant is Tim Megarry (1995), but his exploration of 'society in prehistory' is more a sociologist's migration into archaeological territory than an attempt to apply sociological ideas to archaeological data. On the whole, edited volumes such as the interdisciplinary volume *The evolution of culture* (Dunbar *et al.*1999) and the more social anthropological *Early human kinship* (Allen *et al.* 2008), which both contain papers by Knight and Power, fare better. In these, authors are suggesting new directions for the development of a social anthropology of human origins. This may not be 'mainstream' British anthropology, but it does represent potential. In my view, the theoretical trajectories of these three authors are far too dogmatic to lead the path to a wider subdiscipline of the social anthropology of human origins. Yet they are at least debating some of the relevant issues.

What would a social anthropology of human origins look like?

There might be several logical possibilities for the incorporation of social anthropology into the study of human origins. Each implies a steep learning curve, either on the part of social anthropologists learning about primates, fossils, and so on, or on the part of those in other disciplines coming to grips with social anthropological ideas. To my mind, probably only one is both intellectually sound and really workable: the acceptance of human origins as a specialization within social anthropology. Nevertheless, consider this as one among other possibilities:

1. Human origins as a specialization within social anthropology.
2. Social anthropology to be brought more into the tool kit of primatology, prehistory, evolutionary psychology, etc.
3. Social anthropology as a method within a larger, unified if still 'interdisciplinary' field of human origins studies.
4. The social anthropology of human origins as a separate subject or as a new, fifth field to be added to the four fields of North American anthropology.

The first possibility is my favoured one, mainly because it respects the integrity of social anthropology as a discipline. This discipline is based on ethnography, comparison and grand theory. Some of the grand theory is unique to the field, while some is borrowed from other disciplines and either sits above it or has become embedded into it. Comparison is, at least in my view, the primary essence of social anthropology, and it depends on an understanding of the place of one's own ethnography within a wider constellation of ethnographic data. The stumbling block might be ethnography: this is a requirement for all who call themselves social anthropologists, and for many it could be difficult to place their own ethnography within a spectrum of material related to human origins.

The second is, in some ways, already happening. Nevertheless, the simple borrowing of anthropology ideas and the use of ethnographic comparison or analogy is often problematic, for a number of reasons, not least because of the use of such methods by non-social anthropologists who are unfamiliar with the context of social anthropological usage and social anthropological debate. I have nothing against people from other disciplines using social anthropological data and ideas if they do it well, but this does not really incorporate social anthropology in a meaningful way. It also leaves practitioners of social anthropology out of the circle, except perhaps as invited guests at other people's conferences.

The third is unlikely, though it may in a sense be desirable. It would require a reorganization of university departments and the development of such a new field through course material, as well as probably some reorganization of research groups, funding bodies, and so on. In short, desirable, but far too difficult to achieve in the short term. In time, it may also be problematic for the new discipline, as splits would inevitably occur.

The fourth is equally unlikely, and could not be sustained. Linguistics, archaeology and biological anthropology would have an equal claim to a specialized field of this kind. It is precisely my point that social anthropology should be an equal partner. I would like to see it as a driving force for social considerations in the study of human origins, but not to the extent that a discipline is created beyond all the rest.

A useful analogy might be with linguistics. Only twenty years or so ago, the evolutionary study of language was virtually non-existent. Today it is thriving. There are large international conferences on the origin and evolution of language now every year or two. There seems to be plenty of money for research in proto-language, symbolic behaviour related to early language, and so on, and in several countries. Conference volumes, journal articles and singly authored books on the origin of language, both by linguists and by others, including archaeologists and geneticists, proliferate. If linguists and scholars in marginally related fields can do it, then so can social anthropologists.

I believe that social anthropology can be fully incorporated into the frameworks of both primary research and intellectual debate on human origins. I also believe that the study of human origins should be recognized as a legitimate subdiscipline within social anthropology. How these twin goals can be realized depends on developments both outside social anthropology and within it.

Glossary

accumulation mode of thought My term for an ideology emphasizing the acquisition of property. This ideology is Neolithic and post-Neolithic. The opposite is the **foraging mode of thought**.

Acheulean Stone tool industry of the Lower Palaeolithic. Named after St Acheul, a suburb of Amiens in France.

affinal relative A relative by marriage. Cf. **consanguineal relative**.

alliance Relations in marriage, between individuals or groups. From the French *alliance*.

alpha male Male primate in the dominant social position within a group.

Altimira A cave in northern Spain famous for its Magdalenian (Upper Palaeolithic) rock art, the earliest dated to about 18,000 BP.

ambilocality Postmarital residence in the home of either the husband or the wife.

anatomically modern human (AMH) The species *Homo sapiens* in fully modern form, from about 200,000 BP, including *H. sapiens* before the appearance of symbolic culture.

animism Belief that natural objects, such as rocks and trees, have a spiritual existence.

Anthropithecus Original name of *Pithecantropus erectus*, later *Homo erectus*. It means 'man-ape'.

anthropology The study of humankind. In North America it includes the 'four fields' of cultural anthropology, physical anthropology, anthropological linguistics and prehistoric archaeology. Elsewhere, the term is often used more narrowly, and is synonymous with either cultural anthropology (social anthropology) or physical anthropology (biological anthropology).

antiquarianism The eighteenth-century forerunner of modern archaeology.

archaeology The study of the past through its physical remains.

Ardipithecus A probably bidepal hominin genus with ape-like teeth. It lived in east Africa roughly 4,500,000 to 4,000,000 BP.

australopithecines (*Australopithecus*) The genus which includes 'gracile' forms such as *A. africanus* and 'robust' forms such as *A. robustus* (*Paranthropus robustus*). Australopithecines lived in eastern and southern Africa from about five million to about one million years ago.

Australopithecus afarensis Species dating roughly from 3,600,000 to 3,200,000 BP and found in eastern Africa. The earliest find was 'Lucy', discovered in 1974 by Donald Johanson.

Australopithecus africanus Species found in eastern and southern Africa from 3,000,000 to 2,300,000 BP. The earliest find was 'Dart's child', discovered in 1924 by Raymond Dart.

autochthonous Relating to the relation between land and people. Cf. **indigenous**.

avoidance relationship A kin relationship with required deference and respect, for example commonly between in-laws. The opposite is a **joking relationship**.

avunculocality Postmarital residence in the home of the man's mother's brother. From Latin *avunculus*, 'mother's brother'.

band A hunter-gatherer group.

band cluster A unit of hunter-gatherer social organization comprised of several bands, which might aggregate seasonally or simply share a common identity.

basal hominin sociality The notion of original social traits common to earlier hominins, but from which modern humans have diverged.

'big man' system A political and economic system based on achieved status, where the 'big man' is pivotal to the exchange of goods (through acquisition and redistribution). His role is similar to that of a chief, except that it is based on social action rather than ascribed status. Common in Melanesia.

biological anthropology Modern term for what was once called physical anthropology, used in recognition of the fact that biological studies now include genetics and other sciences, rather than simply the physical properties or dimensions of fossils and living beings.

bipedalism The ability to walk upright, on two legs.

Blombos Cave South African Indian Ocean coastal site excavated by Chris Henshilwood, Francesca d'Errico and others. Important for etched pieces of red ochre (dating from 77,000 BP) and for very early beadwork.

bonding Friendship and co-operation among men, between spouses, etc.

bonobo The 'pygmy chimp', *Pan paniscus*.

BP Before present.

chromosome A cellular structure of DNA.

clade A group of organisms descended from a common ancestor.

cladogenesis The splitting of a species into two clades, as opposed to gradual evolution within one species.

clan A large kin group, composed of several lineages and formed through either patrilineal or matrilineal descent.

cognatic descent A descent system which possesses neither patrilineal nor matrilineal kin groups, or descent through non-lineal relatives in a patrilineal or matrilineal system. Also known as bilateral descent. In a sense, the opposite of **double** (duolineal) descent.

collateral relative A consanguineal relative related though a brother or sister link.

collective representation Any of the collective understandings which people in a given community or society share. The term is derived from Durkheimian sociology.

community A group of people who live together or share common values. It is smaller than a society, but of no precise size.

complex system Lévi-Strauss's term for a kinship structure which has negative marriage rules. For example, one is not allowed to marry a brother or a sister. The opposite is an **elementary system**. See also **Crow–Omaha system**.

concept of the person The cultural perception of what it means to be a 'person'. This differs from society to society.

consanguineal relative A relative by 'blood'. Cf. **affinal relative**.

core In archaeology, a stone from which flakes are removed to produce a tool.

cranial capacity The volume of the cranium.

cranium That part of the skull which covers the brain.

Cro–Magnon Early modern humans of Europe, from a site in southern France excavated in 1868.

cross-cousin Father's sister's child or mother's brother's child. Cf. **parallel cousin**.

cross-relative A collateral relative related through an opposite-sex sibling link.

Crow-Omaha system Lévi-Strauss's term for a kinship structure which has either a 'Crow' or an 'Omaha' terminology (i.e. one in which given kin terms are applied to entire lineages, matrilineal for 'Crow' or patrilineal for 'Omaha'), and in which the marriage prohibitions extended through such lineages are so extensive that the 'complex' structure comes to resemble an 'elementary' one.

cultural anthropology The branch of anthropology that studies cultural phenomena. The term is common in some traditions and countries (e.g. in the United States, in Japan) but less so in others (e.g. in the United Kingdom).

cultural core Julian Steward's notion of the central elements of culture. He perceived these as being those most closely associated with exploitation of the environment.

culture That which is not natural but learned. One may speak of culture in the abstract, or of cultures (plural), though the latter is often regarded as contentious.

culture area A geographical region comprising peoples of similar culture.

'Dart's child' The nickname of the first *Australopithecus* find, a juvenile skull discovered by Raymond Dart in 1924 and described in *Nature* in 1925.

Darwinian The notion that evolution is through natural selection. Cf. **Lamarckian**.

delayed return James Woodburn's term for the economic and social system of 'advanced' hunter-gatherers and non-hunter-gatherers, where time *is* invested in planning ahead in subsistence activity. The opposite of **immediate return**.

demand sharing The customary sharing goods upon request.

descent Relations between the generations in terms of group membership. There are four basic types: patrilineal, matrilineal, double (duolineal) and cognatic (bilateral).

diachronic Literally 'through time'. The opposite is **synchronic**.

diffusionism The diachronic theoretical perspective that stresses migration and diffusion of cultural ideas, rather than evolution.

DNA Deoxyribonucleic acid, the substance which contains genetic information.

double descent A descent system which possesses both patrilineal and matrilineal kin groups. Also known as duolineal descent. In a sense, the opposite of **cognatic** (bilateral) descent.

'Dravidian' A system similar to 'Iroquois' in that it distinguishes parallel from cross-cousins. It differs in its classification of second cousins.

'Dunbar's number' The supposed natural community size for humans, based on comparison and correlations between neocortex size and group size among primates. The number is 150.

duolocality Postmarital residence in two place: the husband and wife each remain in their natal homes.

'early man' Earlier term for the study of human origins. Refers not to any specific period or fossil, but to earlier forms in a broad sense.

Early Stone Age (ESA) Southern African designation of the Palaeolithic prior to the invention of art, ritual, language, etc. (the Middle Stone Age).

ecological anthropology The branch of the discipline that is concerned with relations between environment, technology and society.

egocentric category A category of kin defined through a given individual. Cf. **sociocentric category**.

elementary system Lévi-Strauss's term for a kinship structure which has positive marriage rules. For example, one is obliged to marry into the category that includes the cross-cousin. The opposite is a **complex system**. See also **Crow–Omaha system**.

encephalization Increasing brain size, relative to body mass.

Eoanthropus dawsoni The former scientific name of 'Piltdown Man'.

Eolithic A former name for the presumed 'Dawn Stone Age'. It has been replaced by the term **Palaeolithic**.

ethnicity The characterization of groups by presumed, and/or self-defined, biological or cultural similarity.

ethnology Loosely a synonym for social and cultural anthropology, but often more specifically referring to points of view that emphasize culture history, and especially diffusionism.

evolutionary psychology The field that studies the relationship between natural selection and brain size, cognition and behaviour.

expensive tissue hypothesis The idea that encephalization should be accompanied by the reduction of other expensive tissue, such as gut, which implies a change in diet to richer foods.

fetishism The worship of fetishes.

foraging mode of thought My term for an ideology emphasizing *not* the acquisition of property, but foraging and sharing. This ideology is common among hunter-gatherers. The opposite is the **accumulation mode of thought**.

formalism Within economic anthropology, the view that the 'laws of economics' hold true for all societies. Cf. **substantivism**.

FOXP2 A gene that controls brain and lung development. In humans it also controls speech, and the ability of the brain to formulate complex rules of grammar. A FOXP2 mutation during the evolution of *Homo* is believed to be partly responsible for the development of humankind's linguistic abilities.

functionalism The synchronic theoretical perspective that emphasizes the purpose of institutions or customs, or how things work in relation to each other. Often the term is employed as a synonym for **structural-functionalism**.

genetics The science of heredity.

grandmothering hypothesis The idea that menopause is evolutionarily adaptive and enabled grandmothers to raise children.

great apes Orang-utans, gorillas, chimpanzees and bonobos.

Great Chain of Being In medieval and later thought, a hierarchical, and static, chain from God to lesser beings. It differs from evolutionary understandings, because it presupposes that beings do not evolve into other kinds of being.

hominids (*Hominidae*) In present usage, the Linnaean family that includes great apes and humans. In earlier usage, it was employed for *Homo* and immediate ancestors.

hominins (*Hominini*) The Linnaean tribe that includes humans and human ancestors. In present usage, it includes australopithecines, but used to be defined more narrowly.

Homo erectus The species living in east Africa and later Asia and Europe from about 1,800,000 to 1,300,000 or 1,000,000 BP. *H. erectus* tamed fire, developed techniques for working stone tools and travelled outside Africa to the Far East and to Europe. Sometimes the term is used specifically for the species that migrated to Asia and Africa, with the term *H. ergaster* being employed for the earlier species that evolved in Africa.

Homo ergaster African *H. erectus* or the species which diverged and spread throughout the Old World (see *Homo erectus*).

Homo floresiensis The species of *Homo* recently discovered on Flores, in Indonesia, and dated to about 18,000 BP. This species is sometimes called 'the hobbit', and resembles *H. erectus* but is much smaller.

Homo habilis The earliest member of the genus *Homo*, living 2,300,000 to 1,400,000 BP. The species that developed the use of Oldowan stone tools around 1,700,000 BP.

Homo heidelbergensis Species of *Homo* that lived in Africa and Europe from 600,000 to 250,000 BP and is possibly ancestral to both Neandertals and modern humans.

Homo helmei African *H. heidelbergensis* when classified as a separate species. More modern than European *H. heidelbergensis*.

Homo neanderthalensis, H. sapiens neanderthalensis The Neanderthals. The type find was from the Neander Valley (*Thal*, or in modern spelling *Tal*), in 1857.

Homo rudolfensis Similar to *H. habilis*, and dated at 1,900,000 BP (Skull 1470).

Homo sapiens The only remaining species of *Homo*. Often includes near relatives, namely 'Archaic' *H. sapiens* (*H. sapiens neanderthalensis* and *H. sapiens heidelbergensis*).

Homo sapiens sapiens Fully modern, linguistic *Homo sapiens* (excluding near relatives such as Neanderthals).

human Referring to the genus *Homo*, or more specifically *H. sapiens*.

human origins Broadly, the study of prehistoric humanity and its precursors.

hunter-gatherers Peoples who subsist by hunting, gathering and/or fishing, and do not practise food production (pastoralism or agriculture). More loosely, peoples who have an insignificant amount of food production and subsist mainly by hunting, gathering and/or fishing.

immediate return James Woodburn's term for the economic and social system of small-scale hunter-gatherers, where time is *not* invested in planning ahead in subsistence activity. The opposite of **delayed return**.

incest In social anthropology, sex with a member of a prohibited category of relative (not necessarily with close kin).

indigenous Relating to original occupation. The validity of the term cross-culturally is in dispute, and some anthropologists prefer either not to employ the term or to use instead **autochthonous**.

infanticide The (culturally sanctioned) killing of children, for example to enable older children or male children to thrive.

interpretivism Anti-structuralist, anti-scientist perspective that uses the analogy that cultures are like languages in that they can be 'translated', one to another.

'Java Man' Informal name of the first specimen of *H. erectus*, discovered by Eugene Dubois on Java in 1893. Also known as *Pithecanthropus*.

joking relationship A kin relationship with permitted licence and informality. The opposite is an **avoidance relationship**.

Kanzi A highly intelligent male bonobo born in 1980. Famous for being taught to communicate using lexigrams, he has also picked up some American sign language.

kinship The study of relatedness, including descent, alliance and terminology structures.

Lamarckian The notion that acquired characteristics may be inherited. Cf. **Darwinian**.

Lascaux Rock art site in the Dordogne, France, famous for its Upper Palaeolithic art dated to about 17,000 BP.

Later Stone Age (LSA) The term employed in southern Africa for the most recent stone tool traditions and associated social organization. It comprises modern hunter-gatherers and herders of southern Africa whose lifestyles pre-date the arrival of Iron Age Bantu-speaking populations.

lineage A line of descent (patrilinal or matrilineal). Lineages are grouped into **clans**.

linguistics The scientific study of language in the abstract, or of languages.

'lion man' A statuette with the head of a lion and the body of a man.

lithic In relation to stone tools. Often used as a suffix (as in **Neolithic**).

matriliny Descent through females.

Mesolithic The European and Asian stone tool tradition between the Palaeolithic and the Neolithic. The term means 'middle stone age', but is not to be confused with the southern African Middle Stone Age, which is roughly the equivalent of the European Upper Palaeolithic.

Middle Stone Age (MSA) The southern African stone tool tradition, around 300,000 to 50,000 BP. Associated with early modern and modern humans, and the symbolic revolution.

Modes 1, 2, 3, 4, 5 A classification system for stone tools, designed in the 1960s by Grahame Clark in order to unify African and European classifications.

moiety Literally 'half' (French *moitié*): entailing a division of society into two halves, and a rule that one marries into the half to which he or she does not belong. The division is through either patrilineal or matrilineal descent. Common in Australia and South America.

molecular biology The study of biology at the molecular level.

monogenesis One origin of humankind. Cf. **polygenesis**.

moral philosophy The eighteenth-century forerunner of the modern social sciences.

Mousterian Neanderthal stone tool tradition dating from 100,000 to 35,000 BP, characterized by reshaped flakes. Named after the rock shelter Le Moustier in the Dordogne, This tool tradition falls within the Middle Palaeolithic.

multilinear evolutionism Julian Steward's term for his own theory, based on the idea that different cultures have different environments and histories, and therefore different lines of evolution.

mutual aid The notion that co-operation is the root of evolution. From the Russian *vzaimopomoshch'*.

natural history Essentially, the eighteenth-century forerunner of modern biology. Physics was called 'natural philosophy'.

natural selection The mechanism of Darwinian evolution, through which heritable traits are passed from generation to generation. This can involve either sexual selection (i.e. competition for mates) or ecological selection.

Neanderthal, Neandertal The English name for *Homo neanderthalensis* or *H. sapiens neanderthalensis*.

neocortex The main part of the brain, excluding the brain stem and limbic system.

Neolithic Stone tool industry characterized by polished tools and by ceramics. The term is also employed very commonly for the types of social organization and subsistence lifestyles which characterize this industry. These include permanent settlement, village life and animal husbandry and agriculture. The term means 'new stone age'. See also **Mesolithic**.

neolocality Postmarital residence in a new home. Husband and wife live with neither his parents, nor hers.

ochre Red, orange or yellow mineral pigment believed to be used for decoration or painting.

oestrus The female sexual and reproductive cycle of non-human mammals, including primates.

Oldowan The oldest known stone tool tradition, dated to 2,500,000 BP and associated with *Homo habilis*.

ontogeny Individual development from conception to death. Cf. **phylogeny**.

ontology A theory of being or existence.

optimal foraging theory The perspective which emphasizes economic rationality in the pursuit of subsistence. Found in both biology and social anthropology.

Orang Outang In the eighteenth century, a term roughly equivalent to the modern generic concept of the 'ape', but often believed to be human or nearly human. Not to be confused with the orang-utan of Southeast Asia (*Pongo pygmaeus*).

orang-utan Southeast Asian species *Pongo pygmaeus*.

'original affluent society' Marshall Sahlins's term for hunter-gatherer social life, in which 'affluence' is measured by free time rather than by accumulated wealth. Hunter-gatherers spend *less* time in subsistence-related activities than non-hunter-gatherers.

palaeo-anthropologist A biological anthropologist who specializes in fossil remains.

Palaeolithic The term means 'old stone age'. Divided into Early (including Oldowan and Acheulean, from 3,600,000 or 3,500,000 to 100,000 BP), Middle (including Mousterian, from 300,000 to 30,000 BP) and Late (including several traditions from about 45,000 BP to 10,000 BP).

palaeontologist A specialist in prehistoric life forms, including the study of human origins through fossil remains.

parallel cousin Father's brother's child or mother's sister's child. Cf. **cross-cousin**.

parallel relative A collateral relative related through a same-sex sibling link.

parental investment The idea, within sociobiology, that parents can invest in individual offspring in such a way as to maximize survival of the offspring and ultimately their own reproductive success.

parent–offspring conflict The idea, within sociobiology, that grown-up offspring compete with their parent for reproductive success.

patriliny Descent through males.

'Peking Man' *Homo erectus* fossils discovered at Zhoukoudian, near Beijing, in 1923 and subsequently. Originally labelled *Sinanthropus pekinensis*.

phonetics The study of the objective auditory or acoustic nature of sounds, independent of their place in a sound system (phonemics or phonology).

phratry A very large kin group, composed of several clans and formed through either patrilineal or matrilineal descent.

phylogeny Individual or group evolutionary sequence, generally represented by a tree diagram.

physical anthropology Earlier, and narrower, term for what is now usually called biological anthropology.

'Piltdown Man' A supposed fossil 'discovered' in Kent, southeastern England, in 1912 and exposed as a fake in 1953. Named *Eoanthropus dawsoni*.

Pirahã An Amerindian language of South America, of interest in linguistics because it is supposed to be the only language which lacks the property of recursion.

Pithecanthropus The genus name once used for *Homo erectus*, especially for the type find 'Java Man'. It means 'ape-man'.

Pithecanthropus alalus Ernst Haekel's name for a hypothetical 'missing link'. It is not associated with any fossil.

Pithecanthropus erectus An early name for *Homo erectus*, especially 'Java Man'.

Pleistocene Geological epoch from about 2,600,000 to 12,000 BP (followed by the Holocene).

Pliocene Geological epoch before the Pleistocene. From about 5,400,000 to 2,600,000 BP.

polyandry Where a woman is married to more than one man. Cf. **polygyny**.

polygenesis More than one origin for humankind. Cf. **monogenesis**.

polygyny Where a man is married to more than one woman. Cf. **polyandry**.

potlatch A ceremony involving feasting and the giving away (or sometimes destruction) of one's own property in order to redistribute and to gain prestige. Characteristic of peoples of the Northwest Coast of North America.

prehistory The period before written records.

primate A member of the biological order *primates*, including lemurs, monkeys and apes.

primatologist One who studies primates.

proto-language In my theory of language (derived from Derek Bickerton's), words and phrases only, without simple sentences or rules for word order. Cf. **rudimentary language**.

reciprocal altruism The idea, within sociobiology, that animals help each other and thereby gain advantage for the group or for a smaller unit within the group.

reciprocity Exchange and other relations between individuals and groups. In anthropology, the term is often used in a broad sense to include relationships of giving (generalized reciprocity) and theft (negative reciprocity), as well as balanced reciprocal actions.

recursion In linguistics, the property of embedding one unit into another of the same kind, such as sentences within sentences.

Rift Valley Valley in east Africa, especially Tanzania, Kenya and Ethiopia, noted for the large number of fossil hominins. Also called the Great Rift Valley. Sometimes defined as extending from Mozambique to Lebanon.

rudimentary language In my theory of language (derived from Derek Bickerton's), language possessing only simple syntax. Cf. **proto-language**.

Sahelanthropus The genus of *Sahelanthropus tchadensis*, significant because it predates the divergence between chimpanzees and humans and could represent a common ancestor.

section In Australian Aboriginal kinship, one of four or eight units into which things, including people, are classified. Every person belongs to one of these, and marries a member of one other specific section. In a four-section system, for example, a man belongs to the same section as his father's father and marries into the same section as his father's father did. This happens to be also the section of his cross-cousin.

sectoral canine complex (SCC) A dental characteristic of herbivorous hominids, lost in *Ardipithecus* (therefore indicating an omnivorous diet).

shamanism Religion based on the activities of shamans, ritual specialists with the ability to communicate with the spirit world. Trance performance, healing practice, metamorphosis into animal form and out-of-body travel are common.

signifying Relating to the relationship between a word (or morpheme) and meaning, or by extension, between any object and its meaning.

signifying revolution My term for the revolutionary linguist change to the use of words to signify meaning.

social and cultural anthropology A term which includes both the 'social' and the 'cultural' traditions of anthropology. Growing in popularity in the United Kingdom.

social anthropology The field which is concerned with the study of society in the abstract, and in the comparative understanding of society and societies. It is the preferred term in the United Kingdom and some other countries, whereas 'cultural anthropology' is more common in the United States. In the United States, the term 'social anthropology' sometimes connotes a narrower, British theoretical perspective within cultural anthropology.

social contract The seventeenth- and eighteenth-century idea that the essence of society is a 'contract' among its members to live peaceably together.

social theory Theoretical branch of the social sciences generally, especially sociology. It is sometimes distinguished from empirical studies.

sociality The capacity for being social or sociable. Employed in seventeenth- and eighteenth-century philosophy and reintroduced into biological and anthropological sciences in the twentieth century.

society The largest group of people or animals that share a common cultural tradition, or share a recognition that they are indeed the same group.

sociobiology The study of social relations in a biological framework. More precisely, the discipline or the subdiscipline or theoretical position that treats human culture and society as adjuncts of humankind's animal nature.

sociocentric category A category of kin defined in the same way for all members of society (e.g. a **moiety** or a **section**). Cf. **egocentric category**.

structural-functionalism The theoretical perspective associated with A. R. Radcliffe-Brown and his followers. It emphasizes the synchronic study of society, and the systematic nature of society and social institutions.

structuralism The perspective that emphasizes relations over substance. To a structuralist, things derive meaning only through such relations.

subsection In Australian Aboriginal kinship, a section divided into two, with alternate forms of marriage permissible within it. Cf. **section**.

substantivism Within economic anthropology, the view that the economics is culturally embedded, and therefore that there are no economic laws that hold true for all societies. Cf. **formalism**.

superorganic The cultural forces that exist beyond the control of the individual. The idea, named by A. L. Kroeber, was popular in early twentieth-century American anthropology and still commonly discussed in American anthropology classes.

symbolic Relating to the use of symbols.

symbolic revolution My preferred term for the 'human revolution' of early *Homo sapiens sapiens*, related to full language and to elementary structures of kinship.

synchronic Literally 'in the same time'. The opposite is **diachronic**.

syntactic Relating to sentences, or, more broadly, to grammar.

syntactic revolution My term for the revolutionary linguist change to the use of sentences, and by extension the related change in kinship structure to one which recognized exchange and other relations between groups.

taxonomy Biological classification.

terrestriality Moving from the trees to the ground.

tetradic A four-part system similar to an Australian section system. Hypothesized by N. J. Allen as the primal human kinship structure.

theory of mind The ability to understand another person's point of view, in other words to anticipate the thinking of another person or being. This facility is limited in small children, primates and presumably too in early homins.

therianthrope A creature that is part human and part animal. Common in rock art, where the figure is presumed to represent a shaman.

totemism The phenomenon or religion which entails the representation of groups (or individuals) by animals or plants. The word is derived from the Ojibwa language.

'tragedy of the commons' A dilemma highlighted in a 1968 article of that name by Garett Hardin. It attempts to show that what is best for the individual differs from what is best for the group.

transhumant Referring to seasonal movement, e.g. winter coastal aggregation and summer upland dispersal.

Twin Rivers A site in Zambia with the earliest evidence of pigment use. Dated to 300,000 years and attributed to *Homo heidelbergensis*.

unilineal descent Descent through one line. It includes patrilineal descent and matrilineal descent systems.

unilinear evolutionism Julian Steward's term for (nineteenth-century) theories of social evolution that argue that all humankind has passed through the same line of evolution, albeit some groups faster than others.

universal evolutionism Julian Steward's term for (early twentieth-century) theories of social evolution that argue that all humankind has passed through the same broad stages of evolution: savagery, barbarism and civilization.

universal kinship My term for systems in which everyone in a society is classified by a relationship term and treated appropriately. In such systems there is no concept of someone being 'non-kin'.

uxorilocality Postmarital residence in the wife's home. Also called matrilocality. (Related to female philopatry in primatology, the tendency of groups to form around related females.)

virilocality Postmarital residence in the husband's home. Also called patrilocality. (Related to male philopatry in primatology, the tendency of groups to form around related males.)

worldview A broad perspective on the world by people within their culture. Common in the American tradition. From the German *Weltanschauung*.

References

Aberle, David F. 1961. 'Matrilineal descent in cross-cultural perspective', in Schneider and Gough, pp. 655–727

Abu-Lughod, Lila. 1991. 'Writing against culture', in Richard G. Fox (ed.), *Recapturing anthropology: working in the present*. Santa Fe, NM: School of American Research Press, pp. 137–62

Aiello, Leslie C., and R. I. M. Dunbar. 1993. 'Neocortex size, group size, and the evolution of language', *Current Anthropology* 34: 184–93

Aiello, Leslie C., and Peter Wheeler. 1995. 'The expensive tissue hypothesis: the brain and the digestive system in human and primate evolution', *Current Anthropology* 36: 199–221

Allen, N. J. 1982. 'A dance of relatives', *Journal of the Anthropological Society of Oxford* 13: 139–46

1989a. 'Assimilation of alternate generations', *Journal of the Anthropology Society of Oxford* 20 (1): 45–55

1989b. 'The evolution of kinship terminologies', *Lingua* 77: 173–85

2004. 'Tetradic theory: an approach to kinship', in Robert Parkin and Linda Stone (eds.), *Kinship and family: an anthropological reader*. Oxford: Blackwell Publishing, pp. 221–35

2008. 'Tetradic theory and the origin of human kinship systems', in Allen *et al.*, pp. 96–112

Allen, Nicholas J., Hilary Callan, Robin Dunbar and Wendy James (eds.). 2008. *Early human kinship: from sex to social reproduction*. Oxford: Blackwell Publishing

Ambrose, Stanley H. 1998. 'Late Pleistocene human population bottlenecks, volcanic winter, and differentiation of modern humans', *Journal of Human Evolution* 34: 623–51

2003. 'Did the super-eruption of Toba cause a human population bottleneck? Reply to Gathorne-Hardy and Harcourt-Smith', *Journal of Human Evolution* 45: 231–7

2010. 'Coevolution of composite-tool technology, constructive memory, and language: implications for the evolution of modern human behavior', *Current Anthropology* 51, Supplement 1: S135–47

Ardrey, Robert. 1963. *African genesis: a personal investigation into the animal origins and nature of man*. London: Readers Union

Artemova, Olga Yu. 2009. 'Tribe of Esau: hunters, gatherers and fishers: a cross-cultural study of the alternative social systems' (English summary), in *Koleno Isava: Ohotniki, sobirateli, rybolovy opyt ijeuchenija al'ternativnyh social'nyh sistem*. Moscow: Smysl, pp. 533–58

Bachofen, J. J. 1967. *Myth, religion, and mother right: selected writings of J. J. Bachofen* (translated by Ralph Manheim). Princeton University Press (Bollingen Series LXXXIV)

Bancel, Pierre J., and Alain Matthey de l'Etang. 2002. 'Tracing of the ancestral kinship system: the global etymon KAKA. Part I: A linguistic study', *Mother Tongue* 7: 209–44

Barnard, Alan. 1978. 'Universal systems of kin categorization', *African Studies* 37: 69–81

1979. 'Kalahari Bushman settlement patterns', in Burnham and Ellen, pp. 131–44

1986. 'Rethinking Bushman settlement patterns and territoriality', *Sprache und Geschichte in Afrika* 7 (1): 41–60

1991. 'Social and spatial boundary maintenance among southern African hunter-gatherers', in Michael J. Casmir and Aparna Rao (eds.), *Mobility and territoriality: social and spatial boundaries among foragers, fishers, pastoralists and peripatetics*. New York: Berg Publishers, pp. 137–51

1992a. *Hunters and herders of southern Africa: a comparative ethnography of the Khoisan peoples*. Cambridge University Press

1992b. 'Through Radcliffe-Brown's spectacles: reflections on the history of anthropology', *History of the Human Sciences* 5 (4): 1–20

1995a. '*Orang Outang* and the definition of *Man*: the legacy of Lord Monboddo', in Han F. Vermeulen and Arturo Alvarez Róldan (eds.), *Fieldwork and footnotes: studies in the history of European anthropology*. London: Routledge, pp. 95–112

1995b. 'Monboddo's Orang Outang and the definition of Man', in Raymond Corbey and Bert Theunissen (eds.), *Ape, man, apeman: changing views since 1600*. Leiden: Department of Prehistory, Leiden University, pp. 71–85

1998. 'An anthropologist among the primatologists', *Budongo Forest Project* 1 (3): 1–3.

1999. 'Modern hunter-gatherers and early symbolic culture', in Dunbar, Knight and Power, pp. 50–68

2000. *History and theory in anthropology*. Cambridge University Press

2002. 'The foraging mode of thought', *Senri Ethnological Studies* 60: 5–24

2004. 'Hunting-and-gathering society: an eighteenth-century Scottish invention', in Alan Barnard (ed.), *Hunter-gatherers in history, archaeology and anthropology*. Oxford: Berg Publishers, pp. 31–43

2007a. *Anthropology and the Bushman*. Oxford: Berg Publishers

2007b. 'From Mesolithic to Neolithic modes of thought', in Alasdair Whittle and Vicki Cummings (eds.), *Going over: the Mesolithic–Neolithic transition in north-west Europe* (Proceedings of the British Academy 144). Oxford University Press for the British Academy, pp. 5–19

2008. 'The co-evolution of language and kinship', in Allen *et al.*, pp. 232–43

2009. 'Social origins: sharing, exchange, kinship', in Botha and Knight 2009b, pp. 219–35.

2010a. 'Culture: the indigenous account', in Deborah James, Evie Place and Christina Toren (eds.), *Culture wars: context, models, and anthropologists' accounts*. Oxford: Berghahn Books, pp. 73–85

2010b. 'When individuals do not stop at the skin', in Dunbar, Gamble and Gowlett, pp. 249–67

2010c. 'Mythology and the evolution of language', in Andrew D. M. Smith, Marieke Schouwstra, Bart de Boer and Kenny Smith (eds.), *The evolution of language: proceedings of the 8th International Conference (EVOLANG8)*, Hackensack, NJ: World Scientific, pp. 11–18

Barnard, Alan, and Anthony Good. 1984. *Research practices in the study of kinship.* London: Academic Press

Barnett, H. G. 1938. 'The nature of the potlatch', *American Anthropologist* 40: 349–58

Bateson, Gregory. 1958 [1936]. *Naven: a survey of the problems suggested by a composite picture of the culture of a New Guinea tribe drawn from three points of view* (second edition). Stanford University Press

1987 [1972]. *Steps to an ecology of mind: collected essays in anthropology, psychiatry, evolution, and epistemology.* Northvale, NJ: Jason Aronson

Battiss, Walter W. 1948. *The artists of the rocks.* Pretoria: Red Fawn Press

Bickerton, Derek. 1998. 'Catastrophic evolution: the case for a single step from protolanguage to full human language', in James R. Hurford, Michael Studdert-Kennedy and Chris Knight (eds.), *Approaches to the evolution of language: social and cognitive bases.* Cambridge University Press, pp. 341–58

Biesele, Megan. 1993. *Women like meat: the folklore and foraging ideology of the Kalahari Ju/'hoan.* Johannesburg: Witwatersrand University Press

Binford, Lewis R. 1981. *Bones: ancient men and modern myths.* New York: Academic Press

Bird-David, Nurit. 1990. 'The giving environment: another perspective on the economic system of gatherer-hunters', *Current Anthropology* 31: 189–96

1992. 'Beyond "The original affluent society": a culturalist reformulation. *Current Anthropology* 33: 25–47

Bleek, W. H. I., and L. C. Lloyd. 1911. *Specimens of Bushman folklore.* London: George Allen & Company

Bloch, Maurice. 1983. *Marxism and anthropology: the history of a relationship.* Oxford University Press

Blute, Marion. 2010. *Darwinian sociocultural evolution: solutions to dilemmas in cultural and social theory.* Cambridge University Press

Boas, Franz. 1911. 'Introduction', in *Handbook of American Indian languages.* Washington, DC: Government Printing Office (Bulletin of American Ethnology, Bulletin 40, Part I), pp. 1–83

Boehm, Christopher. 1999. *Hierarchy in the forest: the evolution of egalitarian behavior.* Cambridge, MA: Harvard University Press

2004. 'Large game hunting and the evolution of human sociality', in Robert W. Sussman and Audrey R. Chapman (eds.), *The origin and nature of sociality.* New York: Aldine de Gruyter, pp. 270–87

Boesch, Christophe, and Hedwige Boesch. 1990. 'Tool use and tool making in wild chimpanzees', *Folia Primatologica* 54: 86–99

Boesch, Christophe, and Michael Tomasello. 1998. 'Chimpanzee and human cultures', *Current Anthropology* 39: 591–614

Botha, Rudolf. 2009. 'Theoretical underpinnings of inferences about language evolution: the syntax used at Blombos Cave', in Botha and Knight 2009b, pp. 93–111

Botha, Rudolf, and Chris Knight (eds.). 2009a. *The prehistory of language.*
Oxford University Press
2009b. *The cradle of language.* Oxford University Press
Bowler, Peter, J. 1989. *The invention of progress: the Victorians and the past.*
Oxford: Basil Blackwell
Boyd, Robert and Peter J. Richerson. 2005. *The origin and evolution of cultures.*
Oxford University Press
Boyd, Robert, and Joan Silk. 1997. *How humans evolved.* New York: Norton
Brown, Kyle S., Curtis W. Marean, Andy I. R. Herries, Zenobia Jacobs,
Chantal Tribolo, David Braun, David L. Roberts, Michael C. Meyer and
Jocelyn Bernatchez. 2009. 'Fire as an engineering tool of early modern
humans', *Science* 325 (5942): 859–62
Brown, P., T. Sutikna, M. J. Morwood, R. P. Soejono, E. Jatmiko, Wayhu
Saptomo and Rokus Awe Due. 2004. 'A new small-bodied hominin from
the Late Pleistocene of Flores, Indonesia', *Nature* 431 (7012): 1055–61
Burnham, Phillip, and Roy F. Ellen (eds.). 1979. *Social and ecological systems*
(ASA Monographs 18). London: Academic Press
Burroughs, Edgar Rice. 1963a. *Tarzan of the Apes.* New York: Ballantine
Books
1963b. *Jungle tales of Tarzan.* New York: Ballantine Books
Byrne, Richard W. 2001. 'Social and technical forms of primate intelligence',
in Franz B. M. de Waal (ed.), *Tree of origin: what primate behavior can tell us
about human social evolution.* Cambridge, MA: Harvard University Press,
pp. 145–72
2007. 'Culture in great apes: using intricate complexity in feeding skills to
trace the evolutionary origin of human technical prowess', *Philosophical
Transactions of the Royal Society B* 362 (1480): 577–85
Calvin, William H. 2004. *A brief history of the mind: from apes to intellect and
beyond.* Oxford University Press
Calvin, William H., and Derek Bickerton. 2000. *Lingua ex machina: recon-
ciling Darwin and Chomsky with the human brain.* Cambridge, MA: MIT
Press
Campbell, Bernard G. 1996. 'An outline of human phylogeny', in Andrew
Lock and Charles R. Peters (eds.), *Handbook of human symbolic evolution.*
Oxford University Press, pp. 31–52
Cann, Rebecca L., Mark Stoneking and Allan C. Wilson. 1987. 'Mitochondrial
DNA and human evolution', *Nature* 329 (6099): 31–6
Carsten, Janet. 2004. *After kinship.* Cambridge University Press
Cashdan, Elizabeth A. 1983. Territoriality among human foragers: ecological
models and an application to four Bushman groups', *Current Anthropology*
24: 47–66
Chagnon, Napoleon. 1968. *Yąnomamö: the fierce people.* New York: Holt,
Rinehart and Winston
Chapais, Bernard. 2008. *Primeval kinship: how pair-bonding gave birth to human
society.* Cambridge, MA: Harvard University Press
Clark, J. G. D. 1954. *Excavations at Star Carr: an early Mesolithic site at Seamer,
near Scarborough, Yorkshire.* Cambridge University Press
Childe, V. Gordon. 1941 [1936]. *Man makes himself.* London: Watts & Co.

1969. *World prehistory: a new outline* (second edition). Cambridge University Press

Clastres, Pierre. 1977 [1974]. *Society against the state: essays in political anthropology* (translated by Robert Hurley, with Abe Stein). Oxford: Basil Blackwell

Coolidge, Frederick L., and Thomas Wynn. 2009. *The rise of Homo sapiens: the evolution of modern thinking.* Oxford: Wiley-Blackwell

Corballis, M. C. 2003. 'From hand to mouth: the gestural origins of language', in Morten M. Christiansen and Simon Kirby (eds.), *Language evolution.* Oxford University Press, pp. 201–18

2010. 'The evolution of language', in Michael B. Miller and Alan Kingstone (eds.), *The year in cognitive neuroscience 2009* (Annals of the New York Academy of Sciences 1156). New York: Wiley-Blackwell, pp. 19–43

Cox, Murray P., David A. Morales, August E. Woerner, Jesse Sozanski, Jeffrey D. Wall and Michael F. Hammer. 2009. 'Autosomal resequence data reveal Late Stone Age signals of population expansion in sub-Saharan African foraging and farming populations', *PLoS ONE* 4 (7): e6366 (doi: 10.1371/journal.pone.0006366)

Dalton, George (ed.). 1967. *Tribal and peasant economies: readings in economic anthropology.* New York: Natural History Press

Dart, Raymond A. 1925. '*Australopithecus africanus*: the man-Ape of South Africa', *Nature* 115 (2884): 195–9

Darwin, Charles. 1859. *On the origin of species by means of natural selection, or the preservation of favoured races in the struggle for life.* London: John Murray

1871. *The descent of man and selection in relation to sex.* London: John Murray

Dawkins, Richard. 1976. *The selfish gene.* Oxford University Press

d'Errico, Francesco, Christopher Henshilwood, Marian Vanhaeren and Karen van Niekerk. 2005. '*Nassarius kraussianus* shell beads from Blombos Cave: evidence for symbolic behaviour in the Middle Stone Age', *Journal of Human Evolution* 48: 3–24

d'Errico, Francesco, Christopher Henshilwood, Graeme Lawson, Marian Vanhaeren, Anne-Marie Tillier, Marie Soressi, Frédérique Bresson, Bruno Maureille, April Nowell, Joseba Lakarra, Lucinda Backwell and Michèle Julien. 2003. 'The search for the origin of symbolism, music and language: a multidisciplinary endeavour', *Journal of World Prehistory* 17: 1–70

de Waal, F. B. M. 1989. Food sharing and reciprocal obligations among chimpanzees. *Journal of Human Evolution* 18: 433–59

Donald, Merlin. 1991. *Origins of the modern mind: three stages in the evolution of culture and cognition.* Cambridge, MA: Harvard University Press

Dowson, Thomas A. 2007. 'Debating shamanism in southern African rock art: time to move on …', *South African Archaeological Bulletin* 62 (185): 49–61

Dufour, V., M. Pele, M. Neumann, B. Thierry and J. Call. 2009. 'Calculated reciprocity after all: computation behind token transfers in orang-utans', *Biology Letters* 2009 (5): 172–5

Dunbar, R. I. M. 1992. 'Time: a hidden constraint on the behavioural ecology of baboons', *Behavioural Ecology and Sociobiology* 31: 35–49

1993. 'The co-evolution of neocortical size, group size and language in humans', *Behavioral and Brain Sciences* 16: 681–735

1998. 'The social brain hypothesis', *Evolutionary Anthropology* 6 (5): 178–90

2001. 'Brains on two legs: group size and the evolution of intelligence', in F. B. M. de Waal (ed.), *Tree of origin: what primate behavior can tell us about human social evolution.* Cambridge, MA: Harvard University Press, pp. 173–92

2003. 'The social brain: mind, language and society in evolutionary perspective', *Annual Review of Anthropology* 32: 163–81

2004. *The human story: a new history of mankind's evolution.* London: Faber and Faber

2009. 'Why only humans have language', in Botha and Knight 2009a, pp. 12–35

Dunbar, Robin, Clive Gamble and John Gowlett (eds.). 2010. *Social brain, distributed mind* (Proceedings of the British Academy 158). Oxford University Press for the British Academy

Dunbar, Robin, Chris Knight and Camilla Power (eds.). 1999. *The evolution of culture: an interdisciplinary view.* Edinburgh University Press.

Durkheim, Emile 1915 [1912]. *The elementary forms of the religious life.* London: George Allen & Unwin

Durkheim, Emile and Marcel Mauss. 1963 [1903]. *Primitive classification* (translated and edited by Rodney Needham). London: Cohen & West

Enard, Wolfgang, Molly Przeworski, Simon E. Fisher, Cecilia S. L. Lai, Victor Wiebe, Takashi Kitano, Anthony P. Monaco and Svante Pääbo. 2002. 'Molecular evolution of FOXP2, a gene involved in speech and language', *Nature* 418 (6900): 869–72

Evans-Pritchard, E. E., Raymond Firth, E. R. Leach, J. G. Peristiany, John Layard, Max Gluckman, Meyer Fortes and Godfrey Lienhardt. 1963. *The institutions of primitive society: a series of broadcast talks.* Oxford: Basil Blackwell

Fison, Lorimer, and A. W. Howitt. 1880. *Kamilaroi and Kurnai: group marriage and relationship, and marriage by elopement, drawn chiefly from the usage of the Australian Aborigines.* Melbourne: George Robertson

Foley, Robert. 1992. 'Studying human evolution by analogy', in Steve Jones, Robert Martin and David Pilbeam (eds.), *The Cambridge encyclopedia of human evolution.* Cambridge University Press, pp. 335–40

2001. 'In the shadow of the modern synthesis? Alternative perspectives on the last fifty years of paleoanthropology', *Evolutionary Anthropology* 10: 5–14

Foley, Robert, and Clive Gamble. 2009. 'The ecology of social transitions in human evolution', *Philosophical Transactions of the Royal Society B* 364 (1533): 3267–79

Foley, Robert, and Marta Mirazón Lahr. 2003. 'On stony ground: lithic technology, human evolution, and the emergence of culture', *Evolutionary Anthropology* 12: 109–22

Frazer, Sir James George. 1922. *The Golden Bough: a study in magic and religion (abridged edition).* London: Macmillan and Co.

Freud, Sigmund. 1960 [1913]. *Totem and taboo* (translated by James Strachey). London: Routledge & Kegan Paul

Fuentes, Agustín. 2009. *The evolution of human behavior.* New York: Oxford University Press

Fury, David. 1994. *Kings of the jungle: an illustrated reference to 'Tarzan' on screen and television.* Jefferson, NC: McFarland & Co.

Gamble, Clive. 1993. *Timewalkers: the prehistory of global colonization.* Cambridge, MA: Harvard University Press

2007. *Origins and revolutions: human identity in earliest prehistory.* Cambridge University Press

2008. 'Kinship and material culture: archaeological implications of the human global diaspora', in Allen *et al.*, pp. 27–40

Godelier, Maurice. 1977 [1973]. *Perspectives in Marxist anthropology.* Cambridge University Press

2004. *Métamorphoses de la parenté.* Paris: Fayard

Godelier, Maurice, and Marilyn Strathern (eds.). 1991. *Big men and great men: personifications of power in Melanesia.* Cambridge University Press

Gomes, Cristina M., and Christoph Boesch. 2009. 'Wild chimpanees exchange meat for sex on a long-term basis', *PLoS ONE* 4(4): e5116 (doi:10.1371/journal.pone.0005116)

Goodman, Maurice. 1996. 'Epilogue: a personal account of the origins of a new paradigm', *Molecular phylogenetics and evolution* 5 (1): 269–85

Goodwin, A. J. H., and C. van Riet Lowe. 1929. 'The Stone Age cultures of South Africa', *Annals of the South African Museum* 27 (7): 1–289

Goody, Jack (ed.). 1958. *The developmental cycle in domestic groups.* Cambridge University Press

1959. 'The mother's brother and the sister's son in West Arica', *Journal of the Royal Anthropological Institute* 89: 59–88

Goren-Inbar, Naama, Nira Alperson, Mordechai E. Kislev, Orit Simchoni, Yoel Melamed, Adi Ben-Nun and Ella Werker. 2004. 'Evidence of hominin control of fire at Gesher Benot Ya`aqov, Israel', *Science* 304 (5671): 725–7

Gowlett, John A. J., and Robin Dunbar. 2008. 'A brief overview of human evolution', in Allen *et al.*, pp. 21–4

Gräslund, Bo. 2005. *Early humans and their world.* London: Routledge

Guenther, Mathias. 2006. 'N//àe ("talking"): the oral and rhetorical base of San culture', *Journal of Folklore Research* 43: 241–61

Haddon, Alfred C. (with A. Hingston Quiggin). 1910. *History of anthropology.* London: Watts & Co.

Hallowell, A. Irving. 1955. *Culture and experience.* Philadelphia: University of Pennsylvania Press

1960. 'Ojibwa ontology, behavior and world view', in Stanley Diamond (ed.), *Culture in history: essays in honor of Paul Radin.* New York: Columbia University Press, pp. 19–52

Hamilton, W. D. 1964. 'The genetical evolution of social behaviour, Parts I and II', *Journal of Theoretical Biology* 7: 1–52

1972. 'Altruism and related phenomena, mainly in social insects', *Annual Review of Ecology and Systematics* 3: 193–232

Hardin, Garrett. 1968. 'The tragedy of the commons', *Science* 162 (3859): 1243–8

Hare, Brian, and Suzy Kwetuenda. 2010. 'Bonobos voluntarily share their own food with others', *Current Biology* 20 (5): R230–1

Hawkes, Kirsten, Kim Hill and James O'Connell, 1982. 'Why hunters gather: optimal foraging and the Ache of eastern Paraguay', *American Ethnologist* 9: 379–98

Hein, Jotun. 2004. 'Pedigrees for all humanity', *Nature* 431 (7008): 518–19

Heinz, Hans-Joachim. 1994 [1966]. *The social organization of the !kõ Bushmen* (edited by Klaus Keuthmann) (Research in Khoisan Studies 10). Cologne: Rüdiger Köppe

Henshilwood, Christopher S., and Curtis W. Marean. 2003. 'The origin of modern human behavior', *Current Anthropology* 44: 627–51

Henshilwood Christopher, Francesco d'Errico, Marian Vanhaeren, Karen van Niekerk and Zenobia Jacobs. 2004. 'Middle Stone Age shell beads from South Africa', *Science* 304 (5669): 404

Henshilwood, Christopher S., Francesco d'Errico, Royden Yates, Zenobia Jacobs, Chantal Tribolo, Geoff A. T. Duller, Norbert Mercier, Judith C. Sealy, Helene Valladas, Ian Watts and Ann G. Wintle. 2002. 'Emergence of modern human behavior: Middle Stone Age engravings from South Africa', *Science* 295 (5558): 1278–80

Hirsch, Eric, and Michael O'Hanlon (eds.). 1995. *The anthropology of landscape: perspectives on place and space*. Oxford University Press

Hobbes, Thomas. 1996 [1651]. *Leviathan* (revised student edition, edited by Richard Tuck). Cambridge University Press

Horton, Robin. 1967a. 'African traditional thought and Western science: part I: From tradition to science', *Africa* 37: 50–71

1967b. 'African traditional thought and Western science: part II: The "closed" and "open" predicaments', *Africa* 37: 155–87

Hurford, James. 2007. *The origins of meaning: language in the light of evolution*. Oxford University Press

Ingold, Tim. 1986a. *The appropriation of nature: essays on human ecology and social relations*. Manchester University Press

1986b. *Evolution and social life*. Cambridge University Press

2000. *The perception of the environment: essays in livelihood, dwelling and skill*. London: Routledge

Isaac, G. L. 1978a. 'The food sharing behavior of proto-human hominids', *Scientific American* 238 (4): 90–108

1978b. 'Food sharing and human evolution: archaeological evidence from the Plio-Pleistocene of east Africa', *Journal of Anthropological Research* 34: 311–25

James, Wendy. 2003. *The ceremonial animal: a new portrait of anthropology*. Oxford University Press

2008. 'Alternating birth classes: a note from eastern Africa', in Allen *et al.*, pp. 83–95

Johanson, Donald, and Maitland Edey. 1981. *Lucy: the beginnings of humankind*. New York: Simon & Schuster.

Jolly, Alison. 1996. 'Primate communication, lies, and ideas', in Andrew Lock and Charles R. Peters (eds.), *Handbook of human symbolic evolution*. Oxford University Press, pp. 167–77

Keith, A., G. Elliot Smith, A. Smith Woodward and W. J. H. Duckworth. 1925. 'The fossil anthropoid ape from Taungs', *Nature* 115 (2885): 234–6

Kerns, Virginia. 2003. *Scenes from the high desert: Julian Steward's life and theory.* Urbana: University of Illinois Press

King, Barbara J. 2007. *Evolving God: a provocative view on the origins of religion.* New York: Doubleday

2009. 'Apes, hominids, and the roots of religion', *General Anthropology* 16 (2): 1–8

Klein, Richard G. 2009. *The human career: human biological and cultural origins* (third edition). University of Chicago Press

Klein, Richard G., and Blake Edgar. 2002. *The dawn of human culture.* New York: John Wiley & Sons

Knight, Chris D. 1991 *Blood relations: menstruation and the origins of culture.* New Haven: Yale University Press

2008. 'Early human kinship was matrilineal', in Allen *et al.*, pp. 61–82

Knight, Chris, Camilla Power and Ian Watts. 1995. 'The human symbolic revolution: a Darwinian account', *Cambridge Archaeological Journal* 5: 75–114

Knight, Chris, Michael Studdert-Kennedy and James R. Hurford. 2000. 'Language: a Darwinian adaptation?', in Chris Knight, Michael Studdert-Kennedy and James R. Hurford (eds.), *The evolutionary emergence of language: social function and the origins of linguistic form.* Cambridge University Press, pp. 1–15

Kolenda, Pauline M. 1968. 'Region, caste and family structure: a comparative study of the Indian "joint" family', in Milton Singer and Bernard S. Cohn (eds.), *Structure and change in Indian society.* Chicago: Aldine Publishing Company, pp. 339–96

Kroeber, A. L. 1917. 'The superorganic', *American Anthropologist* 19: 163–213

Kropotkin, Peter. 1987 [1902], *Mutual aid: a factor of evolution.* London: Freedom Press

Kuhn, Steven L., and Mary C. Stiner. 2001. 'The antiquity of hunter-gatherers', in Catherine Panter-Brick, Robert H. Layton and Peter Rowley-Conwy (eds.), *Hunter-gatherers: an interdisciplinary perspective.* Cambridge University Press, pp. 99–142

Kuper, Adam. 1973. *Anthropologists and anthropology: the British school, 1922–1972.* Harmondsworth: Allen Lane

1988. *The invention of primitive society: transformations of an illusion.* London: Routledge

1994. *The chosen primate: human nature and cultural diversity.* Cambridge, MA: Harvard University Press

1999. *Culture: the anthropologists' account.* Cambridge, MA: Harvard University Press

Lahr, Marta Mirazón, and Robert Foley. 1994. 'Multiple dispersals and modern human origins', *Evolutionary Anthropology* 3: 48–60

Lamarck, Jean-Baptiste. 1914 [1809]. *Zoological philosophy: an exposition with regard to the natural history of animals* (translated by Hugh Elliot). London: Macmillan and Co.

Landau, Misia. 1991. *Narratives of human evolution.* New Haven: Yale University Press

Leakey, L. S. B., P. V. Tobias, and Napier, J. R. 1964. 'A new species of the genus *Homo* from Olduvai Gorge', *Nature* 202 (4927): 7–9

Leakey, Richard, and L. Jan Slikkerveer. 1993. *Man-ape ape-man: the quest for human's place in nature and Dubois' 'missing link'*. Leiden: Netherlands Foundation for Kenya Wildlife Service

LeClair, Edward E. Jr, and Harold K. Schneider (eds.). 1968. *Economic anthropology: readings in theory and analysis*. New York: Holt, Rinehart and Winston

Lee, Richard B. 1968. 'The sociology of !Kung Bushman trance performances', in Raymond Prince (ed.), *Trance and possession states*. Montreal: R. M. Bucke Memorial Society, pp. 47–79

1969. '!Kung Bushman subsistence: an input–output analysis', in Andrew P. Vayda (ed.), *Environment and cultural behavior: ecological studies in cultural anthropology*. New York: Natural History Press, pp. 47–79

1979. *The !Kung San: men, women, and work in a foraging society*, Cambridge University Press

Lee, Richard B. and Irven DeVore (eds.). 1968. *Man the hunter*. Chicago: Aldine Publishing Company

Lévi-Strauss, Claude. 1963 [1958]. *Structural anthropology* (translated by Claire Jacobson and Brooke Grundfest Schoepf). New York: Basic Books

1966. 'The future of kinship studies', *Proceedings of the Royal Anthropological Institute for 1965*. London: Royal Anthropological Institute of Great Britain and Ireland, pp. 13–22

1968. 'The concept of primitiveness', in Lee and DeVore, pp. 349–52

1969 [1949]. *The elementary structures of kinship* (revised edition, translated by James Harle Bell, John Richard von Sturmer and Rodney Needham). Boston: Beacon Press

1976 [1973]. *Structural anthropology, volume 2* (translated by Monique Layton). New York: Basic Books

1978. *Myth and meaning*. University of Toronto Press

Lévy-Bruhl, Lucien. 1926 [1910]. *How natives think* (translated by Lilian A. Clare). London: George Allen & Unwin

1975 [1949]. *The notebooks on primitive mentality* (translated by Peter Rivière). Oxford: Basil Blackwell

Lewin, Roger. 1989. *Bones of contention: controversies in the search for human origins*. Harmondsworth: Penguin Books

Lewin, Roger, and Robert A. Foley. 2004. *Principles of human evolution* (second edition). Oxford: Blackwell Publishing

Lewis, Jerome. 2009. 'As well as words: Congo Pygmy hunting, mimicry, and play', in Botha and Knight 2009b, pp. 236–56

Lewis-Williams, J. David. 2002. *The mind in the cave: consciousness and the origins of art*. London: Thames & Hudson

2010. *Conceiving God: the cognitive origin and evolution of religion*. London: Thames & Hudson

Liebenberg, Louis. 1990. *The art of tracking: the origin of science*. Cape Town: David Philip

Locke, John. 1988 [1690]. *Two treatises of government* (student edition, edited by Peter Laslett). Cambridge University Press

Lovejoy, Arthur O. 1936. *The Great Chain of Being: a study of the history of an idea.* Cambridge, MA: Harvard University Press

Lovejoy, C. Owen. 2009. 'Reexamining human origins in light of *Ardipithecus ramidus*', *Science* 326 (5949): 74e1–74e8 (doi: 10.1126/science.1175834)

Lubbock, Sir John. 1874 [1870]. *The origin of civilization and the primitive condition of man.* New York: D. Appleton and Company.

McBrearty, Sally, and Alison S. Brooks. 2000. 'The revolution that wasn't: a new interpretation of the origins of modern humans', *Journal of Human Evolution* 39: 453–563

McBrearty, Sally, and Nina G. Jablonski. 2005. 'First fossil chimpanzee', *Nature* 437 (7055): 105–8

McGrew, W. C. 1991. 'Chimpanzee material culture: what are its origins and why?', in R. A. Foley (ed.), *The origins of human behaviour.* London: Unwin Hyman (One World Archaeology), pp. 13–24

McLennan, John F. 1865. *Primitive marriage: an inquiry into the origin of the form of capture in marriage ceremonies.* Edinburgh: Adam and Charles Black

Maine, Henry Sumner. 1913 [1861]. *Ancient law: its connection with the early history of society and its relation to modern ideas.* London: George Routledge & Sons

Malina, Jaroslav, and Zdenek Vašíček. 1990. *Archaeology yesterday and today: the development of archaeology in the sciences and humanities* (translated by Marek Zelebil). Cambridge University Press

Malmkjær, Kirsten. 2004. 'Origin of language', in *The linguistics encyclopedia, second edition.* London: Routledge, pp. 387–92

Mann, Alan, and Mark Weiss. 1996. 'Hominoid phylogeny and taxonomy: a consideration of the molecular and fossil evidence in an historical perspective', *Molecular Phylogenetics and Evolution* 5 (1): 169–81

Marett, R. R. 1932. *Faith, hope, and charity in primitive religion.* London: Macmillan

Marshall, Lorna. 1976. *The !Kung of Nyae Nyae.* Cambridge, MA: Harvard University Press

Marx, Karl. 1974 [1880–2]. *The ethnological notebooks of Karl Marx (studies of Morgan, Phear, Maine, Lubbock)* (translated and edited by Lawrence Krader). Assen: Van Gorcum

Matthey de l'Etang, Alain, and Pierre J. Bancel. 2002. 'Tracing of the ancestral kinship system: the global etymon KAKA. Part II: An anthropological study', *Mother Tongue* 7: 245–58

Mauss, Marcel. 1990 [1924]. *The gift: form and reason for exchange in archaic societies* (translated by W. D. Halls). London: Routledge

Megarry, Tim. 1995. *Society in prehistory: the origins of human culture.* London: Macmillan Press

Melis, Alicia P., Brian Hare and Michael Tomasello. 2008 'Do chimpanzees reciprocate received favours?', *Animal Behaviour* 76: 951–62

Mitani, John C., and David P. Watts. 2001. 'Why do chimpanzees hunt and share meat?', *Animal Behaviour* 61: 915–24

2005. 'Correlates of territorial boundary patrol behaviour in wild chimpanzees', *Animal Behaviour* 70: 1079–86

Mithen, Steven. 1996. *The prehistory of the mind: a search for the origins of art, religion and science.* London: Thames & Hudson

1998. 'A creative explosion? Theory of mind, language and the disembodied mind of the Upper Palaeolithic', in Steven Mithen (ed.), *Creativity in human evolution and prehistory*. London: Routledge, pp. 165–91

2005. *The singing Neanderthals: the origins of music, language, mind and body*. London: Phoenix

2009. 'Holistic communication and the co-evolution of language and music: resurrecting an old idea', in Botha and Knight 2009a, pp. 58–76

2010. 'Excavating the prehistoric mind: the brain as a culture artefact and material culture as biological extension', in Dunbar, Gamble and Gowlett, pp. 481–503

Monboddo, Lord. 1773. *Of the origin and progress of language*, vol. I. Edinburgh: A. Kincaid and W. Creech; London: T. Cadell

1795. *Antient metaphysics, volume fourth, containing the history of man with an appendix relating to the Fille sauvage whom the author saw*. London: Bell and Bradfute; and T. Cadell

Morgan, Lewis Henry. 1871. *Systems of consanguinity and affinity of the human family* (Smithsonian Contributions to Knowledge 17). Washington: Smithsonian Institution

1877. *Ancient society; or, researches in the lines of human progress from savagery through barbarism to civilization*. New York: Henry Holt

Murdock, George Peter. 1940. 'The cross-cultural survey', *American Sociological Review* 5: 361–70

1949. *Social structure*. New York: Macmillan

Needham, Rodney. 1972. *Belief, language, and experience*. Oxford: Basil Blackwell

Noë, Ronald. 2006. 'Digging for the roots of trading', in P. M. Kappeler and C. P. van Schaik (eds.), *Cooperation in primates and humans: mechanisms and evolution*. Heidelberg: Springer, pp. 233–61

Norenzayan, Ara, and Azim F. Shariff. 2008. 'The origin and evolution of religious prosociality', *Science* 322 (5898): 58–62

O'Connell, J. F., K. Hawkes and N. G. Blurton Jones. 1999. 'Grandmothering and the evolution of *Homo erectus*', *Journal of Human Evolution* 36: 461–85

Opie, Kit, and Camilla Power. 2008. 'Grandmothering and female coalitions: a basis for matrilineal priority?', in Allen *et al.*, pp. 168–86

Oppenheimer, Stephen. 2004. *The real Eve: modern man's journey out of Africa*. New York: Carroll & Graf

Peterson, Nicolas. 1979. 'Territorial adaptations among desert hunter-gatherers: the !Kung and Australians compared', in Burnham and Ellen, pp. 111–29

Pinker, Steven. 1997. *How the mind works*. New York: W. W. Norton & Company

Pinker, Steven, and Paul Bloom. 1990. 'Natural language and natural selection', *Behavioral and Brain Sciences* 12: 707–84

Pufendorf, Samuel. 1991 [1673]. *On the duty of man and citizen* (edited by James Tully and translated by Michael Silverthorne). Cambridge University Press

Quiatt, Duane, and Vernon Reynolds. 1993. *Primate behaviour: information, social knowledge, and the evolution of culture*. Cambridge University Press.

References

References

References 175

References 175

References 175

References 175
References 175

References 175
References 175

References 175

References 175

References 175

References 175

References 175

Radcliffe-Brown, A. R. 1952. *Structure and function in primitive society: essays and addresses*. London: Cohen & West
  1958. *Method in social anthropology: selected essays of A. R. Radcliffe-Brown* (edited by M. N. Srinivas). University of Chicago Press
Rappaport, Roy A. 1999. *Ritual and religion in the making of humanity*. Cambridge University Press
Reader, John. 1988. *Missing links: the hunt for earliest man* (second edition). Harmondsworth: Penguin Books
Reed, David L., Vincent S. Smith, Shaless L. Hammond, Alan R. Rogers and Dale H. Clayton. 2004. 'Genetic analysis of lice supports direct contact between modern and archaic humans', *PLoS Biology* 2 (11): e340 (doi:10.1371/journal.pbio.0020340)
Renfrew, Colin. 2007. *Prehistory: the making of the human mind*. London: Phoenix
Richerson, Peter J., and Robert Boyd. 2005. *Not by genes alone: how culture transformed human evolution*. University of Chicago Press
Roberts, Alice. 2009. *The incredible human journey: the story of how we colonised the planet*. London: Bloomsbury
Rohde, Douglas L. T., Steve Olson and Joseph T. Chang. 2004. 'Modelling the recent common ancestry of all living humans', *Nature* 431 (7008): 562–6
Rosman, Abraham, and Paula G. Rubel. 1971. *Feasting with mine enemy: rank and exchange among Northwest Coast societies*. New York: Columbia University Press
Rousseau, Jean-Jacques. 1973 [1750–62]. *The Social Contract and Discourses* (translated by G. D. H. Cole). London: J. M. Dent & Sons
Runciman, W. G. 2001. 'From nature to culture, from culture to society', in W. G Runciman, *The origin of human social institutions* (Proceedings of the British Academy 110). Oxford: Oxford University Press, pp. 235–54
  2009. *The theory of cultural and social selection*. Cambridge University Press
Sagarin, Edward. 1978. 'On sociological concepts: a prefatory note', in Edward Sagarin (ed.), *Sociology: the basic concepts*. New York: Holt, Rinehart and Winston, pp. vii–ix
Sahlins, Marshall. 1974. *Stone Age economics*. London: Tavistock Publications
  1976. *The use and abuse of biology: an anthropological critique of sociobiology*. London: Tavistock Publications
Salisbury, Richard F. 1962. *From stone to steel: economic consequences of a technological change in New Guinea*. Melbourne University Press
Sapir, E. 1917. 'Do we need a "superorganic?"', *American Anthropologist* 19: 441–7
Sarmiento, Esteban. 2007. 'Twenty-two species of extinct human ancestors', in G. J. Sawyer and Viktor Deak (creators), *The last human: a guide to twenty-two species of extinct humans*. New Haven: Yale University Press, pp. 24–229
Saussure, Ferdinand de. 1974 [1916]. *Course in general linguistics* (edited by Charles Bally and Albert Sechehaye, translated by Wade Baskin). Glasgow: Fontana/Collins
Schick, Kathy D., Nicholas Toth, Gary Garufi, E. Sue Savage-Rumbaugh, Duane Rumbaugh and Rose Sevcik. 1999. 'Continuing investigations

into the stone tool-making and tool-using capabilities of a bonobo (*Pan paniscus*)', *Journal of Archaeological Science* 26, 821–32

Schmidt, Father Wilhelm. 1939 [1937]. *The culture historical method of ethnology: the scientific approach to the racial question* (translated by S. A. Siebert). New York: Fortuny's

Schneider, David M. 1968. *American kinship: a cultural account.* Englewood Cliffs: Prentice Hall

Schneider, David M., and Kathleen Gough (eds.). 1961. *Matrilineal kinship.* Berkeley: University of California Press

Silberbauer, George B. 1981. *Hunter and habitat in the central Kalahari Desert,* Cambridge University Press

Slotkin, J. S. 1965. *Readings in early anthropology.* Chicago: Aldine Publishing Company

Smith Woodward, A. 1913. 'Description of the human skull and mandible and the associated mammalian remains', *Quarterly Journal of the Geological Society* 69: 117–47

Spencer, Frank. 1990. *Piltdown: a scientific forgery.* London: British Museum (Natural History) and Oxford University Press

Spencer, Herbert. 1898. *The principles of sociology,* vol. I. New York: D. Appleton and Company

Steward, Julian H. 1955. *Theory of culture change: the methodology of multilinear evolution.* Urbana: University of Illinois Press

1978. *Evolution and ecology: essays on social transformation.* Urbana: University of Illinois Press

Stoczkowski, Wiktor. 2002 [1994]. *Explaining human origins: myth, imagination and conjecture* (translated by Mary Turton). Cambridge University Press

Stow, George W. 1905. *The native races of South Africa: a history of the intrusion of the Hottentots and Bantu into the hunting grounds of the Bushmen, the aborigines of the country.* London: Swan Sonnenschein

Strathern, Marilyn. 1996. 'The concept of society is theoretically obsolete: for the motion (1)', in Tim Ingold (ed.), *Key debates in anthropology.* London: Routledge, pp. 60–6

Tattersall, Ian. 2000. 'Palaeoanthropology: the last half-century', *Evolutionary Anthropology* 9: 2–16

2009. 'Human origins: Out of Africa', *Proceedings of the National Academy of Sciences (PNAS)* 106 (38): 16018–21

Thomas, Herbert. 1995. *The first humans: the search for our origins* (translated by Paul G. Bahn). London: Thames & Hudson

Trigger, Bruce G. 1989. *A history of archaeological thought.* Cambridge University Press

Trinkaus, Ewrik, and Pat Shipman. 1994. *The Neandertals: of skeletons, scientists, and scandal.* New York: Vintage Books

Trivers, Robert L. 1971. 'The evolution of reciprocal altruism', *Quarterly Review of Biology* 46: 35–57

1972. 'Parental investment and sexual selection', in Bernard Campbell (ed.), *Sexual selection and the Descent of Man, 1871–1971.* Chicago: Aldine-Atherton, pp. 136–79

1974. 'Parent–offspring conflict', *American Zoologist* 14: 249–64